Tales from a Dog Catcher

Tales from a Dog Catcher

Lisa Duffy-Korpics

The Lyons Press
Guilford, Connecticut
An imprint of The Globe Pequot Press

The Lyons Press is an imprint of the Globe Pequot Press.

Text design by Libby Kingsbury

Library of Congress Cataloging-in-Publication Data

Duffy-Korpics, Lisa.

  Tales from a dog catcher / Lisa Duffy-Korpics.
    p. cm.
  ISBN 978-1-59921-498-6
  1. Dogs--New York (State)—New York—Anecdotes. 2. Dog rescue—New York (State)—New York—Anecdotes. 3. Duffy-Korpics, Lisa. I. Title.
  SF426.2.D84 2009
  636.7—dc22

                                 2008042699

ISBN 978-1-59921-498-6

Printed in the United States of America

10 9 8 7 6 5 4 3 2 1

To my mother
Kathleen Rita Finnell Duffy
1941–2003

It was you and I against the world. Through it all you never let on how difficult it was for you, making sure I had the childhood you never had. We both knew we had borrowed time, yet you infused every moment of it with memories that will sustain me forever. While your physical presence is gone, your gentle spirit and unconditional love continue to guide me every day of my life.

This is for you.

Contents

Acknowledgments

$\mathcal{F}$irst and foremost, I would like to thank my wonderful agent, Eileen Cope from Trident Media Group, whose incredible determination, hard work, and unflagging optimism made this book a reality. I would also like to express my sincere gratitude to my editor, Gene Brissie; project manager, Ellen Urban; copyeditor, Melissa Hayes; and to all the great folks at The Lyons Press.

I would like to thank Carol Kline, author and editor extraordinaire, who plucked me out of obscurity and helped open doors for me that I could never have opened myself. Your guidance and friendship through the years have meant the world to me. I would also like to express my gratitude to Jack Canfield, Mark Victor Hansen, Dr. Marty Becker, and all the wonderful people that make up the *Chicken Soup for the Soul* family. Additionally, I would like to thank editor and dear friend, Felicia Hodges, publisher of *Tri-County Woman*, for giving me my first opportunity at being a real, live, working writer!

If it takes a village to raise a child, then it took an entire police department to finish the job! I would like to thank all the members of the Annesville, New York, police department. Even though many years have passed since I was a member of the department, and the names and faces have changed, the memories of those years are never far from my mind. Many have retired, some are gone, and a few still remain, but the support, guidance, and education I received from all of you have had a profound effect on my life. It was a privilege to be a part of this extraordinary organization.

Additionally, I would like to thank the many wonderful people of this small city, a hidden gem along the banks of the Hudson River. Thank you for allowing me into your lives and for entrusting me with your beloved pets. It was never a responsibility I took lightly. While I have lived in many places in my life, this place will always be home.

To my father, John Duffy, who was never too busy to read one of my stories, alway remember that "45 is a big building!" His passion for reading and a way with words are his genetic legacy to me. Thanks go out to my wonderful extended family: Richard and Maryanne Finnell and Linda and Greg Arksey; to the late John Duffy Sr. and the late Alice Turoci; to John, Elsie, Sean, Lina, Ryan, and Maryanne Turoci; to Ellen, Chrissie, and Allison; Tim and Christina; Matt and John Schulz; to Jean Turoci and her family, Ross and Alison Pagliucca; to both Janet Duffys and the O'Connell, Kacanich, and Ocasio families; to Gen and John Privitera; Patrick, Colin, and the late Tim O'Mara; Joe, Diane, Megan, Mallory, and Cara Korpics; and, especially, Maryanne Korpics, who has always been more "mother" than "in-law." I love you all!

Love and gratitude go out to my other parents, Frank and Laila Morgan, and to my cousin, Jane Morgan-Gullery. To my best friend, Luann Nolen, who for over thirty years has been at my side through some of the best and also the darkest of times, and to her family Jeff, Zach, Hannah and Emily, Tony, Joey, and Samantha Spivey. Thank you for opening your hearts and your home to me for so many years. Appreciation goes out to Chantel Haight, Ed Grippe, Ron Tedesco, the Boustani family, the late Richard Krasusky, Sean and Toni Gallagher, and the Marrinan family. And to so many others too numerous to mention . . . please know I have not forgotten you.

Further thanks to colleague, author, and friend Chris Forman for your ever-present encouragement and friendship. Thanks go out to the social studies department, faculty, administration, staff, and students of Valley Central High School in Montgomery, New York.

Finally, I would like to thank my family. To my husband, Jason, for his humor, love, and encouragement, and for being the one who always believed that this book would happen. Thank you for being the one I can always depend on.

And to Charles and Emmaleigh . . . you are, and always will be, my reason for everything.

Bless the Beasts and the Children

$\mathcal{P}$erched atop a hill overlooking the Hudson, St. Bernard's convent provided a panoramic view of the river. The building was a massive, imposing structure. Many years ago, the convent served as a school for orphans, or for children whose parents could no longer care for them. Before the social programs under the Roosevelt administration became available, the school had been filled to capacity. Years before that, many of the children had been put on trains to travel to the Midwest where there were people willing to welcome them into their families, although sadly, too often as little more than indentured servants. At one time St. Bernard's had been meant to be something of a haven, a place that supposedly existed to protect those who could not protect themselves.

City Hall occasionally received phone calls from people who wanted directions to the convent, most likely seeking information about their past. Once in a while you would see someone sitting on one of the old benches that faced the river, staring out into the distance. There was no way of knowing whether this was the last stop on their journey of self-discovery, or the first. I sometimes wondered if coming to look at this enormous grim building would give them the answers they needed. The nuns who lived there now only used a small portion of the building, mostly as a home for retired sisters. Perhaps it was the history of the place, and the fact that it was now so silent and nearly empty, that made it seem ominous to me.

While I often stopped by the grounds when I was in that area of the city to take a moment to admire their magnificent view, my exploration of the convent itself never brought me farther than the main lobby. I had been sent there a few times before when they had called the department to ask if I could drop off some heartworm medicine for a dog that lived in the woods near the convent. For as long as I could remember, a mysterious white German shepherd had roamed the property. In fact, he had become a legend of sorts because he never came to anyone and always seemed so independent. The sisters would grind up the medication and put it in the food they would leave for him.

He had probably lived in those woods for most of his life; to him, it was home. You could ask anyone who lived near the convent if they knew about the white dog, and they would usually say that they had seen him around for years. He never bothered anyone, and nobody had ever found a reason to bother him.

It was windy and raining the day I received the complaint about the white dog, the precursor to a full-fledged hurricane that was heading in our direction. The state was under a hurricane warning, and I knew from experience that animals tend to act strangely before a bad storm. Dogs that never leave their yards will sometimes be found cowering under a car several blocks away. I was surprised that the convent had called in a complaint today, given the fact that the white dog wasn't behaving any differently than he usually did. As old as he was, I figured he had probably seen a few hurricanes in his life, and this one was not likely to be the worst.

Sergeant Murphy called me in before sending me over to the convent. He wanted to make sure I was prepared for the weather. "This is the smallest one I could find," he said, tossing the bright orange raincoat over to me. "Go ahead—put it on, and let's get a look at you." Orange wasn't exactly my best color, especially not fluorescent, neon, glowing-like-nuclear-waste orange.

"Can't I just wear my regular jacket?" I asked. It seemed fairly waterproof and it had a hood. I didn't see why I had to look like a traffic cone. It was just rain.

"Oh no, no, no. This is hazardous weather. You have to be visible. You're not going to a party, you know. Go ahead and put it on."

Sgt. Murphy stood there smiling at me. I looked at him for a second longer, and he stopped smiling and widened his eyes. He looked very innocent like that, with his red hair and blue eyes. Still, he was getting too much enjoyment out of this. Knowing his penchant for practical jokes, I wondered if his enthusiasm about my safety had more to do with making me look ridiculous.

I slipped the raincoat over my head. It was a lot heavier than it looked. The bottom of it fell almost to my toes.

"This is the smallest one you could find?"

"Yes," he said, making a small sound that was somewhere between a snort and a choke. I looked at him without saying anything for a second, and he coughed a few times into his fist.

"Bit of a cold," he said. "It's going around." I could see he was trying to control himself. I turned to look at my reflection in the window that separated the dispatch room from the lobby. I looked like an orange tepee with a head poking out of the top. A small head at that.

"Can you move around okay? You're not going to trip on it?" He seemed sincere. Inasmuch as Sergeant Murphy wanted to have fun at my expense, he also wanted to make sure that I would be safe. It was hard to be angry with him.

I nodded my head. I was getting used to it.

"Okay, then. Off to the convent with thee, woman!" He laughed and turned back to his desk to grab the phone. I walked out to the lobby to leave.

"Keep your radio on, Lisa," he yelled to me as I left. I gave him a quick salute and he responded with the same. When I opened the glass door in the lobby, I could hear the wind beginning to howl.

"Mother will be with you in a moment," the receptionist said, in such a low whisper that I had to lean in closer to hear her. She looked as though she was very busy, although I could see an unfinished crossword puzzle on her desk. When she saw me looking, she quickly flipped open a ledger and slid it over the puzzle.

"You can sit there," she said, pointing at a solitary chair across the room. "It will only be a moment." I walked over to the chair, dripping a trail of water with each step and trying to decide if I should sit on what looked to be real mahogany. Before I could come to a decision, I heard a tapping noise. Turning around, I saw a tall nun in a black-and-white habit standing next to the receptionist's window. It seemed like she had just appeared out of nowhere. She gave me a quick nod and then handed a note to the receptionist, who read it carefully, and then motioned for me to come back to the desk from where only seconds ago I had been banished.

"Mother would like you to pick up that stray dog that is trespassing on the grounds. He looks to have mange or some other disease. We would like you to take him away. Today."

I looked up at the nun who had still not said a word to me. She was very tall and her face seemed like it was etched in concrete.

"The white shepherd—he lives here, doesn't he?" I asked.

The nun just shook her head no and then glared at the receptionist, who looked back at the paper and read it again. "Some of our retired sisters have been feeding him for quite a while. They have been spoken to and will not be doing that anymore. It is in the dog's best interest to be in a place where he will get proper care. The convent is not that place." The receptionist folded the note and slid it toward me.

I couldn't believe they thought an old dog, more a wild animal than a domesticated pet, would be able to find a home where he would get "proper care." This dog had been part of St. Bernard's for years. Now, all of the sudden, he was being banished from the convent. They certainly seemed to do a lot of banishing around here.

"You do realize that there's no place for this dog to go?" I said. "He's old; he's practically wild. If I bring him to the shelter he will be euthanized immediately." I waited for the receptionist to say something, but she just looked down at her desk and shuffled some papers. The tall nun just looked at me and lifted her arm and pointed in the direction of the wooded area of the property. Why wouldn't she speak to me? As intimidating as she was, I was starting to become irritated at being ordered around in this way. I couldn't tell her I wouldn't do it. It was my job, and if an animal was in violation of a city code, then I had to enforce the law.

"I'll do what I can," I said. "But he doesn't come to people, so it's going to be difficult."

I looked over at the window. The rain was starting to come down harder and the sky was getting darker. I had no choice but to try and take him now, before the weather got any worse.

"Why can't you tell me to do this yourself?" I asked the nun, knowing that she would probably consider me disrespectful. I didn't care. She was sending this dog to a certain death, and she didn't seem to care at all. The nun just continued to look at me, her face void of all emotion.

"Vows of silence," the receptionist said to me in a way that seemed to be less harsh than before. "There are certain times every day when they do not speak." The nun turned abruptly and walked away, leaving in her wake a rustling of material and a light scent of something that smelled like bleach.

"Mother Superior is new to Saint Bernard's," the receptionist whispered to me after looking down the hallway to make sure she was gone. "She is very adamant about the dog. A few of our older sisters are very upset about this, but . . . obedience . . . you know." I knew that the Mother Superior was the only person who thought that the convent was no place for a dog, even one that had lived there for years before her arrival.

I got into my car and pulled around to the back, driving up onto the grass. I thought it would be a good idea to make the trip to the car as short as possible—if I was even able to catch the white dog. Any tire tracks resulting from the completion of my duties were just something the Mother Superior would have to deal with.

I threw a leash around my neck, knowing subconsciously that this was too optimistic; he would probably never let me get close enough to use it. I would have to use the snare pole that I'd brought along.

I saw him at the bottom of the hill. He was at least as old as I'd thought, but there was something else: He was shaking. He was absolutely terrified, and I knew it was likely that he'd start to run away as soon as I approached him. Scanning the area, I noticed that someone, some time ago, had built a little lean-to for him, obviously before the current Mother Superior's tenure. Maybe he would run so quickly and so far that he would leave my jurisdiction, and I could tell the nun that there was nothing I could do. I started to head down the muddy hill, slipping and sliding. I looked up at the convent and saw her standing on the terrace, watching me. The wind was whipping her habit around her head and the rain was coming down harder, but she still stood there, making sure that I would do my job.

When I reached the white dog, he was still standing there, shaking. "Run," I whispered. Why was he making this so easy? I guess I knew that he probably couldn't run very fast; he must have been at least fifteen years old. As I stood there, I imagined getting him into the car and bringing him to a wooded area over the city border, into Ulster Valley—somewhere near a place where someone could leave food for him. Maybe I could even bring some and leave it for him each day. As much as I wanted to believe this, I knew it wouldn't happen. He would come back here, to the place where he had lived for over a decade. If it wasn't today, it would be tomorrow, or next week.

I approached him slowly, reaching for my leash. It was gone; it had probably fallen off during my slide down the muddy hill. Looking at the mud that was splattered all over me, I was actually glad that Sarge had made me wear this hideous raincoat. I grasped the snare pole with two hands and twisted it to extend it as far as it could go. I didn't know if it was from the cold rain, or my anxiety over the fate of this dog, but I was shaking so hard, I could hardly reach him with the snare pole. I was finally able to carefully loop the snare around his neck and under his front legs. Slowly, I pulled the wire tighter and started to try and pull him toward me. Instead of thrashing around, he just dug in deeper. I pulled and coaxed. "Come on, I won't hurt you. It'll be okay." I felt the lump in my throat get bigger. I was lying. It wasn't going to be okay at all.

I pulled again and moved him an inch or so, only to slide a few inches forward every time I tried to back myself up the hill. I could hardly see with the rain pelting me in the face, stinging like hundreds of tiny needles. The rain was coming down sideways and my boots were slipping deeper into the mud when I heard the quick blast of a siren. I looked up to see my friend Keith, a police officer at the department, getting out of his patrol car and scrambling down the steep hill, trying not to fall himself.

"We were worried about you," said Keith. "You weren't answering your radio." He was digging his heels into the side of the hill to avoid sliding into me. "Murphy's stressing out about this. He was coming to get you himself but some wires came down on Hilltop, so he's up there redirecting traffic. It's turning into a real mess. Where's your radio?"

I let go of the snare pole with one hand and tried to reach into the opening on the raincoat to check my radio. The pocket on the raincoat wasn't at my waist where it should have been, but almost down near my knee. As I was digging around, trying to find it, I started to slide and grabbed the snare again.

"Never mind . . . forget it!" Keith said. He looked down at the dog and then up toward the convent. "The Penguin's still watching!" he said, smiling.

"She called headquarters, didn't she?" I asked him between breaths.

"Yeah—she had her secretary call and say that if the dog wasn't gone today, she was going to call the mayor." Keith shrugged and carefully edged his way over to me. He grabbed the middle of the snare pole. "Poor guy . . . he never bothered anybody. This dog's been hanging around here since I was in high school." Keith pulled harder, and the white dog rolled over on his side and started to whimper.

"Go open the back of the wagon, and when I get him up there, I'll pull and you push. Together, we can get him in the car." I ran up the hill, my boots sliding down one step for each two I took. The hill was starting to resemble a small waterfall. Keith got him up the hill to the car, but the frightened dog began to whip his head back and forth, panting hard, trying to get out of the snare's grasp. He was looking wildly at me and then at Keith.

"On the count of three!" Keith yelled over the wailing of the wind. With one final tug, the white shepherd was in the back of the car, still panting and crying.

"It's okay . . . it's okay," I whispered. I crawled into the back of the car and slipped the snare off, thinking that maybe now he would calm down and no longer feel threatened. I was shocked when I got a good look at him. He appeared much older than I had first thought, maybe fifteen had been an understatement? Before, I had only caught glimpses of him from a distance, running through the woods or lying next to the river. I could see now, close up, how old he really was. I grabbed a dog biscuit out of the box in the back of the car and put it down near his nose. He didn't even seem to notice it.

Going against all of my training, I put my hand out for him to sniff, hoping that maybe I could pat his head, try to calm him down and show him that I wasn't going to hurt him. This only served to make him pant harder as he tried to move away from me. He wasn't used to petting. Maybe at one time he had belonged to someone, but they had probably mistreated him, and this was why he had ended up at St. Bernard's, where he could remain a safe distance away from humans.

Keith looked over at the dog and said, "You know, you could tell his story to the folks at the shelter. Maybe they can find a place for him to live out his life, where he could be outside . . ." Keith knew as well as I did that with overcrowding at the shelter, the dog's age, and the fact that he was never going to be able to be adopted as someone's pet, the white dog's future didn't look promising. For a moment it seemed to me that history was repeating itself—once again, St. Bernard's was sending away another innocent life for "their best interests," as they had done to the orphans long ago. The difference with the white dog was that the only possible result for him would not be a good one.

"Maybe I can drive him out to Irvington," I said, "or there's that lady up on Ridge Lane who has all that property . . ." Before I could finish my sentence, the white dog started to gasp, and his eyes rolled back in his head. His panting slowed, then stopped.

"Oh no," Keith said softly, staring at the dog. The sound of the wind whistling through the trees seemed to get louder. The white dog was lying still now in the back of the car. He had probably never been near a car, let alone inside one. I leaned over and tried to shake him a bit, but he didn't move. I put my ear down on his chest to see if his heart was beating. He was dead. He had been scared to death.

I put my face in his fur and started to sob.

"Hey, it's okay . . . you didn't cause this," said Keith. "He was old. This was just his time. Come on, come here." Keith rubbed my shoulder. I looked up and saw that he had tears in his eyes, too. "He should have died out there," I said, nodding toward the woods. "He died afraid. He died because of me."

Keith shook his head. "No, that's not why. You know that."

The rain was pelting the hood of the car, and the wind was starting to howl. I looked up at the convent and thought that I may have seen a face in the window, and then it was gone.

Keith directed me to get out of the car. He closed the back hatch and walked over to the driver's side. "I'll take care of this," he said. "Take the patrol car, go back to headquarters, and have some coffee. C'mon . . . the keys are in it." He gently put his hand on my back and gave me a slight push. "Go." Keith stood there with the rain pelting him in the face for a few seconds before he opened the car door. He wiped his eyes with the back of his sleeve. I couldn't tell if it was the rain or something else. I knew that Keith loved animals, and understood that this was just as hard for him as it was for me. "I'll take good care of him. Go now, and get out of the rain," he said.

I felt weak and pathetic, standing there crying in the rain, but I knew I wasn't going to try and stop him. I would go back to headquarters and have some coffee and complete the paperwork. I would go inside where it was warm and dry and look through the files to find any prior complaints from St. Bernard's about the white dog, and close them out. With the storm worsening, the chief would probably pull all the motor units off the street unless there was an emergency. I would likely end up working some overtime. The phones would be ringing off the hook. There would probably be more power outages with the way the storm was picking up. Such was the nature of this job: You were laughing one moment, crying the next, interspersed with periods of panic or the mundane. There would be much to do that night, with no time to think about the life and death of a white dog.

"Thanks, Keith," I said, managing to choke out the words as I took a deep breath and tried to control my emotions. He nodded at me and quickly turned away. I could see that he'd put on his game face. Police officers often have to notify families of the death of a loved one. They witness things on a daily basis that most people could never imagine. They have to make sure that their emotions are in check; otherwise, they wouldn't be able to put on their uniforms and do their jobs. An outsider might say that many cops seem cold and unfeeling, but that's the only way they can do what they do for a living. Sometimes during these routine "animal calls," I would see them react emotionally and let their guard down.

Keith slid into the driver's seat of my wagon and skidded up the muddy hill, the tires spinning and churning up chunks of wet grass and lots of mud. (Although significant damage had been done to the property—enough to require repairs—St. Bernard's never called headquarters to complain, and I never received a memo from the chief.)

One morning about a week later when I arrived at work, the leash I had lost on the muddy hill was sitting on my desk with a note attached from the night dispatcher: *Left at front desk for animal control officer, 1900 hours.*

It was spring before I found the time to return to the convent to see if there were any signs of the damage we'd done to the lawn that night. Before the incident with the white dog, I often stopped by near the grounds of St. Bernard's when I was passing through that part of the city to take a few moments to look out at the river and listen to the trains. It was a scary place in the damp dark days of winter, but come spring it was an entirely different atmosphere. It took several months for me to return because I still felt so badly about what had happened on that day during the storm. It was avoidance, perhaps they call it denial, whatever it was I just knew that it was quite a while before I felt comfortable enough to even get close to St. Bernard's. I parked over near some benches, not too close to the entrance. I didn't want to chance running into Mother Superior again.

I looked over at the convent. With the sun shining through the trees, the building looked less intimidating than I remembered. I had to admit, the location was perfect. They honestly had the best view of the Hudson in the city.

"Do you see him?" Startled, I turned to see a very frail, elderly nun standing next to me. She was so small and pale. I thought that she was probably the oldest person I had ever seen this close. Her skin seemed almost translucent, with spidery blue veins close to the surface. Her eyes, however, were bright and clear.

"See who?" I asked, thinking perhaps she meant the security guard or the groundskeeper.

"Snowball, our dog," she whispered, smiling conspiratorially. "Mother had him taken away a while ago. I couldn't imagine not seeing him every day; it brought me such sadness."

"I'm sorry," I said. "I didn't want to do it, but I had to . . ." The old nun put her finger up to stop me from talking and smiled.

"He's back," she whispered.

I started to say something, but stopped myself. It occurred to me in that moment that the important thing for me to do was listen.

"I prayed and prayed, and Our Lord answered my prayers. He is so clean now, and he can run again. He's even allowed me to get close to him sometimes." I looked at her and then followed her gaze;

she was looking down the hill that ran close to the river. The sunlight was bouncing off the water, almost sparkling. It was beautiful, but there was no white dog.

"You won't tell Mother, will you?" she asked, still smiling.

"No. I won't tell anyone," I said softly, finding myself smiling back at her.

"Bless you, dear," she said, and reached out for my hand, grasping it harder than I thought her capable of. She turned around and slowly made her way back to the building. I watched her walk away and then stood there for a few more minutes, even though I felt a little ridiculous, looking and hoping to see any sign of a white dog.

Glancing over to where my car had torn up the landscaping nine months before, I saw that the area I had damaged was now a perfect blanket of grass. There was no evidence that anything had ever happened there.

I thought of the elderly nun looking out over the hill, and the peaceful smile on her face as she told me about the return of the white dog. Looking up at the convent, it seemed much less gloomy than it had that day, in the driving rain. This place had once been a shelter. Regardless of how cruel they seemed now, the intentions of those who had worked with the orphans had been pure. They believed they were providing the only possible solution at the time for those children. Perhaps that was one of the reasons that the former children of the orphan trains returned to St. Bernard's: to see it as it is now, and not how it was in their memories.

A place where a tragedy had occurred in the middle of a dangerous storm was now nothing but a lovely grassy hill—a lovely spot for a picnic, or a place for someone to sit alone and gaze at the river.

It was a perfect place for a wild white dog to spend eternity.

The Few, the Proud, the Pekingese

"I don't want another phone call from these people. Leave that school crossing and get on up to Crompond Avenue, before that dog tears up the house again," Sergeant Bennett told me.

You could always tell when it was Sergeant Bennett's shift. He ran the department the same way he led his soldiers when he was in the Marines; he meant business. Everything ran smoother. No one hung around gossiping and drinking coffee, which had been known to happen once in a while on a quiet shift. There were fewer cops in the building doing paperwork, and more cops out on the road. The Records staff rarely came out of their office. Even the floor looked cleaner.

The good thing about Sgt. Bennett being a no-nonsense kind of person was that unlike some of the other sergeants, he wouldn't send me out on just any animal call that came in without first ascertaining whether or not it was the kind of problem that could be resolved quickly, without wasting time. Some animal calls required me to drive out to a location to take a complaint, where I'd have to listen to several opinions about the complaint before then driving out to a second location to deal with the actual problem. What could have taken ten minutes had now taken an hour. Sgt. Bennett was keen on time management. This meant he would sometimes screen my calls in an effort to make the best use of my time. He could tell when it was the type of complaint that was more about revenge than anything to do with animals. He could detect those like he had radar. However, if there was a real crisis involving an animal; he sent someone regardless of rank. Sometimes he even went himself. Unlike some, he took the job of animal control officer seriously, not only because he knew the real importance of having a service such as this available in a city of over 20,000 people within four square miles, but also because when he was younger, he had done this job himself.

He was the only sergeant in our department who knew the New York State agriculture & market laws like the back of his hand. Some members felt that animal calls were beneath them, and they would ignore them or put them off until I was on duty, sometimes resulting in some pretty serious situations. Also, the laws pertaining to animal complaints often differed from the common types of laws that the police enforced on a daily basis. What I did day in and day out was sort of a mystery to some. Not so for Sgt. Bennett, who took every call seriously. If there was a valid animal call that needed attention, he would send someone, whether it was a police officer or an animal control officer. Having Sgt. Bennett as the shift leader made everyone stand a little straighter—and knowing that he knew my job inside and out made me want to do it to the very best of my ability. When Sgt. Bennett was on the desk, you were in the marines.

"Ten-Four, Sarge; en route to 543 Crompond," I replied. I put my car in drive to get over to the other side of town from where I had been handling a school crossing.

At the first hint of cold weather, most of our school crossing guards would begin to call in sick. The colder it got, the sicker they became. So year after year, everyone from patrol officers, parking meter collectors, community service officers, and sometimes even parking attendants, was scheduled to sit at school crossings at one time or another, at least until the weather warmed up. It never failed to surprise me what miraculous recoveries were made at the onset of spring. Today, however, there was a nip in the air which meant that we were already short of crossing guards.

Officer Nick Catalano, my replacement, had just shown up.

"Ahh, a nice quiet school crossing," said Nick. "Now I can drink my coffee in peace while you get eaten alive by a ferocious poodle!"

"It's a Pekingese," I said.

"Same thing." Nick smiled at me and then took a big gulp of his coffee.

It was rare to get pulled off a school crossing for an animal call, but I knew the situation all too well, having been to this home several times. It wasn't a dangerous situation by any means. It was, however, an extremely loud experience that I wasn't looking forward to this early in the morning.

"I've had enough, I tell you, enough-a this dog. I am-a having her a-taken away . . . no more!" Mr. Bonerbo was adamant. The Bonerbos lived at the top of Crompond Avenue in a very large stone ranch. The house seemed to go on forever, and the landscaping appeared to be constantly in the process of being changed. Statues, fountains, and koi ponds abounded. It would have been almost like living in a Tuscan paradise were it not for the nonstop, never-ending screaming and yelling that went on in their family.

"Fine, fine . . . he-a bite me for the first and last time. Get him out-a here!" said Mr. Bonerbo. He was talking about their Pekingese, Rafael. Rafael seemed to fit in well with the family dynamic. I had been called to this house several times before when the dog had destroyed some new furniture, terrorized the landscapers (who practically lived there due to the perpetual redesigning of the yard), and now, finally, for biting the patriarch of the Bonerbo family.

"Could you sign this form so I can take Rafael with me?" I pushed the surrender slip across the marble counter toward Mr. Bonerbo. I was actually pretty lucky today. It was sometimes difficult to pin one of them down to talk to you. I would get a call to report to their home to take a complaint, and once I arrived there was nobody there to talk to. Sometimes I wondered if they called headquarters and by the time I got there, had already forgotten about it because they seemed to be in a constant state of movement, much like their landscaping. A door slammed, and another one of the Bonerbo men raced in.

"Why do you have-a this *polizia* car in back of mine. I have to go now," he said.

"She is-a here because I called her here, and she will leave when I say it's-a time. Do you hear me?" Mr. Bonerbo was starting to get red in the face as he yelled at his son . . . or his brother—I wasn't sure who was who in this large family. All I knew was that from the minute I arrived until the minute I left, the fighting would get louder and louder until I wanted to scream myself. At some point it would turn from English into Italian, and that's when I would usually make my getaway. This time, however, I was going to be taking Rafael with me—a dog that made this family seem peaceful in comparison.

"If you could just sign this form, then I'll take the dog right now. There is a surrender fee of ten dollars. And you should probably fill out a bite report, too."

"Fee, I will pay fee . . . I will pay, what you say, one hundred dollars—fine. No bite report, as-a you say . . . This go to State of New York, right?"

I opened my mouth to try and tell him it wasn't one hundred dollars, it was only ten, but before I could get a word in, he started talking again.

"The State of-a New York know too much about-a my business anyway. Just take-a the dog now before my wife comes back from—"

Mr. Bonerbo was interrupted by the loud slamming of a door. "Why, why, why you do this again, Antonio? You call the *polizia* for a little dog?" Mrs. Bonerbo had come home. She was holding a bag of groceries and she didn't look too happy at the moment, but then again, I couldn't remember any of them ever looking too happy.

"Look, Maria . . . look at my hand. This little beast bit a chunk of my hand!" He held out his hand to his wife. It seemed like more of a scrape to me. "Oh, Santa Maria," he went on. "What kind of animal does-a this to the hand that-a feeds him?"

Mrs. Bonerbo was consoling her husband, who had limped over to her so she could get a better look. I wondered what had happened to his foot.

"Um, I just need someone to sign this," I said. "It's not a hundred dollars . . . just ten." I was going to give it one more shot before leaving and coming back later. I didn't think they would miss me. I picked up my clipboard and took a step back away from the counter. All of the sudden, it was quiet.

"You can no leave!" Mr. Bonerbo was looking at me; Mrs. Bonerbo was holding his hand.

"No, you stay for lunch," agreed Mrs. Bonerbo. "You way too skinny. Stay . . . sit." She walked into the kitchen and started to unload the groceries.

"No, thank you. I mean, maybe another time," I said. "I really appreciate the invitation, but I, uh . . . I have an appointment." It was a bit early for lunch. I reached for my snare pole, thinking that the sooner I could get crazy Rafael out of the house, the sooner I could recover some of my hearing.

Mrs. Bonerbo grabbed my snare pole and leaned it against the wall. "Sit. It only take some small minutes. You take a sandwich with you. I make it now." Mrs. Bonerbo started slicing bread. I sat down on a stool next to the marble counter. I could hear a girl and a boy yelling at each other in the background. "Mind your own business!"—and then the response: "I'm telling! No . . . yes . . . okay, okay . . . just stop. Hey, that hurts!"

It seemed that there were several dramas going on at once. I wondered if the yelling stopped when everyone was sleeping. I wondered if anyone here actually slept.

I had some concerns about Rafael. First of all, if he was a habitual biter, then the shelter would not allow him to be adopted. No matter; my job at the moment was to get him out of this house. I stood up and started to look around for the little dog.

"Oh, don't worry about Rafael," said Mr. Bonerbo. "I had Salvatore put him in the car for you. He is-a one wild dog. It no safe for a little girl to do that kind of thing herself."

I smiled at Mr. Bonerbo. I was almost out of there, and with a sandwich to boot. I said my farewells, and with the sound of arguing still behind me, I approached my car and started to open the back hatch to slide the snare pole in. Rafael leaped out at the glass like a mad wolf. I quickly slammed the hatch just in time. Thank goodness for the metal grill that divided the backseat from the front! I was really going to need it today.

I carefully opened the driver's-side door and slid into the seat. I looked in the rearview mirror and saw Rafael, looking back at me. He was such a pretty Pekingese. It looked like he needed a little grooming, but his beautiful apricot coat was shiny and healthy. I had to stop myself from getting sidetracked. What I had in the backseat was not a fairly young purebred Pekingese, but the demon dog of the Bonerbo house. I started the car and began to drive.

Every time I glanced in the rearview mirror, Rafael was looking back at me. At a red light, I looked back at Rafael again. He was looking at me. Then the oddest thing happened: He started to wag his tail. I continued driving down to the riverfront, then up to where many of the city council members lived, in an expensive neighborhood commonly known as "Mortgage Hill." I looked in the rearview mirror again. Rafael looked back. If I hadn't known better, I would have sworn he was smiling at me.

I decided to conduct an experiment. I would take this dog on a quiet ride to the quietest place I knew. A few minutes later, I pulled into the park and drove to a shady spot under a tree, near the lake. I turned around and faced Rafael again. Rafael was sitting up now, wagging his tail a mile a minute. During our entire time in the car, this dog—who up till now I had never heard *not* barking—had not uttered a sound. I got out, opened the back door, and leaned in. I thought that perhaps I would try and get Rafael to come to me, maybe tempting him with a biscuit.

Before I could reach for the box of dog biscuits I kept in my car, Rafael trotted over to me and stood up on his hind legs, his tail wagging the whole time. He put one paw on my chest and then the other. I carefully picked him up and held him, a bit worried that the dog was warming up for the kill. Instead, Rafael put his head on my shoulder and wiggled a little closer. He licked my chin and snuggled back into my neck.

Rafael, the demon dog of Crompond Avenue, was nothing but a cuddle bug!

It occurred to me then that perhaps what this dog had needed all along was a place where there was no screaming and yelling twenty hours out of the day. Maybe the damage to the furniture and the bad behavior had been Rafael's way of saying "Get me out of here!" I decided I would forgo the ride down to the shelter and keep Rafael with me for the rest of the day, just to see what happened.

Rafael cried when I put him back in the rear of the wagon, so I moved him up next to me on the front seat, and there he stayed, his tail wagging happily while I went on with the necessary business of the day. I knew I would soon have to deal with the problem of explaining to Sgt. Bennett why I had spent the day with the wild Pekingese, and also, what I was planning to do with him. I hadn't figured that out yet.

Officer Lloyd was waiting for me in the parking lot. He and Sgt. Bennett had been friends for years; they were even hired at the same time. Just like Sgt. Bennett, Officer Lloyd was a stick-to-the-rules kind of guy. They had been working the same shift for over twenty years. If you found one of them, the other wasn't far behind.

"I've been thinking about you today, hon. What happened up at the Bonerbos' house?" asked Officer Lloyd. "You never radioed that you were en route to the shelter, so I was thinking maybe you'd been eaten by that ferocious dog of theirs?" He stood there, tall and thin, leaning on his car. He had that Irish grin on his face that usually meant he was up to something. Officer Lloyd hadn't been thinking about me; I was sure of that. He enjoyed knowing exactly what was happening on any given day, and in a city of four square miles, it was easy to keep track of the activities of the members of the department. The radio transmissions left nothing to the imagination, and if it was a particularly slow day, Officer Lloyd seemed to enjoy occupying himself by busting my chops. He had likely been watching me. He knew that I'd had the Pekingese with me all day. He knew I hadn't called out that I was en route out of the city limits to drive down to the shelter, and while many others wouldn't give it a second thought, not so Officer Lloyd. He didn't miss a thing, and now he was waiting to see me sweat it out as I tried to explain.

"Okay, this is what happened . . . Do you have a minute?" I said.

"Oh, yeah . . . I have a minute. Let's hear it." He really seemed to be enjoying this.

I opened the door of the car, and Rafael jumped into my arms. I turned and faced Officer Lloyd. "This dog is a victim of a bad home environment, that's all. He is not a bad dog; he was just miserable up there with all the constant yelling and shouting."

"Hmmm . . ." Officer Lloyd stopped leaning on the car and took a few steps toward me. "So what you're telling me is that this dog, the one we've received numerous phone calls about, is actually not a bad dog."

"Yes," I said. I turned Rafael to face Officer Lloyd. "He is a victim."

"So now you're a dog psychiatrist?" Officer Lloyd was smiling at me like I was the one in need of a psychiatrist. At that moment, my radio went off. The dispatcher said I had a complainant in the lobby, which meant I had to go inside and take a complaint, and I had to do it immediately.

"Okay, hon, tell you what—you go inside and take that complaint, and I'll keep an eye on this dog. Bennett won't like you bringing this dog inside, and I can't see you explaining this to him like you did to me. Let me handle this for a bit. Go ahead."

"Thank you," I said, handing Rafael over to Officer Lloyd. The dog continued to wag his tail. Officer Lloyd hadn't seemed too bothered about holding on to this dog for me. I couldn't remember the last time he had volunteered to help me with an animal in my custody. Actually, I couldn't remember *any* time he had offered to help me with an animal. Sure, he had picked up coffee and lunch for me a few times when I was stuck on a call. He had even driven by my apartment once toward the end of his midnight shift, shining the floodlight into my window and using the PA to shout "Wake up!" (although I thought that this had been more for his own amusement than anything else). Either way, at this moment I had no other choice but to trust him.

I turned and went inside to take my complaint. At least I didn't have to figure out what to say to Sgt. Bennett just yet. He was a by-the-book kind of guy, and this situation was anything but straight out of the book.

It was an average kind of complaint—just some neighborly disagreement over exactly what the term *Curb your dog* means . . . or more accurately, which curb. I promised to go and speak to the complainant's neighbor the next morning, making sure not to mention where the complaint had come from, and that seemed to be a reasonable solution to the problem. Most people really don't want to involve the police over things like this, but they don't know how to approach it themselves. Having a neutral party speak to the "offenders" usually solved the problem, and did no damage to the neighborly relationship. Much of my job—at least for the simpler complaints—was really just mediation.

I went back outside to get Rafael from Officer Lloyd, but they weren't there. I walked around the building, peered into his police car, and even crossed the street to check the parking garage. No Officer Lloyd and no Rafael anywhere. I went over to my car, grabbed my clipboard, and filled out the rest of my daily report. They must have gone inside. It was now or never. It was time for me to go inside headquarters and face the music.

Someone had gotten Rafael a bowl of water, and the little dog was happily lapping away. Sgt. Bennett crossed his arms and peered at me over his bifocals. This was not good.

"You know what you did now, don't you?" he asked.

"Um, yes . . . I think I do."

"You *think* you do. Well, that's good. I always encourage thought." He stopped looking at me and looked back down at Rafael. Nobody spoke for a moment.

Finally, I took a deep breath and began.

"I think that I took a dog with a history of being uncontrollable and a biter, and I didn't bring him down to the shelter like I was supposed to because I knew if I brought him there, he would be euthanized." I looked directly at Sgt. Bennett, waiting for his reaction. He nodded for me to continue.

"I also think that this is a perfectly safe and sweet little dog that would really do well in a quieter, less chaotic environment. That is what I think."

He kept looking at me for a moment, still peering at me over his glasses in an unsettling way. "So, you did what you thought you *should* do, not what you were *supposed* to do," Sgt. Bennett said. "You did not perform your duties within the guidelines of the existing law, given the responsibilities of your position. Am I correct in this assumption?"

I swallowed, making sure not to break eye contact. It was really difficult. "Yes, sir."

"Well, then." Sgt. Bennett leaned down and scratched Rafael behind the ear. The dog's tail started to wag like crazy. It was quiet save for the sound of Rafael lapping up the water.

"He's not as smart as my dog, you know. I had a Border collie for years. Smartest dog on the planet. There will never be another like him."

"Yes, sir."

"Somebody threw that dog out on the road, just dumped him off. I don't like to think what could have happened to him if I hadn't found him when I did."

"Yes, sir."

Sgt. Bennett stood up to his full height and once again crossed his arms. He looked at me for a minute, which seemed like an hour, and then asked, "Do you understand the ramifications of your decision?"

"No, sir. Not yet," I responded. I had started to worry that I was going to get in trouble, but something in his voice had changed. I wasn't so sure anymore.

"Officer Lloyd is now on the phone with his wife. Due to your actions today, this dog will be going home with Officer Lloyd to be spoiled by his wife, and even though he would never admit it, by him as well."

I hadn't moved yet; I wasn't sure this was really happening. Officer Lloyd and his wife had lived alone in their house since their youngest son had gone off to college. He often commented on how quiet it was around his house. Too quiet.

"Your shift is over, Officer Duffy. You can go home now." Sgt. Bennett removed his glasses and put them in their case. "You can return the surrender fee to the Bonerbos tomorrow. I will leave it up to you to decide what to tell them."

"Yes, sir," I replied.

He turned to pick up his briefcase and go home.

Officer Lloyd came up from downstairs, dressed in plain clothes, and scooped up Rafael like he had known him since puppyhood. "Time to go home, puppy—have some treats," and then he looked up, surprised to see us standing there, looking at him.

"I'm just trying to, you know, get him used to the way my wife will talk to him."

"Oh yeah, of course," laughed Sgt. Bennett.

Officer Lloyd looked at Sgt. Bennett. "Oh, give me a break, Bob."

"Okay, Joe. Why don't you go home and have some treats yourself?"

Officer Lloyd started walking toward the exit, saying, "Real funny. Ha ha ha." He stopped right before he reached the door and turned around to look at me. "This is all your fault, you know."

I smiled at him and said, "Yes, I know."

He smiled back and then carefully opened the door with one arm, holding a sleepy Rafael in the other.

Sgt. Bennett gave me a nod, and held the door open for me. We walked out the door together. Standing there in silence, waiting for the light to turn red so we could cross the street, he said, "You'll sleep better tonight now, won't you?"

"Yes, sir," I answered.

"Me, too," he said.

I watched Sgt. Bennett cross the street, every crease in his uniform as sharp as it was when he'd arrived that morning. He was a former Marine. He ran the department by the book.

And he also ran it by his heart.

Rescued by Love

On most days you could find him sitting on the wall in front of Saint Mary's Church next to the sign that read SAINT MARY'S—A CHURCH FOR EVERYONE. No doubt the pastor had meant to attract a larger membership with this billboard invitation, but I'm not sure he was prepared for Bobby. A towering six-footer, weighing in at over 250 pounds, Bobby was, at thirty-something, a very large child.

He had lived in Annesville for as long as I could remember. When I was a child, I always saw him around town. Sometimes I had even been a little scared of him. He could be friendly and outgoing one minute, and the next thing you knew he was cursing and yelling at you for no apparent reason. As I grew older I learned that this was just his way. A lot of people were like that, but since he spent his life on the streets, he was just more visible than others. On his good days, Bobby was like the city's official greeter. He spent most of his time waving and smiling at the people driving by, and shouting "Hey, pal!" to those he recognized.

Bobby called me Goldilocks. He knew me because, as the police department's animal control officer, I was as visible around town as he was. My regular duties were to uphold the leash law, patrol for loose dogs, and issue tickets. Bobby had appointed himself my unpaid assistant, and he took his job seriously. One time he found a litter of newborn kittens in a garbage can and made it his job

*Originally published in condensed form in *Chicken Soup for the Cat & Dog Lover's Soul* ©1999.

to find a home for all of them—including the last one, which, at his insistence, I ended up taking home myself.

Another time he waved me down in traffic, ran over to the patrol car, and banged on the hood. "Hey, Goldilocks, there's a big dog up the street gonna get hit by a car! You gotta go get 'im, now!"

I think Bobby had been responsible for saving more than a few dogs from meeting with disaster. That was why I decided that he should have his own leash. If he was going to be the deputy animal control officer, it was the least I could do.

"Which color do you like?" I asked, while holding out an array of leashes. I had just come from the pet store where the chief had given me money out of petty cash to resupply my leash inventory. Due to the nature of my job, I went through them pretty quickly. "Hey, this is great. Thanks, Goldilocks!" Bobby looked like I had offered him a million dollars. As difficult as he could be sometimes, there was something really innocent about him.

"Red. I pick the red one." I handed him the red leash, and he examined it carefully. I looked at his hands while he was running it through his fingers. The backs of his hands were covered with small, circular scars. Perfectly round. Perfectly intentional. I had always wondered why Bobby had chosen to live most of his life on the streets of Annesville. Something about those scars answered my question.

Having found the leash acceptable, Bobby put it in his pocket. He started chewing on his lip, thinking hard about something. "Goldilocks, do you know stuff about hamsters?"

"Not really, Bobby." I said. "I'm sorry. Why? Do you have a hamster?"

A slow smile crept across his face. "Yeah."

"Where are you keeping it?" I asked. As far as I knew, Bobby spent his time moving around between a variety of places. He had a few relatives he would live with off and on, mostly off. I knew for a fact that he had been thrown out of more than one group home. I wondered where he could be staying that would allow him to keep a hamster cage.

Still smiling, Bobby reached his hand into his jacket pocket and pulled out a tiny brown-and-white hamster. "His name is McClusky. I named him after Mr. McClusky." McClusky's was a market in the middle of town. I had noticed that Bobby's jacket had MCCLUSKY'S MARKET—SERVING YOU SINCE 1945 emblazoned across the back. I made a mental note to myself to make sure I gave McClusky more of my business.

At first I had loved being the dog catcher, but as time went by, the job began to get me down. It wasn't the animals; it was the people. I dreaded having to deal with negligent owners—especially those who no longer wanted their dogs. In our town the city provided a dog-surrender service with the local animal shelter. For a ten-dollar fee, I'd pick up a dog whose owner could no longer keep him, and, more important, I'd collect information about him (good with children, medical history, favorite toys, etc.) that would make it easier for him to be adopted.

Unbelievably, sometimes the people most capable of paying this fee chose not to, abandoning the dog to be picked up as a stray instead. They gave up their best opportunity to increase the dog's chances of finding another home, just to save a measly ten dollars. There had been times when people had purposely let their dogs run loose, in hopes that I would pick them up and do their dirty work for them.

I knew that there were many people who struggled to take care of their pets, whether it was finding the money to pay for medication to extend the life of their animal (even if only for a little while), or even to buy food. Those were rarely the people who tried to manipulate the system. What was really disheartening were those people who considered their dogs to be toys that had outgrown their use. Several times I went to pick up a surrendered dog who the people claimed was a stray. Sometimes they didn't even bother to hide the dog's bowl. I wasn't angry that they were insulting my intelligence, or even that they were trying to pull the wool over my eyes just to avoid spending ten dollars. What would bother me for days was the memory of driving away from their beautiful, expensive homes and perfectly manicured lawns, while their dog cried and howled in the back of my car, watching the only home he had ever known grow smaller in the distance. At first I felt crushed by this kind of behavior, but as time passed I toughened up. Lately, I had become so cynical, I was afraid of what was happening to me.

One October when the nights were already dropping below freezing, it occurred to me that I hadn't seen Bobby for a while. During the cold-weather months, Bobby usually spent his nights at the Salvation Army shelter, so I stopped by and asked about him. No one had seen him. I looked at the phone call log at headquarters to see if he had been making his usual calls to report animals, or sometimes, just to talk. No calls were recorded.

"Will," I said, "can I ask you something?" Will, the senior dispatcher, was busy typing up complaints. I was always impressed by the speed at which he did this. The only problem was that he really didn't like being interrupted. I knew I was taking a big risk. He sighed dramatically and looked up at me.

"Yesss! What can I do for you, Officer Duffy, who should be outside doing her job and not in here bothering me?" Will was tough . . . on the outside. His bark was worse than his bite.

"Wow! How did you get all that out without taking a breath?" I said, smiling. Will crossed his arms and leaned back in his chair, glaring at me. "Okay, Will, I'm sorry to bother you, but I need to know if Bobby has called here anytime in the last few weeks. I haven't seen him anywhere, and that's not normal."

Will rolled his eyes. "There's nothing normal about that guy. But go ahead, go look at the logs. I can't stop you," he said, returning to his typing.

"I already did that," I said quietly.

Will spun back around in his chair to face me again. "Well, then, I guess he hasn't called. Maybe he started yelling and carrying on at the group home again. They've kicked him out a bunch of times for that."

The phone rang and Will grabbed it on the first ring, whipped the report he was working on out of the typewriter, and slid in a new sheet, almost simultaneously. If there was such a thing as a dispatcher decathlon, Will would get a gold medal.

"ACO!" Will shouted at me as I went to get my jacket. I looked back. Will put his hand over the mouthpiece and said, "If he calls, I'll put a note in your mailbox."

"Thanks, I appreciate that." I walked over to the door to go back outside.

"I'll just address it to Bleedin' Heart, the dog warden!" Will called after me.

About a week later, I got a call at headquarters. It was Will's first shift back on days. I was getting ready to go cover a school crossing, but before I could leave, Will snapped his fingers to get my attention. "Lisa, it's him. I'll put it through on the sergeant's desk." I hurried over to pick up the phone.

"Goldilocks," he rasped, "I need you to come." It was Bobby. He sounded like he had a bad cold.

"Bobby! Where are you? Everyone's been looking for you!" I looked up to see Will and a few of the officers watching me. I heard someone get shushed. "Shall I speak up?" I asked loudly, for their benefit. Everyone suddenly became busy, except for Officer Farrell, who smiled and nodded yes.

"Bobby, where have you been? You don't sound good."

"I'm okay. I'm out in back of the chair factory. Just come now."

Within a few minutes, I was turning the car off the main street onto a gravel road behind the old chair factory. The road stopped abruptly, and I found myself in a large field strewn with debris, in the middle of which sat a rusting station wagon on cement blocks. I approached the car, my shoes crunching with each step in the frozen grass. I bent over and knocked lightly on the passenger window. Bobby was curled up tightly in the front seat with his windbreaker thrown over him. Lying next to him was a chocolate Labrador puppy with long gangly legs and ears that he had yet to grow into. The dog looked up at my knock with bright eyes and a thumping tail. I peered in to get a closer look. The front of the car was filled with empty Styrofoam cups and potato-chip bags. The back of the wagon was covered in soft blankets. Neatly stacked boxes of dog biscuits and a bag of dog food were lined up next to two jugs of bottled water and two chewed rubber balls. A worn-out red leash lay next to them.

"Bobby, are you okay?"

His eyes fluttered open. "Goldilocks," he croaked. He struggled to sit up and get his bearings. He looked at me and I could see his nose was red and his eyes bleary. He untangled himself and climbed from the car, wincing as he stood.

"Come on with me, Bobby. Get in the patrol car and I'll bring you to the Salvation Army, or the hospital. Okay? It's warm there," I urged.

"No, I'm okay. Social Services says I'm gonna lose my check if I don't go into housing. You gotta take Brownie."

It was true. I couldn't think of a single facility that would allow him to keep his dog. He was only out here in the cold because the Salvation Army didn't allow pets. He started unloading the puppy's supplies and carrying them over to the patrol car. Brownie watched every move he made with adoring eyes. I grabbed a jug of water out of the car and started to give him a hand, feeling helpless all the same.

Everything was packed up, except for Brownie. Bobby knelt down and put his hands on each side of the puppy's head. They looked at each other for a long moment, and then Brownie started to lick Bobby's face. In one quick movement, the man picked him up and placed him gently in the front seat of the patrol car. He turned to me, his eyes even redder than before. "Here," he said, handing me a ten-dollar bill. "For the dog pound." I stared openmouthed at the money. I couldn't believe it. Bobby was paying the surrender fee, even though it was probably all the money he had in the world.

I put out my hand and touched his arm. "Bobby, don't worry about the fee. They'll understand."

He looked at me. "No, Goldilocks. You told me ten dollars to get a good home, 'member? A home with a kid to play with would be good for Brownie." He turned from me suddenly and started to walk back toward the rusty station wagon. I knew better than to try to convince him to come with me. He had a mind of his own and treasured his independence, often at the expense of his health and safety.

"Bobby! I'll find him a great home," I called after him, my voice catching in my throat. He made a noise, but didn't turn around. As I drove away, Brownie put his muzzle on my lap and fell asleep. There were times I couldn't see the road through my tears.

Brownie was taken home that evening by a police officer who fell in love with him the moment he saw me carry him into the precinct. A year later his Christmas photos featured his little boy and Brownie sitting together in front of a fireplace. Everything that Bobby had wished for Brownie had come true. I tried to return Bobby's money, but the abandoned station wagon was always empty. Later, I heard that he had gone to a group home in another city and was doing fine. Not being able to return Bobby's money, I did what I considered the next best thing: I dropped the ten-dollar bill into the Salvation Army donation box.

I missed Bobby, and wished I could have told my trusty assistant what a wonderful job he'd done. He had rescued cats and dogs—and my faith in people, too.

The Lions of Bear Mountain

"Where is the animal?" I asked, peering through the haze that obscured my vision. Squinting, I attempted to focus on the woman in the doorway who had made the call, my eyes watery from a bad cold.

"Where is the *what*?" the woman asked me while she tried to balance the phone on her shoulder, a mug of coffee in one hand, and an *Architectural Digest* magazine in the other. She didn't have any hands left to hold the door open.

"Where—is—the—an-i-mal—you—called—about?" I asked again. This time, I made sure to enunciate each word carefully.

"Oh . . . it sounded like you asked 'Where is Deanamo?' There's no one named Deanamo here." She looked me up and down, taking in the uniform. I was starting to wonder if she even remembered calling the police station.

"I know. I have a cold. It's difficult to talk," I said, trying to dig around in my pocket for a tissue. "You called us about a wild animal in your garage?"

"Oh, yeah. Come in," she said, while letting the door go. I caught it with the tip of my shoe, but not until after it had slammed into my shoulder. "Ow," I said loudly. The woman had begun talking, but wasn't facing in my direction anymore, thus missing my injury. I followed her into the kitchen where she continued talking, although I wasn't sure it was to me because she wasn't looking in my direction. "So anyway, I told Aaron to take the trash out, you know, put it out in the trash can that we keep out in, you know, in the . . ."

"Garage?" I suggested, trying to accelerate the discussion while she paced around in the kitchen, opening and closing drawers and rambling on. Stopping abruptly and looking at me, she hesitated, and stood there for a moment like she had forgotten why I was there. "You want to see the garage?" she asked.

"No—I mean, yes . . . I don't know. Is the animal in the garage?" I was starting to feel like I'd had enough of this woman. My head was pounding, and I wasn't sure if it was just due to a cold anymore.

"Yes, it's trapped in there, in the trash can. I could hear it all night, scratching and making a racket." She stopped looking in drawers and turned to stare at the door to the garage.

"Okay, then, let's have a look." I started to walk over to the door, anxious to solve her problem and be on my way. I was thinking that after this call, I should probably stop somewhere to pick up some cold medicine.

"No! You can't open the door from in here! What if it's one of those mountain lions?! It could get in the house!" I looked at her carefully for a minute, trying to sense if she was kidding around or not. She was totally serious.

"We don't have any mountain lions around here that I know of, ma'am. If you just open the garage door for me, I can find out what kind of animal is in there. It's probably a stray cat or a raccoon or something."

"Oh, it's much bigger than that. It sounded like a very large animal, maybe a bear. It could be a bear. Don't you have to call for backup or something?"

"This is a small city, ma'am. It's not the type of place you would usually find bears. We're not even near any woods or mountains."

"Yes, we are," she said, folding her arms in front of her chest, then changing her mind and putting her hands on her hips. "We live right next to Bear Mountain."

"You must be thinking of the Bear Mountain Extension, off Bear Mountain Parkway, the highway that passes through the city."

"Yes, right off of Bear Mountain. Where bears live."

I sighed. All I wanted was to find out what was in the garage, get rid of it, and have her sign off on the complaint. Bear Mountain did indeed exist; however, it was clear across the river, and the only bears that lived there resided in a small zoo. I thought of mentioning this, but there are times when losing an argument really means you've won. This was one of those times.

"Well, why don't I go into the garage and find out exactly what kind of animal is in there?"

She didn't seem too happy about her victory; if anything, she seemed even more agitated than before. "I don't know why Aaron talked me into moving all the way up here in the country. This kind of thing never happened in the city."

"You know what I can do? I can just go outside and go through the garage . . ." I started to edge over to the front door.

"Aaron and I argued about moving upstate. I told him that it was too dangerous." She seemed to be getting even more frantic, and began pacing back and forth. I had the feeling that she was no longer listening to me.

"We're only like thirty minutes north of New York City," I said, trying not to sound as aggravated as I was feeling. "It's not really upstate. It may be a possum or something. Can you let me in the garage from outside?" I sneezed.

"You sound like you have a cold," she said, taking a break for a moment from her fear of mountain animals.

"I do," I said.

"You do what?" she asked.

"I do have a cold. I need you to open the garage," I said.

"Can you do it?" she asked in a shaky voice.

"Yes, I suppose so. Is there a garage door opener?"

"Yes," she said. "I'll go get it."

She started racing around the kitchen again, opening and closing drawers. Finally, she looked behind her and grabbed a bunch of keys off the counter.

I followed her outside and over to a car in the driveway. She opened the driver's-side door and crawled inside. She seemed to be looking under the seat. I stood in the driveway watching the car's lights go on and off. A stream of windshield wiper fluid shot up from the car. The horn honked. Finally, she got out of the car with a garage door opener in her hand.

"Here it is," she said, waving it in the air. I felt like letting out a small cheer, but stopped, silently reminding myself that I was a civil servant, and sarcasm wasn't part of my job description. I knew that part of the reason I was cranky was because I felt so rotten, although this particular complainant wasn't making things any easier.

Slowly she aimed the garage door opener at the garage. She carefully pressed the button, and you could hear the motor kick on. The door started to open. I made my way into the garage and went over to a group of trash cans. This was one of the neatest garages I had ever seen. A counter connected to the wall. Shelves lined the walls, and next to the trash cans was a workbench, also connected to the wall. The trash cans seemed to be color-coordinated to match the workbench counter. There was not a tool in sight, and it looked like the only work ever done on this surface might have been the use of paper towels to clean it. I could hear some faint scratching from one of the cans. I lightly stepped on the pedal that opened the lid and peered over the top. It was with little surprise that I saw a baby skunk looking back up at me. I backed away from the trash can and turned to tell the woman that it was not a mountain lion or a bear, but she was nowhere to be found.

"Hello," I called out.

I heard a quick blast of a horn and noticed that she was sitting in the car. She rolled down the window and stuck her head out. "Is it a bear?"

"No, it's a—"

"It's a mountain lion!"

"No, it's a baby skunk. He must have gotten in your garage when it was open and somehow fell off your workbench and into the trash can."

"Oh my God! Oh my God! How are you going to get it out of there?!" She seemed really upset by the baby skunk. I wondered what she would have done if it *had* been a bear or a mountain lion. I sort of wished it had been.

"You should call for backup! Maybe the fire department has some equipment for this. I knew moving up here was a bad idea. Oh my God, of all things!"

While she continued to rant and cry, I walked back over to the trash can and slowly tipped it over on its side. The tiny skunk walked out of the can, out of the garage, and over to the yard where it waddled off into the distance.

I walked over to the car. The woman was digging through the glove box, still muttering to herself. I heard the words *upstate* and *skunk*. The rest was unintelligible. I waited for a moment and then knocked lightly on the window. She jumped up, startled.

"Where is it? Did you capture it?"

"It's gone—probably went back to where it came from. Everything's okay now. Can you sign this complaint form, please?"

She got out of the car, straightened her shirt, and ran her fingers through her hair. "Sure . . . um . . . thanks. Wait!" She had been reaching for the pen, but suddenly turned and crawled back into her car where she started digging once again for something in the backseat.

"Ma'am, what are you doing? I have a pen right here." I knew now that when I'd thought this was going to be an easy call, I had been incredibly mistaken. I should've expected this. I was surprised to find that I was no longer aggravated or frustrated. I was somewhere beyond that. Maybe I had found that state of mind that Buddhists seek. Maybe I had a high fever and was starting to hallucinate. I sneezed again and started to look in my other pocket for a tissue.

"Here it is!" The woman had climbed out of the car and was standing in front of me. She even looked like she might have been smiling, but I wasn't sure. She was too blurry.

"You could have used my pen," I said, handing her the clipboard and pointing to the signature line. "If you could please sign here . . ."

"Oh, I wasn't looking for a pen. I was looking for this." She thrust her arm out in my direction. I jumped back, startled. Perhaps this was it, the day when a crazed citizen ends it all. If only I had taken a sick day.

"Tissues. You need tissues. I always keep little packets of them in my car for my allergies." She shook the packet at me as I squinted to make it out. "Thank you." I said quietly.

She took my pen and signed the complaint form. "You're welcome. Like I said, I always keep tissues around because of my allergies. They're much worse now that we moved all the way up here to the boondocks."

"Yes, they must be," I said, while in the distance I could hear a siren, highway traffic, and the tinkling music of an ice cream truck.

"You should probably leave your garage doors closed when you're not using them, so this won't happen again," I said. "And so you won't have to have me come over and disrupt your routine again anytime soon."

"Yeah, that's for sure. I, um, need to get back to . . . finish my . . ." She looked over to her house, and I realized that there probably wasn't anything she had to get back to.

"Have a nice day," I said, and nodded at her as I turned to walk back to my car. I went to open the driver's-side door and looked down at the pack of tissues in my hand.

"Ma'am," I called over to her. The woman was picking a lone dandelion off her lawn. She looked up. "Yeah?" she asked.

"We're having our annual ten-K run on Saturday. It starts at nine a.m., and afterwards there's a street fair downtown. It's a lot of fun. Sometimes I help give out water to the runners. They're always looking for help."

She looked at me, thinking.

"Free T-shirts for volunteers," I added.

"A real old-fashioned country fair?" she asked.

"Not really . . . um, yeah . . . sure," I answered.

She stood there in her driveway, a hint of a smile starting to form on her face. "Okay. Yeah. That sounds like fun. I'll bring Aaron too."

"Great. Just go over to the parking lot near the bank. That's where the volunteers meet."

I walked back over to my car and got in. I started the car and looked over to the house. She was standing on the front lawn, smiling and waving at me. I waved back, and before I put the car in gear, I opened the packet of tissues and took out a few, starting to put the rest in my pocket. Deciding against it, I opened the glove compartment and dropped them in. This way I would always know where they were when I needed them.

Knowing where things are makes life a lot easier, and sometimes, finding out where things are makes life a lot happier. It can make the difference between a place where you live, and a place that you can call home.

He Who Barks Last

"Listen to this!" he said as he slammed down a cassette player on the counter in the main lobby of the police department. This was not, by any means, Mr. O'Connell's first complaint about excessive barking on his street.

"I know there's a law against this—don't think I'm not aware of it!"

Mr. O'Connell knew a lot. He knew that the city ordinance stated that "anything in excess of ten minutes of consecutive barking" meant a ticket and a fine to the owner of the dog responsible for the barking. He also knew which dog was doing the barking, and, most important, whom that dog belonged to. It was his neighbor, or more aptly, his nemesis, Mr. Fred Riley.

He looked at me over the counter, where I had slid open the glass panel to take his complaint. Seeing that he had my full attention at last—not to mention the attention of the entire dispatch room, the people waiting in the lobby, and Daryl, the day janitor, who was leaning on his mop, waiting to see what would happen next—he hit the PLAY button on the tape recorder. The sounds of barking filled the lobby. Mr. O'Connell glared at me the entire time the barking played, which was probably about a minute even though it seemed a lot longer.

"Highly unusual, isn't it?" he said after he had hit the STOP button.

"How is it unusual?" I asked.

"Can't you see what he's doing?" he shouted, leaning in toward me, obviously irritated at my question.

"Barking?" I asked.

"Now, Missy, you listen here!" Mr. O'Connell started shaking his fist at me.

"Okay, that's enough of that!" said Sergeant Freeman, getting up from behind the sergeant's desk and approaching the counter. "There's no reason for yelling at our ACO. If you want some help with your problem, then you'd better settle down."

Sgt. Freeman looked like a peaceful kind of guy when he was sitting behind the desk. But once he stood up and revealed his full height of six feet, four inches, he made another impression entirely.

Mr. O'Connell seemed to step back a moment, but then he started wagging his finger at Sgt. Freeman. "Listen, Billy, I knew your father, and *he* would have done something about this! He wouldn't have played politics with this kind of noise. Why, he—"

"*Mr. O'Connell!*" Sgt. Freeman shouted. He was starting to look very angry, which made Daryl stop leaning on his mop and get to work on the lobby floor. The spectators in the lobby suddenly found something interesting to look for in their purses and newspapers, and I visibly winced, because Sgt. Freeman had projected his very angry voice almost directly into my ear.

Sgt. Freeman took a slow breath in, and then blew it out slowly. He turned to look at me. "I'm sorry. Are you okay?"

"What?" I said, feigning deafness.

He rolled his eyes; he was used to me. He turned back to Mr. O'Connell. "Mr. O'Connell," he said again—however, this time he spoke a lot more softly. "I know you knew my dad, but you see, I knew my dad, too. He would have tried to resolve your problem within the letter of the law, without any favoritism or politics, just like I'm trying to do. The problem is," Sgt. Freeman added, "we have been down this road a hundred times before, and I'm starting to think that this is not about a barking dog. This is about hating Fred Riley."

Patrick O'Connell had lived on Constant Avenue for most of his adult life. Unfortunately, for that entire time, so had Fred Riley. They lived side by side in almost identical houses—older, two-story homes, built in the early 1900s but separated by an eight-foot fence. The story was that while their wives had always been friendly, and their children had played together, the two men had never seen eye to eye on anything—especially politics. Patrick O'Connell was a staunch Republican, and Fred Riley was a lifelong Democrat. If Mr. Riley parked his car on the road, Mr. O'Connell would be the first to call in the morning to complain that he was violating the opposite-side-of-the-street parking rules that went into effect at 6:00 AM. Sometimes he would call at 6:01.

Mr. Riley would call on the Fourth of July to complain that Mr. O'Connell's barbecue grill was generating too much smoke. Mr. O'Connell would call on Halloween and complain that Mr. Riley was sending "hooligans" over to harass him when kids came over to trick-or-treat. Both of them would call the station and complain that they couldn't hear their individual television shows over the barking of each other's dogs.

Sometimes the complaints were valid. One or the other would periodically block the other's driveway with their car, "accidentally" pick up each other's newspaper, and shovel the snow off of their sidewalks by flinging it onto each other's property. During election years, they would take each other's political signs off their front lawns. It seemed to be a seasonal type of mutual harassment, with different types of antagonism depending on the time of year. The barking complaints, however, were always the same. The animal control officer before me had actually warned me about the two men, even giving me a list of what she thought were their top-ten favorite complaints about each other. *Barking dog* was at the top of the list.

I used to wonder if the only reason those two kept dogs as pets was just to bother each other. Once they had both retired, it seemed they finally had all the time they needed to buckle down and begin new, full-time careers of driving each other crazy.

"Oh, so that's how it's going to be," said Mr. O'Connell, raising one bushy eyebrow.

I nodded at Sgt. Freeman to let him know I could take it from here. "Mr. O'Connell," I began, "I have investigated this barking complaint several times. I've sat outside your house every time you called, to listen. Yes, Mr. Riley's dog barks, but not excessively, and even though he's not in violation of the barking code, I have still spoken to him about it and asked him to be more aware of the situation, just as I have spoken to you about *his* complaints regarding *your* dog. There's not much else I can do."

He leaned in and began to question me. "Have you ever timed how long that infernal noise goes on?"

"Yes. I have a stopwatch for that very purpose. The longest was perhaps a minute and a half."

"Do you realize that this barking is going on at all hours of the day and night, not just during your workday?"

"I've come in early to sit in front of your house," I said. "I've stayed late to sit in front of your house. I've switched shifts to the four to twelve and the twelve to eight, just so I can sit in front of your house and time the barking."

"Have you questioned other witnesses?"

I could tell Sgt. Freeman was getting frustrated at this point.

"There are no other witnesses," I said. "I've spoken to every homeowner on your block, including the folks who live directly behind you and Mr. Riley. No one else has ever heard long periods of barking."

"What about this tape? What about that?"

Sgt. Freeman sighed and looked over at the stacks of paper sitting on his desk, waiting for him. He looked back at Mr. O'Connell. "Pat, c'mon—that could be any dog, anywhere. You could have taped that off the television for all I know. There's no way you can prove that this barking came from Fred Riley's dog."

"Hmmph," Mr. O'Connell grumbled. I thought he was starting to see that he wasn't going to win this battle. Then, he stood up straight and smiled, and I knew he was going in for the kill. "From my reading of the City Municipal Code, I understand that I can bring a complaint against the defendant by making you take my complaint by deposition." He stood up even taller and beamed. He knew he had a point. Apparently, one of the TV shows he had been able to hear above all that barking was *Matlock*.

I occasionally took depositions for violations of the municipal code; however, in most situations, any tickets I wrote had to be based upon my direct observation, especially code violations. Dangerous dog complaints or more serious and repeat infractions were another story. The reason we had tried to limit the taking of depositions in these types of complaints was standing right in front of me. People who hated each other would take any opportunity to make trouble for each other. That was often the problem with dog complaints; people sometimes used them as a tool to make life difficult for each other. It ate up time that could have been better spent upholding the law and helping others. I had dealt with people who had actually let their neighbor's dogs off their chains, enticed them with dog biscuits, and then turned around and called the police, complaining that there was a loose dog on their property.

One time, someone went into the mayor's yard and did exactly that. It seemed that he were angry about a policy the city council had initiated, and which the mayor had supported. This person wanted to make it seem like the mayor thought he was better than everyone else by ignoring the leash law. The poor dog hadn't had much experience running loose before, so he merely walked over to the curb in front of his house and sat down, waiting for someone to come get him. He probably would have gone back into the yard of his own accord had there not been a chain-link fence with a gate, keeping him out.

"Go ahead, Lisa . . . I want you to give me a ticket," said the mayor when I went to see him in his office at City Hall. He was one of the nicest people I have ever known, and it was a rare sight to see him sitting still—he was always so busy running all over the city. He was also a teacher at the high school and remembered me from there, as well, although I had never been in his class. (He taught the more advanced math classes, and long division was my limit; anything more complicated than that wasn't my concern. That's what calculators are for!)

"Mr. Johnson, I can't give you a ticket," I said.

"No, really, Lisa . . . please give me a ticket. I don't want anyone to think it's favoritism. Really, it's okay. I want one."

The mayor of the city that employed me was begging me to give him a ticket. Talk about an awkward situation!

"Mr. Johnson, it's not that. I mean . . . I wouldn't give a ticket to anyone in this situation. Someone trespassed onto your property, unchained your dog, led him out of your fenced-in yard, and then, your dog didn't even run loose. He just sat in front of your house until we called you and you went home and let him back in. I, um, really don't think *you* are the one who deserves a ticket."

"Oh," he said. "I guess you have a point."

This was probably the most unusual discussion I had ever had in City Hall, and even though I really admired Mr. Johnson, I wanted to get out of there and get back to work. Even though I had done nothing wrong, being there felt like the equivalent of being called to the principal's office and having the principal say, "Oh, I just wanted to say hi and see how you liked the sloppy joes at lunch today." You would still want to get out of there as quickly as possible. It was just the nature of the thing.

By requesting to write out a deposition, Mr. O'Connell had played his trump card. Even though this barking complaint had, through the years, required many hours of manpower just to prove that it was *not* a valid complaint, I knew that Mr. O'Connell was within his rights. If he wanted to sign a deposition against Mr. Riley, I would have to take it. I would have to serve Mr. Riley with a summons. He would refuse a fine and ask for a court date. It wouldn't be the first time. However, even though they had both sued each other for several reasons over the years, this would be the first time that they'd be able to get the city, and me, to do their dirty work for them.

Sgt. Freeman looked at me and shook his head. "Just take his deposition." He went back to his desk and sat down.

Guy, the day dispatcher, put his hand over the phone and called over to Sgt. Freeman. "Sarge, this lady wants to know if there is some law prohibiting people who, uh, are too, um . . . plump . . . from wearing two-piece bathing suits at the park's public pool. Do you wanna take this?"

Sgt. Freeman stood up, put on his hat, and said, "I'm going to lunch. I'll be available on radio," and walked out the door.

I looked back at Mr. O'Connell. "I'll be right with you, Mr. O'Connell. Just wait at that door and I'll let you in." Mr. O'Connell picked up his tape recorder and tucked it under his arm. He then pulled a notepad out of his back pocket and began flipping through the pages. He looked over at Guy and grinned.

"My notes," he said.

I went over to the file cabinet behind the dispatch desk and pulled out the forms I would need. Guy answered the phone on the first ring.

"Police Department—Wells," he said. Then, turning to me and putting his hand over the mouthpiece, his eyes sparkling, he said, "I don't expect you'll be taking your lunch now too?" Considering that this was a professional workplace, I responded to him in the way that was to be expected in a situation like this. I stuck my tongue out at him. Then I went off to sit with Mr. O'Connell to take his deposition.

The day had arrived. The docket had been crowded, and the court-room was packed with people, all waiting to have their say about a variety of issues. A drug raid had netted a large group of prisoners who were awaiting indictments, which also pushed us further back. On top of that, it seemed like the air-conditioning wasn't function-ing at full capacity.

Mr. Riley and Mr. O'Connell had both shown up early, each of them carrying briefcases. I didn't even want to imagine what they were carrying in them. They were seated on opposite sides of the courtroom and glared at each other from time to time. Appearing in court was not one of my favorite aspects of the job. I liked to think that I was helping animals and the people who cared about them, and also helping to prevent the abuse of animals. Being in court made me feel more like I was being used as a pawn in a decades-old feud; sort of like the Hatfields and McCoys, with a canine twist.

It was obvious that the court was going to have to break for lunch before my famous barking case was going to be heard. Don, the court officer, came over to me. "You should probably tell those two to go and get a bite to eat and come back. There's no chance that their case will come before the judge before lunch."

Great, I thought. *This is not going to be pleasant.* I made my way over to where I had seen Mr. O'Connell sitting with his briefcase, but he wasn't there. I thought maybe he had gone to the bathroom, or someone else had told him to come back after lunch. I turned to go over to Mr. Riley, and that's when I saw the two of them standing together. What's worse, it looked like they had a hold of each other, one grabbing the other's shoulder.

"Oh no!" I said. I rushed over there, glancing over at Don. He spotted them at the same moment and started to push his way through the crowd to where they were standing.

"Mr. O'Connell, maybe you should come with me," I said. "This is not the place to settle this. Well, I mean, this *is* the place, but, uh, not like this . . . not now. I mean, when court resumes . . ." I motioned for Don to hurry up. I could see the top of his head as he tried to navigate through the large crowd that was heading for the exit. It was so loud that I couldn't hear what the two men were arguing about. Then I noticed that neither one of them seemed to be arguing. It actually looked like Mr. Riley was holding on to Mr. O'Connell's arm not to hurt him, but to hold him up.

Mr. O'Connell looked gray. He was trying to catch his breath, but he was clearly having a hard time. Mr. Riley was shouting at him.

"Pat, we have to call the medics! I'm not saying it's something serious, but remember when Al had this same thing? I know Al was a diabetic, but still . . . it could be . . ." Mr. Riley didn't look much better himself. As pale and gray as Mr. O'Connell looked, Mr. Riley looked redder than a beet.

"Fred, don't tell me I'm having a heart attack!" said Mr. O'Connell. "You don't know anything. Look at you—you're the one with high blood pressure. Yes, I know about it . . . the wife told me. It's my business right now! I'm calling *you* an ambulance."

Mr. O'Connell didn't look like he could stand up, let alone call anyone, but he wasn't going to let Mr. Riley see that.

Mr. Riley was starting to sweat. "Patrick O'Connell, don't let pride be the cause of your death! I'm getting you some medical attention. I'm just hot. It's hot in here, that's all. Why is it so damn hot?!"

Before I could even reach for my radio, Don had already grabbed his, calling headquarters for an ambulance. He told me to start clearing people out of the way before the ambulance crew arrived.

The case of the barking dog had to be rescheduled twice, but on the third nonappearance, the case was dismissed. I had heard through the grapevine that Mr. O'Connell hadn't had a heart attack—more "like a warning," was what his doctor had told him. However, had he not gone to the hospital when he did, the doctors wouldn't have found out that he needed medical intervention. Mr. Riley's blood pressure had been dangerously high, almost to the level where he could have been at risk for a stroke. He was also fortunate, because his doctor was able to adjust his medication before anything more serious could happen.

I never received any more dog barking complaints from either Mr. O'Connell or Mr. Riley. There were never any more complaints about cars, newspapers, or political signs being moved or stolen, either. I would occasionally see one or the other walking their dog or going to get their mail and I would wave. They would look at me sheepishly, give me a small wave, and then go back about their business. It was sort of like nothing had ever happened—except something had.

I would like to say that Mr. O'Connell and Mr. Riley became the best of buddies and put all their years of bad blood behind them. I'm not exactly sure what happened after that day in court, when they both became so worked up with anger that they put their health at risk, but I do know that as long as I worked there, they never called or came to the police department to complain about each other again.

My theory was that after all those years of feuding, things had changed. Children grew up and moved on with their lives, careers ended, and the retirement years began. Simple tasks that had once been easy, like climbing stairs and mowing the lawn, began to become increasingly difficult. The neighborhood changed as older families moved south and younger families moved in, many too busy to invest time in getting to know their neighbors as people used to do in the old days. Annesville was becoming somewhat of a bedroom community, home to the many commuters that took the Metro-North back and forth to the city for work. The entire city was changing, and for Mr. Riley and Mr. O'Connell, maybe the only thing that had stayed the same was their shared hostility. It had always been there—dependable, comfortable, and unchanging. If something had happened to one of them, then *everything* would have changed.

Whether it was a combination of their frustration and hostility, the poor air-conditioning in the courtroom on that hot day, or just simple fate, they were brought together on a day where, instead of pulling each other down, they were forced to hold each other up. Rather than risk losing each other, they finally agreed to disagree.

In the end, it seems that maybe this is what saved their lives.

Groundhog Day

$\mathcal{M}$r. Woolcott was much more than just a building super-intendent. He seemed to play many roles. He was the plumber, carpenter, social worker, nurse, teacher, detective, and premier playground negotiator at Lincoln Heights, a large development of apartment buildings at the northern end of the city. If this apartment complex had been designated a town unto itself, Mr. Woolcott would have been the mayor. His jovial nature and gentle humor made him one of my favorite residents in the city, and sometimes, even though I had no active complaints in the area, I would stop by to bring him a cup of coffee and talk a while. It was surprising to learn that this gentle man had served as a soldier during World War II, at a time when African American units were still segregated.

"I met Patton once, you know," Mr. Woolcott told me one early-spring morning, sipping his coffee while overseeing the painting of the new parking-lot lines.

"You met Patton?!" I was astonished. He said it like he had bumped into him at the grocery store. It was just his way to be laid-back about having met Patton. He liked to tease me, so I wanted to clarify what he had just said.

"You're kidding, right? You really met Patton?"

"Yes, Officer, I did. I was very young and it was a long time ago, but I remember it well. Something like that you don't forget too easily."

As many times as I'd asked him to call me by my first name, Mr. Woolcott insisted on referring to me as "Officer." Being called that by a former World War II veteran was a little embarrassing. After all, I was a civilian employee, and the dog warden at that! Even though I had peace officer status, it didn't seem right that this tall, stately former military man would address me this way. But again, that was his nature.

"Now, Patton . . . I did say Patton, right?" His eyes gave away his amusement. He was trying to maintain a serious demeanor, but he knew I was studying history, and that World War II in particular was one of my biggest obsessions.

One of the painters walked up just then and drew him into a discussion regarding the appropriate distance between the lines on the parking lot. The plan had been to try and create more parking spaces by readjusting the lines to be a little closer to each other, while still providing a reasonable distance between the spaces. Mr. Woolcott turned and quietly discussed this with the painter, who in my opinion had interrupted one of the most significant conversations of my life. However, this was the way Mr. Woolcott was. He gave everyone his undivided attention, and work always came first.

When he was done talking to the painter, he offered him a soda, telling him to just go into his office and help himself. Simple things like this drew people to Mr. Woolcott. He never made you feel like you were any less important than anyone else. I thought that growing up when he did, and going to fight a war overseas only to return home to a country that still treated him as a second-class citizen, may have played a role in how he treated others. He cultivated this kind of respectful behavior among the children who played in the playground at Lincoln Heights. He mediated their arguments, stopped their fistfights, and was always available to comfort a crying child or apply a Band-Aid to a scraped knee. I always wondered if they knew how lucky they were to have him there.

"Yes . . . Patton . . . that's what I was talking about, right?" he asked again, holding his chin in his hand like he was struggling to remember. He knew how to get me.

"Yes, yes, Patton. Go on." I wanted him to tell me the story quickly just in case my radio went off and they sent me on a call. Downtime was rare in nice weather, and I wanted to hear his story.

"We were in segregated units, as you know, and Patton—well, he wasn't one to think too highly of Negro soldiers from what I've heard. That's how they referred to us then. First it was colored, then Negro; now it's black. I don't know why everyone gets their boxers in a twist over a word." He looked at me and could see that I was anxious for him to continue. "But that's neither here nor there. Anyway, we were all sitting down at the mess hall, and in walks Patton, just like it was nothing. He said something about how well we were doing, something sort of like he thought he'd been wrong in thinking that we weren't as capable as the others, but I simply don't remember exactly what he said. I was so young and overwhelmed at the sight of him.

"I know it wasn't an apology—I don't think generals make apologies—but what I remember most is him laying a hand on my friend's shoulder, and taking a few minutes of his time to come in and do that. It meant the world to me at the time . . . still does."

Mr. Woolcott glanced over at the painter for a moment and then turned back. "Years later I saw a TV movie about him; seems he had a dog he took everywhere with him. When the general died, that dog was inconsolable. Never the same again. There's got to be something good about a man whose dog loves him that much, don't you think?" He took a long sip of his coffee.

I nodded in agreement. I definitely believed that animals could sense who they could trust.

He looked out over the parking lot and saw that the current line being painted on the pavement looked a little shaky. He called over to the painter. "Hey, Mr. Larry . . . are you sure you grabbed a soda and not a beer?!" He nodded at me. "Nice chatting with you, Officer, as usual," and went over to address the issue. After all, this was *his* parking lot. And knowing Mr. Woolcott, it had to be perfect.

Several of the people I came into contact with in the city knew how much I loved history. I think they may have thought it was a little odd that a dog catcher, barely into her twenties, would be willing to hear stories about World War II, Korea, and the Vietnam War, but I think they looked forward to talking about it with someone as willing to listen as I was. Sometimes people are uncomfortable listening to others describe their experiences in war. I liked to think that maybe it was good for both of us.

It had been some time since I'd had a call from Mr. Woolcott. Months had passed, and it was one of those early fall mornings with a perceptible chill in the air, the kind of day that hints at colder days to come. When I walked into headquarters and pulled open my mail drawer, I saw that Mr. Woolcott had called sometime in the early hours before my shift.

Even with his friendly demeanor and popularity in the community, Mr. Woolcott kept his home life very private. I had only recently learned that his wife, who had been struggling with medical problems for a while, had suddenly died. I heard about it when I ran into one of his grandchildren outside of headquarters. I felt badly that I hadn't been able to attend the funeral service, and often thought of stopping by to offer my sympathies. However, since I hadn't heard from him in a while, I figured that maybe he didn't want visitors. In all honesty, I was a little nervous about seeing him.

From what I'd heard, Mr. Woolcott was not the same man anymore. Since his wife's death, he rarely spoke or went outside of his apartment unless he had to. Although he continued to do his job, he was no longer the storytelling, multitasking, razor-sharp wit he'd once been. In fact, he'd become something of a hermit.

This was why I was surprised to see that he had requested I come to the building as soon as I started my shift. I wondered what I would find when I got there.

I pulled into the lower parking lot at Lincoln Heights, just as the note had directed. Standing in a spot of sunshine was Mr.

Woolcott. He looked as though he had dropped twenty pounds since I'd last seen him. He had always been one to stand up straight, like the former military man he was. Today he was sort of hunched over, looking at something on the ground.

"Hello, Mr. Woolcott. Um . . . how are you today?"

I was nervous, and didn't know what to say. Merely saying "I'm sorry for your loss" didn't seem like enough. Those words sounded so empty to me, even though I really meant them. He probably heard things like that a lot these days, and from the looks of him, it hadn't seemed to make things any better. Our usual rapport had been one of gentle teasing. Obviously, things were different now.

He lifted his head to look at me. He hardly looked like himself. His eyes, bloodshot and rheumy, seemed to have sunk into his face. Even his usual crisply ironed clothes seemed to droop off of him, wrinkled and unmatching. I knew I was looking at the face of grief.

"Mornin', Officer. Sorry to . . . uh . . . summon you here so early, but I came across this little fellow earlier this morning, and I thought . . . maybe I would, uh, give you a call."

Lying at his feet was a groundhog, or at least that's what I thought it was. I hadn't had many opportunities to see them up close, but from what I gathered, this was what we were looking at. He was lying in the parking lot, unmoving. I nudged him lightly with my foot, and he didn't budge.

"First I thought it might be a possum. You know how they play dead. But I think this is a woodchuck or one of those, uh, you know . . ."

"Groundhogs?" I finished his sentence. It looked like he was having some difficulty speaking. The Mr. Woolcott I remembered had always spoken in a clear, confident voice. I hoped he wasn't getting sick now too. Maybe he had suffered a small stroke, which would explain his halting way of speaking. When I got back to head-quarters, I thought I'd call the police surgeon, affectionately known as "Doc" to all of us there. Doc would know what to do.

Looking down at the groundhog, I figured this was probably a case for the snare pole. I could hook it around his middle and tighten the wire enough to pick him up and put him in a crate in the back of the wagon.

"I'll take care of it, Mr. Woolcott. I'll be right back." I jogged over to the car and opened the back hatch. Nothing. No crates of any kind. What was I thinking? Then I realized that I had taken them out to bleach and hose down yesterday on Lower South Street where we gassed up the police cars, near the kennels. (Well, to be honest, kennel in the singular sense—one broken and rusty kennel, to be perfectly accurate.) The crates were still sitting there, drying at the moment, no good to anyone. Sometimes I thought those comments at headquarters about my being a blonde were sort of valid. Thinking that I could quickly drive down there and pick them up, I turned and looked at Mr. Woolcott.

He was standing there silently, staring at the dead animal. This was not good. I couldn't leave him there alone, staring at even more death. That was absolutely not an option. I would have to put the groundhog directly in the back of the wagon. I took the snare pole out of the car and rolled out a plastic bag to protect the bottom of the car. I could never be sure what kind of diseases or bacteria a wild animal might spread to a domesticated cat or dog. I transported people's pets in this car. Granted, much of the time they were irresponsible people's pets, yet the animals themselves didn't deserve to catch anything through my negligence.

It occurred to me that I should have been better trained for this job, rather than basically hearing "Here's a book, here's the keys . . . go get 'em!"—which pretty much summed up most of my preparation for becoming an animal control officer. What I worried about most was rabies. The state sent regular notifications about how many domestic and wild animals had been diagnosed with rabies in the Northeast. Raccoons were leading the way, with more and more cases of rabies each year. At the moment, the majority of cases were in Pennsylvania, but they were migrating toward New York, and you couldn't be too cautious.

Walking back over to Mr. Woolcott, I noticed that he had squatted down next to the groundhog. He seemed to be examining it more carefully. "You know, Officer, there you are one minute, going about your business, and the next . . ." He snapped his fingers in the air. "You're gone."

I stood in front of him, gripping the handle of my snare pole. I knew Mr. Woolcott wasn't talking about the groundhog. "I'm going to get him out of here for you, Mr. Woolcott," I said softly. "So you won't have to look at him anymore."

He struggled a bit to stand up, putting his hands on his knees to brace himself. Mr. Woolcott had always seemed so strong and tall, almost ageless to me. I could see in the harsh light of the day that things had changed. I knew he had been in the war, so I had an idea that he was up there in age. I had just never really thought about it before, much as I didn't think about the dogs and cats that I pulled off the road after being hit by cars, or the old wheezing dogs who died in my arms, or worse yet, a beautiful young beagle who had been shot for no other reason than a cruel prank. I'd tended the beagle's wound as well as I could, wrapping gauze tightly around his abdomen, but he still bled to death on my lap while I raced to the animal hospital. I didn't think about those things while they were happening, and sometimes not for hours afterward. It was when I was finally home by myself that I would pull my knees up to my chest, wrap my arms around them, and sit in my rocking chair and cry.

I loosened the wire on the top of the snare pole and carefully slipped it around the groundhog's head, then maneuvered it under his front legs. I knew that some other dog wardens and animal control officers just used the snare pole to wrap the wire and then tighten it around the neck of the animal. While it was a fact that you could control a live animal this way, I thought it was cruel and not something I would do unless absolutely necessary. I preferred to grasp the animal under their front legs and pull up, guiding them along while still being safe and humane in the process. Even though this particular animal wouldn't notice how I went about picking him up, it was something that I felt strongly about. It seemed more dignified to me.

When I went to pull the snare to tighten it, nothing happened. I pulled again, and still, it wouldn't move an inch. Great! Now my snare pole was broken. It had been around for quite a while, probably years before I'd taken the job, but still . . . it had worked fine just last week. No crates, no snare pole. And when I looked up at Mr. Woolcott, he was staring at the dead groundhog with tears in his eyes. This was definitely not the way I'd wanted this to go.

"You know, sir, you don't have to stay with me. I can take care of this myself. I know you must have plenty of things to do. Don't let me get in your way." I hoped that if I could encourage him to be busy, he would snap out of it, return to the way he'd been before. At the very least, he wouldn't have to stand around with one more thing reminding him of death.

"Maybe I could go up to the house and get a sheet to wrap him in?" He turned and looked in the direction of his apartment building. "I think I might have a sheet we could use. I don't know, though; she wouldn't want me to use the new ones. She just bought those."

I had to make a decision and get out of there, not so much for me, but for Mr. Woolcott's sake. I had wanted to make this as easy on him as possible, but I felt that I was just making it harder. Could this day get any worse?

"I haven't changed the sheets since she left in the ambulance. I can't use those. My daughter says they . . . the sheets . . . that they should come off the bed, but I said no . . . I can't. I just closed the door and left it that way. I sleep on the couch now."

He stood there, so sad, so defeated. Now I felt like I was going to cry, and that was the last thing he needed.

"No, that's fine. You should leave them there," I said. "There's no reason you have to take them off until you're ready." Here I was, giving advice on grief. I had spoken without thinking; I just wanted him to feel better. He was so sad, and if he wanted to leave her sheets on their bed, then why not? I thought that if it were me in his place, I would've done the same thing. But still, it wasn't my place to give him any advice, and I worried that I was overstepping my bounds. I was here to pick up a dead groundhog, and the sooner

I did that and took it away, the sooner Mr. Woolcott could go on with his day.

The gloves! I had forgotten about the lead-lined gloves, guaranteed to be impenetrable. The chief had spent a small fortune on them. He had told me they used these gloves at the San Diego Zoo to handle primates. He had been very proud of them, until the very first time I'd used them and a wildcat had bitten clear through them to my hand, which had resulted in a large blood loss and a trip to the emergency room. I could still remember the chief looking sadly at the gloves, momentarily reminding me of a little kid with a broken toy. I still had them in my wagon, and even with the punctures, they would help protect my hands when I picked up the groundhog and put him in the car.

I put them on and carefully picked up the groundhog. I thought that after all this time he would have been cold, but he wasn't. Then again, he had been lying in a spot of sunshine the entire time I'd been there. I held him as far away from myself as I could and looked at him carefully. He wasn't breathing. His eyes were shut. He didn't move at all, and his fur seemed matted where he had been lying for so long.

"What are you going to do with him?" Mr. Woolcott asked.

The usual procedure I followed was to bring the animal to the Department of Public Works, and they would take it from there. Unless it was someone's pet and we could trace the animal to an owner, the policy for animals that died within city limits was out of my hands once I delivered them to the DPW. If the animal died in transit or was going to be euthanized, then the shelter down-county would be responsible for disposing of the body. My knowledge as to what happened after either of those destinations was reached was limited. I didn't want to know any more than I had to.

"I'm, um, going to take him to the woods . . . take him back to his . . . home."

As soon as I said it, I knew it was exactly what I was going to do. It seemed to be the most appropriate thing, and Mr. Woolcott seemed to brighten a little at my answer. That in itself made my decision definite.

I carried the animal over to the car. He was heavier than he looked. I placed him on the plastic in the back and closed the hatch. I would grab my clipboard to have Mr. Woolcott sign off on the complaint. I hoped that in some small way, getting the groundhog out of there in a humane way would somehow help a little, although I doubted it would make much of a difference.

I opened the car door and slid onto the backseat to pick up the clipboard from where I had left it. I sat down for a minute and was thumbing through complaint forms to find a blank one, when I suddenly felt something odd. The car felt like it had, well, sort of bounced. Maybe the parking brake was releasing? I looked up through the grill to make sure it was fully engaged. It seemed fine. Suddenly, I heard someone shouting. It didn't register right away who it was; after all, shouting was a regular occurrence in this city. Then I realized that the shouting was coming from Mr. Woolcott.

"Officer Duffy . . . ma'am . . . Stand down. Stand down! Uh, I mean . . . Lisa! *Get out of the car!*"

Startled, I pushed open the door and scrambled out of the backseat. It was the first time I had ever heard Mr. Woolcott call me by my first name. That surprised me so much that I dove out of the car and skidded onto the ground like I was making a landing on a runway. From my dignified vantage point, lying on my stomach on the ground, I looked over at Mr. Woolcott to see what he had been yelling about. Had he snapped? What I saw surprised me more than anything.

He was laughing. Not just smiling, or even chuckling. He was laughing out loud—so hard that tears were streaming down his face.

The recently deceased groundhog of Lincoln Heights had risen from the dead. Not only was he alive, but he was doing flips! The groundhog was leaping around the back of my car like he was the ball in a pinball machine. The velocity at which he was performing his acrobatics was causing the car to actually rock back and forth. Every few seconds he would seem to stick to the window as if he had suction cups on his feet; then he'd fling himself backward and begin the somersaults again. That groundhog was alive; more than that, he was a gymnast groundhog. And from the looks of it, he was ready for the Olympics.

"That is . . ." Mr. Woolcott took a deep breath, trying to pull himself together. "That's the funniest thing I've seen in a long time!" Mr. Woolcott could barely get the words out. He was laughing so hard he was bent over, holding on to his ribs. "Are you okay?" he wheezed between bouts of laughter. He walked over to give me his hand to help me up.

"I'm fine," I said. I hadn't really checked, but I felt all right. I thought I may have had some type of skid mark on my stomach, but I wasn't about to check out there in the parking lot. The overwhelming feelings I had at that moment were relief and happiness—relief for having gotten out of the car before the crazy groundhog landed on me, and happiness to see that Mr. Woolcott was acting more like his old self.

"I'm sorry . . . I'm laughing so hard . . . It's just that, well, that groundhog and the car, and . . . it's so funny . . ." And he was off again, with more peals of laughter.

In the background the car was still shaking. You could hear the groundhog banging around in the back of the police wagon—a consistent *thump-bang . . . thump-thump-bang-bang*.

". . . And . . . and the way you hit the ground like someone had just shouted 'Incoming!' You sure you're okay now? Thank goodness . . . Well, it's all really rather funny!"

I looked down at my uniform. Outside of being covered in dirt and gravel, which was nothing out of the ordinary for me, I was fine. I started to laugh. The situation in the car was hysterical. The groundhog seemed energetic after his long nap. This was definitely not the type of groundhog that needed some caffeine to get him going when he woke up. What had been wrong with him? Had he been in a coma? Had he had a rough night at a party with the other groundhogs? I had no idea. I had never come across something like this before.

I said good-bye to Mr. Woolcott and drove slowly away from Lincoln Heights. Thanking a higher power for the steel grill that separated me from the backseat, I drove as steadily as possible toward the park near the southern part of the city. Blue Mountain Reservation abutted the city park, and continued for miles into open woods that belonged to the county. Pulling over to a shady area near some dense bushes, I got out of the car and opened up the back of the wagon. I was prepared to jump up on the hood of the car if I had to, but as it turned out, it wasn't necessary. My crazy groundhog walked over to the edge of the bumper and looked down at the ground like he was assessing how far he would have to jump.

"Don't worry about that, little guy," I said. "That's nothing after what I've seen you do." He jumped out of the car and seemed to stretch a little before he methodically made his way into the bushes, not looking back once. "There you go," I said. "After everything you put me through, you don't even say good-bye." If people knew how much I talked to these animals, they might think I had a screw loose.

I thought about what Mr. Woolcott had said to me right before I drove away to return the groundhog to the woods.

"I haven't laughed like that in . . ." Mr. Woolcott hesitated and looked down at me kindly, lowering his voice. "I haven't laughed like that in months."

Mr. Woolcott seemed a little better. While he still looked like a man who had recently been through a difficult time, at least now he was smiling. A glimmer of the man I knew was still in there somewhere. And I hoped for his sake, as well as for his children and grandchildren, and even for the residents of Lincoln Heights, that he would continue to come back to us, a little more every day.

My Fair Charlie

$\mathcal{I}$ should have known better than to bring the cat trap into my apartment. Anxious to see if the grades for my last course had come in the mail, and not wanting to leave the cat in the hot car, I had placed the cat carrier in the middle of my living room floor and walked out to the mailbox.

It was a mistake. When I returned to my apartment, I had no idea that I would be walking into a hostage situation.

I had picked Charlie up from behind the senior citizen apartments downtown, on South Street. In the beginning, it had seemed as though everything would be fine. Some of the residents had been leaving food and water for the stray cats in the alley behind the building for years. That all changed the day Charlie appeared. He was a very large orange-and-white-striped tabby who didn't want to share food or water with any other cat. To make matters worse, he really didn't want much to do with the people leaving the food or water either. He would sit and hide in the bushes until some poor soul would leave a bowl of food, and as soon as they turned around, he would leap from his hiding place with a loud howl and attach himself to the back of the unsuspecting Good Samaritan. It seemed that this cat didn't care about the kind of impression he was making.

Something had to be done. I knew that with this kind of attitude, the future did not look bright for this particular cat. When you bite the hand that feeds you, it's unlikely that you'll get a second chance.

I set out a Havahart trap for him, designed to catch animals in a humane way so that they can be relocated safely. As luck would have it, the next day I was able to pick up a very large, very angry, hissing, yowling feline to bring to the shelter.

"Why do you call him Charlie?" I asked Mr. Gomez, the day-time janitor of the building, when I went to pick up the trap.

"Well, I've been trying to catch this cat for months. He's been a regular nuisance and has the residents scared to come outside. The more I try to catch him, the sneakier he gets." Mr. Gomez was uncharacteristically disturbed by this cat. He was the sort of man who seemed to have a handle on whatever kind of situation came his way. He cut a trim figure in his carpenter pants and polo shirt with the word MANAGEMENT scrolled across the back. While we were probably the same height, there was not an ounce of fat on Mr. Gomez. He was five feet, five inches of pure, wiry muscle. The only telltale sign of his age was the slightly graying hair at his temples. I was surprised that a wild cat seemed to be getting him so worked up.

"I can see him watching me from the bushes, waiting to jump. Doesn't matter what time of day, he's always slinking around, watch-ing. It reminds me of my days in Vietnam. He's like Charlie, you know—like the Vietcong—always watching you, ready to pounce." Mr. Gomez stopped talking all of the sudden and just stared out into the bushes. I had a feeling that the Vietnam War wasn't that long ago for him. We stood there for a few moments in silence.

"Sorry, um . . . Well, anyway, glad to see you got him," said Mr. Gomez. "Get him—and all the trouble he makes—out of here. He is one bad cat."

I had rarely seen a dog or cat that could be labeled *bad*. Most of the "bad" animals I had come in contact with were that way because they'd been abused by bad human beings. I had come across a few aggressive animals that seemed to support my belief that some ani-mals *are* just born that way—the ones that won't break eye contact with you, that exhibit aggressive behavior without provocation—yes, I had seen that before. I had come across a dog that seemed to intentionally commit murder by luring less-street-savvy dogs out into the middle of busy roads where they would meet a tragic end (although I'd yet to prove this theory).

I had read that sometimes with purebreds, aggressive behavior can be a result of overbreeding. Then there was always the nature versus nurture argument. Are there really any bad people or animals, or does society have more to do with it than anything else? How do you explain the Jack the Rippers or the Charles Mansons? Were they just born bad, or did something cause them to become that way? Likewise, was Charlie the cat inherently evil? I was glad that the bars on the trap kept me from finding out firsthand.

I put the trap down on the floor, wondering if it was even worthwhile to go and get my mail. It would probably contain nothing of value. Perhaps one of those envelopes telling me I might have already won $10 million. *How long were they going to take to mail the grades?* I thought, my mind wandering.

I turned to pet my own cat, Shebee, a beautiful black-and-white domestic shorthair with round yellow eyes, a pink nose, and black lips. She had come to live with me when she was just ten weeks old, part of a litter of kittens from my cousin's cat.

This particular kitten loved to ride in the car. One night when it was dark, she had run out of the garage and tried to leap into my cousin's car as he was shutting the door. Her tiny head was accidentally slammed in the car door. Thanks to the quick actions of a veterinary technician, she survived. However, afterward she had a hard time keeping her balance and adjusting to life in a litter. While the other kittens were growing into cats, Shebee seemed to be stuck in an arrested kittenhood.

When I moved into my first apartment, little more than a remodeled garage, my grandfather, who lived upstairs from my cousin, had placed an aluminum roasting pan along with a small bag of cat litter in the back of my car when I was leaving his house. "What's this for?" I asked him. He smiled at me with his mischievous grin. "It's for this little girl," he said, placing the little black-and-white kitten into my arms.

"I don't know if I have time for a pet right now. This is my first apartment, and with work and school . . . I don't even have any furniture!"

My grandfather continued to smile, and then started to chuckle in the way he often did when he spoke to me. He always seemed to find me amusing. "She needs you," he said simply.

I found myself driving home to my new apartment with the little kitten perched on my shoulder, meowing constantly all the way home.

My friends often joked with me, saying, "You don't even live in a two-car garage!" They were right. It was a former one-car garage, and a small one at that. The garage door had been replaced with a large picture window, which would have been nice had it not been directly at eye level with the street, only five or so feet away from it. To make matters worse, my apartment sat on the corner of a four-way intersection. Cars had to stop directly in front of that picture window in order to obey traffic law.

I had a large shade on the window, but I had started to dress in the bathroom, just in case. I knew that people outside of my family and friends were aware that I lived there, because on more than one occasion I had woken up to find a dog tied to my door. These facts, combined with living in such a small city, and, of course, being just twenty-one years old, meant that I was unintentionally getting my fifteen minutes of fame.

When I first moved into the apartment, I made the grave mistake of changing my clothes in front of my closet. But after a day or two it seemed that I was drawing a small crowd to my picture window on some evenings, like they were waiting for the drive-in movie to start. It was a bit unsettling because I realized that maybe my large window shade hadn't been doing the job I thought it had. After that, I began to change in the bathroom.

One day I had come home from work to find that my landlords had knocked out the window and were in the process of putting up Sheetrock. They planned to replace the picture window with a normal-sized one. "We thought this would be a good idea," they told me.

I loved the Donohues; they were one of the nicest couples I had ever met. They invited me to dinner with their family sometimes, and once a year, they invited all of their tenants over for a party. At one of these parties I discovered that one-third of a glass of homemade dandelion wine caused memory loss, especially in someone whose only prior drinking experience had involved a sip of a friend's beer. Only a few blocks away, I realized I'd forgotten my way home. One of the cops on duty that night picked me up and drove me home. (I'd yet to live that one down!)

I remembered the first night I spent with Shebee in my new apartment. I was lying on my mattress, on the floor of my empty apartment, with only the light of a black-and-white TV illuminating the darkness. As much as I had been excited to live on my own, I found that every noise made me nervous. I turned over onto my side, away from the door. I was trying to ignore the fact that the lock I had on that door, one of those little slide locks (the kind usually used on cabinets, not on front doors), was the only thing separating me from the dark street outside. Thinking that maybe it was best if I kept my eye on the door, I turned back over. I was startled by two round yellow eyes looking directly into mine. Shebee rubbed up against my face, purring louder than any cat I had ever heard before, and curled up next to me. All of sudden it was apparent that what my grandfather had really meant was "*You* need *her*."

Looking through the junk mail again, hoping to see that maybe I had missed the envelope from school, I could hear Shebee meowing loudly. I looked over at her. She was sitting on my couch just staring up toward the ceiling. "What's wrong with you?" I asked. Maybe Charlie was making her uncomfortable, so while still trying to open my mail with one hand, I bent down to pick up the trap.

It was very light. Too light.

It was empty.

"Oh no!" I looked around the apartment. How had Charlie gotten out of the trap? It was a pretty tricky process to open one of those Havaharts. It was fairly impossible to open it from the inside, and the only *person* around who could have opened it from the outside was me . . . which left only one other suspect.

"Shebee! Did you let Charlie out?" Of course I didn't expect her to answer me (although maybe in my near hysteria, I did). If she had indeed opened it, I had no idea how she'd done it. I followed her line of vision up to the ceiling, and that's when I saw Charlie; actually, I heard him first. He was perched in the narrow space between the tops of my kitchen cabinets and the ceiling. When I made eye contact with him, he started howling and yowling for all he was worth. *Great*, I thought. *How am I going to get this wild cat off the top of my cabinets, back into the trap, and out of my apartment without killing myself in the process?*

"Hi, Charlie," I said in my sweetest voice. This was the voice that I used to get pit bulls and rottweilers to stop fighting with each other and to come over to me. Much of my success at handling animals without getting bitten came from the soft way I spoke to them. They seemed to respond to it. Maybe it was because they knew I wouldn't hurt them, or maybe it was because they had never been spoken to kindly by a human before. Either way, this magical tool that had served me so well in the past was failing when it came to getting Charlie to come down off the top of my cabinets.

I tried to climb up on the table to see if I could somehow pull him down. No luck there; he was having none of it. The closer I got to him, the louder and scarier he became. "Okay, then," I said. "We will just have to wait you out."

I closed my own cat in the bathroom with some food and water and put out small bowls of the same for Charlie, in the middle of the floor. I waited. I couldn't even look up at Charlie without setting off his rumbling growls. Not only did he not want me near him, but he also didn't even want me *looking* at him. I couldn't stay in my apartment for the rest of the day, as I'd only been on my lunch break. I figured that since I had my own cat safely ensconced in the bathroom, where she would often choose to sit on the windowsill anyway, I could go back to work and deal with this when I came home.

By the time my shift was over and I'd filled out my reports, it was already 4:30 PM. When I returned to my apartment, I found Charlie still sitting on top of the cabinets, the food and water untouched. This was not good. Actually, this was very bad. It was bad enough that I had somehow let this wild cat loose in my house, but who was I going to call about it—the animal control officer? What a mess. If this got out, it would give the cops at headquarters more ammunition with which to torture me. I was still recuperating from the dandelion wine episode. The only thing to do was continue to wait him out.

It wasn't easy going to sleep the first night that the enemy was watching me. He seemed not to care at all about my Shebee; I was the one he couldn't stand. I had put a bowl of dry cat food and a bowl of water up on top of the cabinets as far away from Charlie as I could so at least he would have something to eat. I couldn't let him starve; after all, my own stupidity had helped to create this situation.

In the middle of the night I could hear Charlie crunching away on his cat food. If I looked up at him, he would stare back and start to growl. Okay, fine. If this was the way it was going to be . . . There were married couples that lived like this for years. The longer Charlie lived on top of my cabinets, the longer Charlie would live, period, due to the fact that as a hostile animal, there was no chance that anyone at the shelter would adopt him. He was a likely candidate for euthanasia. This thought also contributed to my letting him hold me hostage for a while longer. Eventually he would have to come down . . . I hoped.

I left the door open on nice days. I left all the windows open, including screens, when I went to work. Eventually I felt comfortable enough to let Shebee out of the bathroom while I was at work, since Charlie paid her no attention when I was around. He primarily had a problem with me.

Soon it got too cold to do that anymore. It didn't matter; every day when I came home, there was Charlie, holding court on top of my cabinets. As wild as he seemed, he still crept down at night to use the litter box. I found this a bit odd. I would hear him scratching in the litter box, and I would be careful not to glance over in his direction. Even more strange was the fact that he was a lot neater about this than my own very domesticated cat, who flung litter everywhere when taking care of her business. As soon as he was done, he would leap back up to the top of my cabinets.

A week went by, then two. Friends would stop over to get a look at the cat that was holding me hostage, but he didn't like them looking at him, either. As long as nobody looked in his direction, everything was fine. He ignored us and we ignored him. It was really strange, but it worked.

Then, one night I felt Shebee kneading her paws at the bottom of my bed before she curled up to go to sleep. She usually slept right next to my head, but I didn't think anything of it. I had worked all day and attended night classes until 11:00 p.m., and I was more than a little tired. Then, all of the sudden, I thought about it. I slowly lifted my head off the pillow to see Charlie, lying between my ankles, about to go to sleep. He looked at me and growled. I put my head back down and stared up at the ceiling for a bit, and since there was really nothing else I could do, I went to sleep.

This continued for almost three months. Charlie would sleep in my bed and occasionally sit in my chair and watch TV. He never let me touch him, and he still didn't like me looking at him, but he used the litter box, ate and drank, and was pretty much a polite, albeit uninvited, guest. From time to time I would try to corral him in the trap, with no success, causing him to once again retreat back to the cabinets. I finally decided to let him be and see what happened.

One day, while I was sitting in my chair, reading, Charlie jumped off the top of the cabinet onto the counter, and then gracefully leapt to the floor. He went over to his food bowl, now on the floor next to Shebee's. He walked past me, turned around, rubbed against my leg, and sat down. Since he didn't move, I decided to take the biggest risk yet. I put my hand down and lightly patted his head. He didn't growl but made an even odder noise: a faint purr. I couldn't believe it. *By George, he's got it!* I thought. This was the feline version of *My Fair Lady*. Charlie had purred!

As a few more weeks went by, Charlie began to warm up more and more. He had no desire to go outside like Shebee loved to do. He was content to sit on the chair, have his meals, and especially, to watch the one channel we got on my black-and-white TV. The thought occurred to me that maybe Charlie would be fine staying exactly where he was, but I knew that my landlord had only allowed me to have one cat in my small apartment. Even that was really too much for the size of the place. Maybe I could find another home for Charlie now that he had turned over a new leaf? One with low expectations, a soft lap, and a working TV.

It occurred to me that Charlie would be the perfect pet for a senior citizen, but how would I find just the right home for him? How could I go back to the senior citizen building where Charlie had earned himself a reputation for guerrilla warfare? I would have to get past Mr. Gomez first, and that could be a problem.

I decided to give it a try, and went to visit the building in December.

"Hi, Mr. Gomez, what's new?" I asked. Mr. Gomez was busy hanging Christmas lights in the lobby, half of which was decorated with red and blue lights and a gold garland, while the other half was decorated with a three-foot-tall menorah.

"The residents love their lights," Mr. Gomez said while searching for a longer extension cord in the box he had taken from the janitor's closet. "I just don't know why they didn't put enough outlets in this lobby. Every year I have to search for more extension cords, even though I know I bought them last year. I think Four-B is sneaking some of them out of here; you should see her window. It glows from three blocks over. You gotta have a bunch of extension cords to get that kind of power." Mr. Gomez looked up at me from his box. "Of course, you don't want to be listening to this. What can

I do for you? Any more problems with those cats? I haven't heard anything."

"No, Mr. Gomez, no problem with the cats. In fact, I think I have an idea that may help one of those cats—and maybe one of the residents too." I smiled at him. Sometimes my smile worked all by itself, although it didn't have that kind of effect on Mr. Gomez. He had known me since I was twelve.

"Okay, what is it?" Mr. Gomez stood up and crossed his arms, his attention temporarily taken away from his extension cords, or lack thereof.

I explained to him about Charlie and his amazing metamorphosis during the months he had been living at my apartment. I said I thought he would be an exceptional pet for someone who just needed some company and was rather limited when it came to going out—someone who was probably living right here in this building.

"I don't know . . . You say this cat has turned his attitude around. That's not the cat I remember. Why can't you just bring him to the place you always bring them, that shelter down-county?"

"He's older, Mr. Gomez. He also has a history of being less than affectionate, especially with people who are active. I can't imagine him living with a family who has young kids. The fact is, he would probably just be sent to the back."

"To the back?" Mr. Gomez started to pull on the side of his mustache. "You mean the point of no return, don't ya?"

I nodded my head. He knew exactly what I meant.

"I just don't know . . . I mean, there's Betty Cox up on Five, whose husband just passed about six months ago. She's lonely and her kids live clear across the country." He looked up like he could actually see the fifth floor through the ceiling. Then he turned to me again. "She's the one who was feeding those cats most of the time anyway. I don't know . . . You know I called him Charlie because he reminded me of the VC in 'Nam . . . you know that's not good."

"I know, Mr. Gomez, but I think *this* Charlie deserves a second chance, and I think he would have a perfect home here, with Betty . . . up on Five."

"Second chance, hmmm?" Mr. Gomez looked at me and a smile started to play at the corners of his mouth. "I know about those. After I came home from the war, there was no living with me. Even my own mother couldn't stand to have me in her house. I drank too much, got into fights, and lost more than a few jobs. I was no good to anyone."

I watched him. Although he was right there in the lobby with me, he also seemed to be somewhere else, far away.

"But my wife . . . I don't know how she did it. If I had been in her place, I wouldn't have put up with it. She never gave up on me, and then we had our Anne Marie. It straightened me right up." Mr. Gomez turned to look at me like he'd just remembered I was there.

"You know my Anne Marie; you two went to school together. She's almost done with her coursework now. How about you?"

"Pretty soon, Mr. Gomez—thanks for asking. I have about a year left." This was a city, but with the way everyone knew everyone else, it was more like a small town. I had left college because I couldn't afford it, and since I worked for the police department, I was given the opportunity to go back to college at night, with a 50 percent tuition break. It was rough at times, working full-time during the day and going to school full-time at night, but it was definitely worth it. In a way, this had been my second chance.

"All right, okay . . . I'm not promising anything, but let's go up to Five-A and see how Betty would feel about giving this cat a home."

I ended up driving Betty over to my apartment so she could meet Charlie on his own terms. I wasn't sure if his new peaceful demeanor would hold up under the stress of transporting him in a carrier across town. Betty was a petite woman with silver hair. She was very polite, and a good sport about riding over to my apartment to look at Charlie. However, there was a visible sadness about her. You could tell that she had been through a lot.

Once we arrived, she entered my apartment and looked around. "Oh, isn't this cozy. It's just perfect for one," she said. Many people called my apartment cozy, but I had a feeling that Betty really meant it.

Betty sat down in my chair, and within a few minutes, Charlie jumped up into her lap. Betty seemed a little nervous at first, especially considering that her last experience with this cat had ended quite differently. There was no need for any worry, because Charlie began to purr almost at once. It was almost like he remembered her. Maybe he hadn't been upset about having to share the food with the other stray cats; maybe he hadn't wanted to share Betty.

"I don't know if this is a good idea," Betty said, not taking her eyes off Charlie as she stroked his back. "I've been through so much the past year, and I don't know if I need a pet right now." I watched Betty start scratching Charlie behind his ears. He closed his eyes like he was going to fall asleep, although his purring seemed to get louder. I looked at them for a moment and then it occurred to me. I glanced over at my own cat sitting on the windowsill, taking in a ray of sunshine.

"He needs you," I said.

So Betty took Charlie home with her. The cat that had held me hostage for almost four months had a new lease on life. Shebee seemed relieved to have her home back to herself, and nobody mentioned the dandelion wine incident at work anymore. I now had a normal-sized window that offered me some of the privacy I had been missing, and I had been able to resolve the Charlie situation without being known as the animal control officer who had been controlled by an animal. Most important, however, was the fact that Charlie had undergone a total transformation. Like Mr. Gomez, who hadn't been a bad man—just a good man going through a bad time—Charlie had also needed some time, and a place that felt safe enough to finally let his true personality shine through.

I ran into Betty at the grocery store a few months after she had adopted Charlie. She was in the pet food aisle, carefully choosing a bag of cat food for Charlie. "He really seems to favor the beef," she said, smiling at me.

"My cat does too," I told her. I smiled, thinking that since this was the only cat food Shebee would eat, it was the only thing on the menu the entire time Charlie had been "in rehab" at my apartment. Betty looked different than I remembered, but then I realized that I had never seen her look happy before. She was one of those people whose smile changed her entire face. She must have been very beautiful when she was a young woman.

"I want to thank you so much for Charlie. He's been a lifesaver for me. He follows me from room to room, never leaves my side."

I reached out to shake her hand. "I'm very glad for you, Mrs. Cox. You really helped a lot. I don't think Charlie would've made it anywhere else."

Betty took hold of my hand, but didn't let go right away. "Remember when you told me that he needed me? This may seem silly to you, because you're still so young, but I realized after a while that I'm the one who needed him." She let go of my hand and touched the side of my face. "Thank you," she said.

She turned, and with a little wave, continued on with her shopping. I stood there for a moment, watching her roll her cart away, before I turned around and started walking in the direction of the cat litter, wiping one eye with the corner of my sleeve.

Betty had been only partially right. I was, indeed, still pretty young, but I didn't think she was silly, and I understood exactly what she meant.

I understood very well.

The Serial Killer of Main Street

$\mathcal{H}$omicides, while not unheard of in the history of our small city, were not a common occurrence. There was, however, one homicidal maniac that roamed our streets, free to come and go as he pleased. You couldn't tell when you met him, because he seemed like a normal, average, everyday black-and-white Great Dane mix. But even though I could never prove it, I knew that underneath that biscuit-loving, tail-wagging demeanor lived the heart of a cold-blooded killer. His name was Manny, and no matter what anyone told me, I truly believed his intentions were deadly.

The previous ACO had warned me about Manny on my very first day of work. We had spent it driving around the city together while she filled me in on the things I would need to know. She pulled over to the side of a street and looked up a hill toward a house sitting up in the woods. "Manny lives there. Black and white . . . Great Dane mix . . . pretty dog, but I think he may actually be evil." She went on to tell me a little about his behavior, and I thought that there was no possible way a dog could be capable of such intentions. I was wrong.

Manny lived on Main Street, a busy road that was partly commercial, but with some residential areas located in between the businesses. Many of the homes on this street were built up on the steep hills that overlooked Main Street. This meant that any effort to give Manny's owners a warning about his behavior involved five separate flights of stairs just to get to the front door. I had come pretty close to catching him a few times, but this dog had the vision of a hawk. He was a predator like one, too, but he didn't pose a threat to humans. He never bothered people; he also never bit or attacked another animal the entire time I worked as an animal control officer. What Manny did was worse: He committed premeditated murder.

Sometimes, on slow days, I would actually stalk Manny until he had to go home. "You have to eat sometime, Manny," I would say to myself, waiting. I would sit in my car, preparing to make my move. I figured if I waited near his house, when I knew he would be coming home for dinner, I could grab him. But this never worked because somehow, he always seemed to know when I was getting close. I would follow him into the woods near his house up on the hill and watch as he miraculously vanished. I would then go to his home and knock on the door in an effort to talk to his owners, but it seemed that they were never home when I attempted to contact them. Sometimes I'd see a curtain move aside and something I thought was a face, only to see it was Manny himself, peering out the window from inside the house. Once, thinking it was one of his owners trying to avoid a fine, I marched right up to the window to stand there, arms crossed in an effort to look at least marginally intimidating. It was Manny. I felt like he was mocking me. I looked for doggy doors, open basement doors or windows, yet I never managed to find out how he got into his house so quickly when only moments before, I had been chasing him down Main Street.

I tried many times to ticket his owners for a loose-dog violation, because Manny was always roaming around town, doing as he pleased. I knocked on their door, called them, left messages—all to no avail. I served them tickets on my own observation, even though I couldn't get close enough to Manny to put him into my car to take down to the shelter. They simply paid their fines. Somebody must have finally told them to try and fight the ticket, because they actually went to court. I had never really seen them up close before. They were a young couple, and looked nice enough—not like the type of people who would be harboring a fugitive from justice or anything, but wasn't that always the case? Since I had been unable to physically seize their dog and transport him to the shelter, they said I had no proof that their dog was loose, and the case was dropped.

I tried to fine them for an unlicensed-dog violation, but as luck would have it, Manny *was* licensed, and it was renewed every year. Next, I researched the dangerous dog action laws. Since Manny wasn't really attacking people or animals, there was little I could do to even enforce that. What Manny did, rather, was entrap other animals. He caused their deaths without actually being directly responsible for them—at least not visibly. This dog, had he been a human, could have been Stalin.

Main Street was an extremely busy area. It was the best way to get to the highway north or south out of the city, and also the route you needed to take to reach grocery stores, fast-food restaurants, and the mall. Annesville had once been a thriving commercial area, with local shops and even a large department store. The mall killed the city. Why should people compete for parking, put money in a meter, and, of all the inhumane things, attempt to parallel-park, when it was much easier to just go to the mall where everything you could ever need was safely encapsulated in a temperature-controlled, rain-proof building?

Even though the downtown area was struggling from this loss of revenue, the roads that ran through the city were still highly traveled. This meant that when a dog or a cat was loose in this area, they often ended up being hit by a car. It seemed that the number of dogs being hit by cars on a particular stretch of Main Street was increasing. I started to park on a side street during the day to see if I noticed anything out of the ordinary. I finally started to suspect this was more than a coincidence when I noticed Manny sitting on the yellow line, smack in the middle of Main Street.

He would sit there for a while, and then get up and cross back and forth, never even getting close to a speeding car. He was truly talented at this dangerous balancing act. It was almost like he enjoyed it. Perhaps it was like the canine equivalent of bungee-jumping or skydiving. The thing was, Manny never got hit. He never even came close. I would watch him do this perilous dance with death, yet every time I tried to get out there to grab him, he would fly out of my reach and vanish up into the hills. Of course, I would get honked at and end up trying to get back across the street without getting hit myself. (You would think the badge and the blue uniform would've helped, but it didn't.)

Then one day, I decided to hide my car on a different side street and really observe Manny at his risky street maneuvers. I knew that some humans were twisted enough to enjoy doing this kind of thing as well, especially after a few too many drinks. Maybe Manny was just a thrill seeker. I watched Manny sit on the yellow line, and then right before a car came, he would fly over to the side of the road. He'd look both ways, return back to the yellow line once the coast was clear, sit for a bit, and then cross the street again. I noticed that Manny was staring at something across the street, slowly edging his way backwards to the yellow line. I watched him do this several times until I saw him start to go across the street again, turning his head every so often to make sure of something. I saw he was staring at another dog, a beagle mix that I'd never seen around town before.

Manny looked both ways before crossing over to the other dog. It was then that I witnessed his modus operandi. He would slowly back up, wagging his tail to get the other dog to follow him. Once he'd tempted his victim to the yellow line, he would fly back across the street, leaving the less-streetwise dog stuck in the middle of the road.

"No!" I yelled. I flung open my car door, and after waiting for what seemed an interminable amount of time, I was finally able to cross over to the yellow line where, luckily, this dog seemed to be frozen in fear.

"It's okay, puppy—don't move...don't move." I scooped him up and tucked him under my arm. Cars were whizzing past on each side of the road. This time, a Good Samaritan, seeing what I was trying to do, slowed down and let me cross. My heart was pounding with the near miss. I looked around to see if I could spot Manny anywhere. Out of the corner of my eye I caught sight of his hindquarters as he hightailed it into the woods. This dog didn't want to make friends; he wanted to start his own canine genocide campaign.

"Canine genocide . . . hmmm . . . now that's something I've never heard anybody say before," said Guy, my favorite dispatcher. By the time I had returned to headquarters with the beagle, his owner was already there, filling out a missing dog report. He had somehow slipped out of his collar while chained in his yard, and he'd taken off. I gave the owner a warning since this was the first time I had seen this dog loose, and I also told her about the situation I had found him in. She was crying when she left. I was pretty sure that she would do everything she could to make sure her dog was safe in the future.

"I think you're getting a bit obsessed with this dog." Guy was always watching others to analyze whether or not they may be in need of some psychological help. He had been taking some college psychology courses, and I think we were his lab.

"I know, Guy, but there have been about ten dead animals on that one section of Main Street this year alone, and it's not like dead squirrels. It's been purebred shepherds, Labrador retrievers, poodles with bells on their collars. These are not your average run-around-the-street animals. These are naïve house pets that are being drawn out into the middle of a busy street by a homicidal canine maniac!"

Guy pulled on his chin and looked to be in deep thought. I could imagine him looking just like this someday, talking to one of his patients. Maybe he was practicing. "Well, what are you planning to do?" he asked. "Arrest him? Tell him he has the right to remain silent? I think you could do that; you do have peace officer status, right?" He couldn't help himself.

"Quit it, Guy. Tell me you don't feel bad about all those innocent animals being hit by cars in the same exact place. It's not a coincidence."

Guy stopped smiling and looked at me intently. "I know that, but all those other pets are loose, too; it's not like they are entirely innocent—or at least their owners aren't."

Guy definitely had a point. As insane as my serial killer theory sounded, it was true that any owner who allowed a dog to run around unleashed and not under direct control was breaking the law. It seemed the only thing I could do was stage a sort of stakeout to try and thwart as many of Manny's attempts as I could. Then, I could ticket the owners of the other dogs in hopes of keeping them off the streets and away from the likes of Manny. It seemed unfair when the real criminal I was trying to catch was Manny. I had learned that because of the way they were written, some laws didn't always make the most sense when applied to real-life situations.

"Ask Sarge if you can mix your shifts up a bit so you can watch at different times of the day," Guy suggested. "Maybe if you catch enough of the other animals running loose, and warn the owners about your . . . *homicidal maniac dog*"—Guy took a moment to make the universal gesture for air quotes—"then things will get better. It won't totally solve the problem, but it's something you do have power over, and it may help."

"Thanks, Guy. That's actually very helpful," I said. "Do you want me to make a coffee run?" He really had been a big help. In my opinion, Guy was one of the smartest people at the department. He had a tremendous amount of common sense, combined with a very dry sense of humor. He was able to handle some of our most difficult callers without ever losing his temper.

"Hey, no problem," Guy said with a smile. "I'll put it on your bill." The phone rang and he grabbed it on the first ring. "City of Annesville Police, Dispatcher Wells," followed by a whisper to me: "Black, no sugar . . . on a new diet." He winked and continued with his phone call. "What is your current location, ma'am . . . ?"

I took Guy's advice about how to handle the Manny situation. And so it began—the great stakeout of the 1400 block of Main Street. The people in the deli on the corner were great about it. They would bring me coffee in the morning and sometimes a cold soda during the day. They were just as interested as I was in trying to thwart Manny's murderous goals. Several times a week, I would grab a dog from the side of the road right before they were about to cross over to meet Manny on his yellow line of death.

A large majority of the time, these pets had tags with their names and owners' phone numbers on them. There were no first warnings. I would take the animal down to the shelter so that their owners would have to drive down-county and pick up their pet themselves. If it happened more than once, I would increase the fine to a second violation. Hitting people in their pocketbooks was a double-edged sword: Sometimes it acted as a deterrent, but sometimes, it resulted in the owner just giving up his pet to the shelter. So far during my stakeout, it was working in our favor. I was writing a lot of tickets, which made the chief happy, and things seemed to be improving on Main Street.

There was one problem that I had yet to resolve. On three separate occasions I had grabbed Sadie, a beautiful golden retriever who lived on a cul-de-sac off of Main Street, after finding her sitting on the side of the road watching Manny's maneuvers. I could never catch him, he was too fast, but Sadie knew me and would come when I called her. She was a beautiful dog with all of her vaccinations up-to-date and her license always renewed on time. The problem was, her owners let her run free. As many times as I took their dog down to the shelter, wrote out tickets, and increased their fines, they would still let their dog off her chain in the morning for a run while they got ready for work. Each time they did this, she went off to take her chances with Manny, who actually seemed to be aware of her schedule. At least I now had the aid of others in the department who helped me catch the owners when they were at home to give them a ticket.

The number of tickets I was writing continued to add up, while the amount of dead and injured animals I was picking up off of Main Street had decreased, to zero casualties in over two months. My system was labor-intensive, but it was working. The only holdout seemed to be the golden retriever from the cul-de-sac up the hill.

"She loves her run," said the owner of the retriever, a woman in her thirties, when I went to their home holding Sadie on the end of my leash. "It's only for a few minutes each morning, and then we bring her right back inside or tie her up in the shade in the back." The owner was pretty and had short dark hair, cut professionally. She worked in the city and took the train, so she was usually rushing around when I knocked on her door. I knew I was disrupting her morning routine, but I felt like I had to get it through her head: Not only was she breaking municipal code, but she was also risking the life of her pet, which she really seemed to love.

"I don't have time to let her run in the park in the evenings; this is the only chance she gets. Weekends aren't enough. I keep an eye on her." She told me this while she was standing in the doorway with a towel wrapped around her head, wearing a bathrobe, still dripping from a shower I had obviously interrupted. The fact that you couldn't watch your dog while you were taking a shower seemed lost on her.

"Maybe she would be better living with someone else, then. A friend or a relative with more property—someone who doesn't live near a major road?" I suggested, knowing perfectly well that she would never accept this solution.

"No, I could never live without Sadie. I promise I'll do better, honestly; the next time you see me, you won't have to give us a ticket or bring her home to us. I promise . . . I will never let her off her chain again." She seemed chastened, like this time she finally understood.

Thank goodness, I thought to myself. It seemed as though Manny was going to be out of business for a while. The number of tickets I had written had died down now that the word was out. All of the effort I'd put toward preventing Manny from continuing his killing spree had taken up a great deal of time. There were a lot of other problems that needed my attention now.

It was about three weeks later that I woke up to a beautiful morning. You could tell it was going to be a warm day, but without an ounce of humidity. My general feeling of optimism faded when I heard Guy's voice over the radio advising me to respond to the 1400 block of Main Street for a possible incident involving an animal.

The beautiful sunshine meant nothing to me as I stood over poor Sadie, lying dead in the middle of Main Street. She was still warm when I got there, but she had no pulse, no sign of life in her at all. Her injuries were so severe that the Department of Public Works had decided to take care of removal without my even having to ask. They didn't always do this for me, but in this case, it would have been too difficult for me to do alone. Her owner had been right; I wouldn't be bringing her home to them again.

I drove up their driveway and parked the car. I hated these calls, but this time I was more angry than upset. In an odd way, it made it easier. I knocked on the door, and the owner opened it immediately. She looked like she was dressed for work and was just about to leave. She smiled at me. "I know, I know . . . I promised, and I feel so bad—honestly, I do. It's just that she was barking and barking at the door, so I just thought a little run around the yard would be okay . . ."

I didn't say a word. I was worried that if I opened my mouth I would either start saying things that could get me fired, or I would start to cry. I put out my hand toward her. She was trying to look behind me, checking to see if Sadie was in my car.

"Oh, you're probably going to give me another ticket, right? Okay . . ." She reached out, and I laid Sadie's collar and tags in her hand. Her smile seemed to fade as she tried to figure out what I was doing.

"Where is she? Is she down at the shelter? Why did you take her collar off?"

I looked at her for a moment. Then I turned around and walked away.

"What is this? What happened . . . where is she?" I could hear her voice break with the realization of what had happened to her dog. "Oh no, no . . . she can't be . . . she's dead, isn't she?"

I didn't turn around to offer her any comfort or to tell her how bad I felt for her, or that Sadie had died so quickly it was likely she hadn't felt a thing. I didn't tell her any of those things because none of them were true. I just got in my car and drove out of her driveway and away from her house. In my rearview mirror I could see her standing there, crying, holding Sadie's collar in her hands. I had never reacted this way before after a dog had died. I had always tried to make the owner feel better somehow. This time was different. I was too angry with her. She didn't deserve my condolences. Sadie had deserved better than her.

I didn't see Manny again for quite a while. It was almost like he knew I was waiting for him. Either that, or he had won. The one dog he had never been able to tempt to cross the street had finally done it. Even my ticket blitz had all but stopped now because the word had spread that loose dogs were getting ticketed more than usual. I thought that as time went on, I would finally start to get over what Guy claimed was my "obsession" with Manny; he was just a dog, after all. He wasn't capable of manipulation and planning. I had worked myself into a frenzy over this dog. All I wanted now was to move on and do my job.

Several weeks later I was driving home from the grocery store. It was one of those gray days that signal the beginning of winter. The clouds looked like they held the possibility of snow. That would be nice—the first flurries of the year. After all, it was already November. I was driving down Main Street, and out of the corner of my eye I saw a flash of white and black. I glanced over quickly, and there was Manny, sitting on the sidewalk and watching the traffic. I didn't have my patrol wagon, and I wasn't in a uniform. It was a Saturday, and I was simply going home to make some lunch and finish a research paper. But then a thought occurred to me: Manny didn't recognize my car right now, and, out of uniform, he probably wouldn't recognize me. I pulled over and parked on the side of the road right next to where he was sitting.

This was probably the closest I had ever gotten to him. He didn't look like a killer, but he also didn't have the warmth about him that I'd seen in almost every dog I had ever come into contact with. I got out of the car and quietly closed my door.

What am I thinking? What am I going to do if I am able to grab him—drag him into my car? I knew it made no sense, and that if Guy knew what I was doing right now, he would take out his psychology textbook and look up what type of medication I should be taking. I couldn't stop myself. All I could see when I looked at Manny was beautiful golden Sadie, lying in the road with all the life taken out of her.

I walked closer, to where I could almost touch him. He turned his head to look at me, and at that moment, you could see it registered. Uniform or no uniform, he knew who I was. He turned to run and I lunged for him, falling on the sidewalk for a second. I scrambled to get up. I must have looked like a crazy person, which I probably was at that moment. He ran up into the hills and I followed him. He ran around a tree and I ran around a tree. He kept running, occasionally turning to see how close I was, but he never barked at me once. He wasn't threatened enough by me to bark, but he knew enough to run, that was for sure.

I kept climbing and climbing, and he kept weaving in and out of my reach. It was like he had read some manual on guerrilla warfare, on how to avoid the enemy. I was struggling to breathe. The cold air and the sudden physical exertion were causing my asthma to act up. I couldn't do it anymore. I sat down with a thump on the ground. Manny was nowhere to be found, and I was a crazy lady sitting in the woods, wheezing, with leaves in my hair.

"This job is getting to me," I said to no one in particular. I thought then that perhaps Guy could add *talks to herself* to my pending diagnosis. I stood up and brushed myself off. Trying to get the leaves and twigs out of my hair and to regain some of my dignity, I carefully edged my way down the hill and back to the street. A man sitting on a bench at the bus stop watched me emerge from the woods and walk over to my car, still covered in dirt and leaves, like some small version of Bigfoot. He looked at me for a moment and then went back to reading his paper. His reaction was to be expected. In this city, odd things happened on a daily basis.

I went home, put away my groceries, and took a hot shower. I called my cousin to see if she wanted to go out later. She would help me put my real life on the front burner and all of this in perspective. She always told me that I took a lot of things personally that were sure to cause me endless frustration, and this quest for Manny was one of them. Perhaps reading too many fairy tales as a child had made me this way. I had to get it through my head that not every story had a happy ending. Sometimes there would be no justice. Even in my job, with the small power I possessed to try to change things for the better . . . no matter what I did, there would be times when it would never be enough. I had to realize that much of the time—not only in my job, but in my personal life as well—that was just the way things went.

I never saw Manny again. Nobody did. His owners were renters, and when their lease was up, they moved away, taking Manny with them. I tried to find out where they'd gone so I could call the town or city they moved to, to give them a heads-up on Manny, but that information wasn't available. All I could hope for was that Manny had had enough of his sick game, or that they had moved far enough away from a city that he would no longer have access to a major road. Guy still insisted that I was giving too much power to a dog, and that as tragic as all of it was, it was just an unfortunate coincidence.

Although Guy's reasoning sounded logical and made perfect sense, I will always believe that Manny—even though he was just a dog—knew exactly what he was doing.

Odd Blessings

"**I** just can't have all these cats roaming around here anymore." Mrs. Lucas looked very tired, and not only could I see that these cats were wreaking havoc on her yard and garden, but I could also smell them.

"I've been taking care of my mother-in-law by myself since my husband died, and she won't stop feeding them. I feel bad, but it's . . ." She looked around at her yard and sighed. It was obvious that she was stressed for many reasons, and the aroma that seemed to emanate from every direction probably added to it.

The house on Lower South Street was a tiny old colonial that looked to be in need of massive repair. It always bothered me to see what happened to older couples when one of them passed away, especially when the women were left alone. They were at an age when their physical strength was starting to ebb, and given their generation, they had usually depended on their husbands to be the providers. They rarely had enough money on their limited incomes to hire someone to make repairs. They had played by the rules of the day, staying at home to take care of their families, and then, after a lifetime of caring for others, suddenly there was no one around to take care of them. It was like a cruel joke: At an age when they should have been able to relax and look back on a satisfying life, they were too often forced into nearly impossible situations. If there was ever anyone that looked to be at the end of her rope, it was Mrs. Lucas.

"I love her, really. But I have to have them removed before she wakes up from her nap. She walks to church every morning and then comes home and falls asleep for a few hours. She used to take long walks and stop by the bakery, the fish market . . . but now she only has the energy to go to Mass and back." Mrs. Lucas sighed. "I don't know how she even has the energy to do that at her age." Mrs. Lucas was whispering as she tiptoed into the kitchen, so I did the same as I followed her. She motioned for me to sit down at the small kitchen table. "Can you please start today?" she whispered.

I nodded. "Just sign these surrender forms and put *stray* in this column here," I whispered back, pushing the booklet toward her and handing her a pen. The animal shelter was always giving me grief about this. The usual fee to surrender a dog or cat was ten dollars, unless the animal was a stray. In this case, it would have cost Mrs. Lucas over two hundred dollars. Too often I had found that this fee—or the inability to pay it—got in the way of doing the right thing.

"It seems your city has an awful lot of strays," Maureen, the receptionist at the shelter, said to me once as she stamped my forms. "The streets must be teeming with cats and dogs. I can't imagine there's much room left for vehicular traffic. Must be quite the mess." Maureen hadn't been looking at me at that moment, which was a relief, since her stare could ignite paper. She was one tough cookie.

Although she was the receptionist, in reality, Maureen ran the place. Camouflaged by a very fit, petite frame and a lovely face, Maureen was about five feet, ninety pounds of pure steel. The board president of the shelter often stayed inside her safe, air-conditioned office, but not to avoid any of the more unfortunate realities of the position. I thought it more likely that she stayed in there to avoid Maureen.

I had reached a peaceful coexistence with this czar of the animal shelter early on, when Maureen had learned I was taking college courses at night. Maureen had one degree and was only a few credits shy of her next. A few times I was taking a class that she had already finished, and she gave me her textbooks so I wouldn't have to buy them myself. Maureen was a little scary, but wicked smart. I could never figure out why she stayed on as a receptionist when she could have easily found a position somewhere else that was more suited to someone with not one, but two degrees. She possessed a bachelor's degree in political science and a master's in business management, yet, Maureen continued to work at the shelter.

"When you're a parent someday, you'll know why" is all she would tell me. I knew she was raising her children alone, and that she'd been working at the shelter for a long time. I figured that for the time being, she felt this job was best for her situation. As smart as she was, it wasn't my role to question her decisions. I also couldn't imagine what would happen at the shelter if she ever left. I guessed that people would probably try to get away with all sorts of shenanigans, like not closing the door fast enough when the air-conditioning was on, or taking the leash off a dog before she said to, or possibly even speaking without permission. Yes, without Maureen, things could get pretty ugly.

As it was, she knew when I was bypassing the system and still allowed me to do it, although never without some reproach. "Trying to save the world one dog at a time isn't going to teach people responsibility, Lisa." She would look at me over her tiny spectacles, which I sometimes thought she wore more for effect than anything else.

There were times when I waived the fees because the owners of a dog would refuse to pick the dog up at the shelter, and then after seven days, that dog—who had no clue as to what he was doing there and why he couldn't go home—would end up being put up for adoption, or, too often, slated for euthanasia. Nobody wanted that, least of all the people at the shelter. But with the number of dogs and cats being held at the shelter, which had contracts with multiple cities and towns in the county, there just wasn't enough room. Most people wanted puppies and kittens. They wanted purebreds with papers. Most people who went to the shelter to adopt an animal were not looking for a large pit bull/rottweiler/shepherd mix with rotten teeth. They also wanted younger dogs, another fact that had caused Maureen to admonish me on several occasions.

"Oh, what do we have here from ACO Duffy? Ah, of course ... another three- to five-year-old terrier mix, who—at such a young age, mind you—already has cataracts and gray hair. It must be that rare, accelerated aging disease again. Your city should really test its water ... that might be the source of the problem."

She was right, of course. She always was. But I noticed that even though she saw right through my embellishments, she still wrote the information down on the dog's registration card, exactly as I had stated it. Inside her tiny body was a great big heart; it may have been surrounded by several layers of igneous rock, but I knew it was there nonetheless.

The shelter was crowded, that was true, but unlike other shelters in the area, this particular shelter was immaculate. The animals were vaccinated and neutered or spayed for a fraction of the usual cost when you adopted a pet. People were screened carefully to ascertain whether or not they were responsible or capable enough to care for an animal. Black cats were never adopted out several weeks before or after Halloween, to prevent their possible abuse by people with questionable intentions. There was never a rash of kennel cough or any other type of condition that easily spreads in places like that.

And as much as driving down to the shelter was definitely not the highlight of my day, I really liked all of the people who worked there. Most of them shared the same type of dark humor you often find in hospitals and police stations; this is a common defense mechanism in places where tragedy and joy intermingle on a regular basis. However, even when they were kidding around, you could see that they loved the animals they worked with, and caring for them was their primary concern. They were passionate about their jobs, and it showed.

Mrs. Lucas started to sit down at the kitchen table, but stopped halfway to her chair. "Are you sure you wouldn't like a cup of tea?" she asked.

"No, thank you," I said. I was worried that we were running out of time. We had no way of knowing when her mother-in-law would wake up from her nap.

Mrs. Lucas sat down slowly, wincing as she lowered herself into the chair. "Maybe if you only took a few each day, she wouldn't notice. Then, when there are only one or two left, I could say that they must have left on their own . . . gone somewhere else."

"That's a good idea," I said, thinking that a few stray cats every other day was much more believable than twenty or so at the same time. While Mrs. Lucas had been explaining her problem, I had already been trying to figure out how to handle this issue with Maureen. Also, the vision of me driving a wagon filled with all of those cats down the highway was a little disconcerting.

Then I had an idea of my own. "Have you ever tried to remove the food after she's left it? Maybe the cats would just move on if they didn't find any food here."

Mrs. Lucas had already started to nod her head before I'd completed my sentence. "Yes, I already tried that, but it's like she knows what I'm thinking. She actually got herself up and outside around midnight a few weeks ago to check and see if I'd taken the food away. Then she became confused in the dark and tripped on the back step. I can't do that. I can't let her fall again. She's ninety-one, you know."

"You're absolutely right—you can't let that happen again. Let's just go with your plan: You let me know when she usually naps, and I'll come over at that time and try to take a few each day."

Mrs. Lucas smiled. She looked exhausted. I had to get these cats out of here, and I would start today. I knew that if I left the Havahart traps in hidden areas with food in them, I would probably be able to trap at least two a day. I wasn't that concerned about the shelter finding them homes, as they all seemed to be very friendly and in good health, which wasn't the norm for cats that lived outside. This was a different kind of situation, and I told myself that the shelter would probably spay and neuter them and adopt them out. It was one of those rare times at the shelter when the cat building was fairly empty. Maybe it would be okay. Maybe it was fate.

With what seemed like an unusual amount of effort, Mrs. Lucas took the pen I handed her. "I would usually make us some tea . . . I feel so rude. It's just . . ." She looked toward the back bedroom where you could hear the slight snoring of her mother-in-law. She ran her fingers through her hair. It seemed thinner since the last time I had stopped by a year or so ago to drop off some cat food someone had donated to me. (I knew that her mother-in-law had been feeding the cats, even though I had never met her personally.) Caretakers are often exhausted; I could see that Mrs. Lucas was overwhelmed with her responsibilities, and all of these cats weren't making her job any easier. It seemed as if she had aged ten years in one. I made a mental note to talk to the director of the senior citizen program, to see if they had a respite program for caregivers.

"It's fine, Mrs. Lucas—don't worry about it. I'm going to try and take a few today." I looked out the window and noticed that two chubby cats were actually lying on the hood of my station wagon, sunning themselves. "I just need you to sign this form, and then—"

"My kitties! You're giving away my kitties!" Neither one of us had heard the elderly woman coming out of her bedroom; it's like she appeared out of nowhere. "I knew you were going to get rid of them, and I was right!" Mrs. Lucas's mother-in-law looked to be even older than ninety-one, but she had the vocal cords of someone much younger. She was pumping her fist in the air and yelling at Mrs. Lucas, and then all at once, she started to cry. Her shoulders heaving with sobs, she said, "My kitties . . . you can't take my kitties away."

Mrs. Lucas stood up. She looked so worn-out standing there in the sunlight that was streaming through the window. "Oh, Mother, I'm not getting rid of all of them . . . please don't cry."

I stood up abruptly, almost knocking over my chair. I opened my mouth to speak, thinking that perhaps I could find something to say that sounded professional, about code violations or city ordinances, something to take the pressure off Mrs. Lucas. I felt

I needed to do something to help alleviate the tension. But when I looked more carefully at her mother-in-law, I closed my mouth. The elderly woman in front of me was hunched over so badly that it took every ounce of energy she had just to lift her head and look at us. Her entire back was a huge hump, and every movement she made seemed to cause her incredible pain. Nonetheless, she lifted her head and looked directly at me.

I recognized her all at once, but could see that she didn't remember me. How could she? I had never told her my name.

"Miss Aggie," I whispered.

Mrs. Lucas turned to me, surprised. "Yes—how did you know that? Mom's name is Agnes Lucas, but everyone has always called her Miss Aggie, ever since she was a little girl. Have you met before?"

It was all I could do to nod my head. The woman in front of me was someone who had helped me through one of the most difficult times of my life, yet she didn't know it. I couldn't speak. I couldn't move. And I knew that no matter how hard it was on Mrs. Lucas, I couldn't take away any of her cats today.

When I was fifteen years old, I started going to the bakery very early every morning. I would get up before sunrise and rush to get dressed so I could get to the Imperial Bake Shop when they opened at 5:00 a.m., to get a fresh tea biscuit and hot chocolate. The biscuit would still be warm as I walked down the quiet sidewalks, the streets virtually empty of traffic and everything so silent that you could hear the trains all the way from down by the river. I felt like the city belonged to me. When it was cold out, I would slip into Saint Ignatius Church before school. There I could eat my breakfast in the warmth of the back pew, unnoticed by anyone—or at least, so I thought.

Miss Aggie went to church every morning. I noticed her because she walked everywhere, all over the city. While I saw several elderly women around town on a daily basis, Miss Aggie stood out in my memory for a special reason: She had a very large hump on her back. She was so bent over that you would think walking anywhere, least of all, all over town, would be incredibly painful. Some of the children were afraid of her, while others would make fun of her, yelling out cruel things. But she never took it to heart. She would smile back and tell them that she'd pray for them. Soon it seemed that even the meanest children would wave and say hello to Miss Aggie when they saw her. I found myself often looking for her when I walked to and from school, not only because of the curious picture she made, briskly marching about town with what seemed to be a considerable handicap, but because it was a handicap that we shared.

I had been diagnosed with scoliosis as a toddler, and had worn a brace since the age of twelve in an effort to straighten a spinal curve that seemed to be getting worse despite the doctors' efforts. Years and years of trips down to a special hospital in the city to try and resolve the problem had finally proved to be useless. The decision had to be made to schedule surgery to repair the curve with a steel rod, fusing the stubborn vertebrae that seemed to have a mind of their own. The surgery would be painful and a bit dangerous, and even afterward, it still wouldn't be over. I would have to wear a body cast for six months after the operation. All of this came at the age when I'd be learning to drive, going to dances, talking to boys. This was not the kind of thing a girl just approaching the age of sixteen wanted to hear.

I remember Dr. Friedman giving us the news at the hospital in New York City. "The bracing hasn't worked," he said. "We gave it a good try, but with a curve as severe as hers, surgery is the best option; in fact, I think it's our only option."

I was looking out the window at the East River, as I'd done many times over the years. I remembered that in the beginning, my mother had had to pick me up so I could look through the window. I hadn't realized the reason behind our visits until I was about six years old. Up until then I thought it was for the cherry lollipops.

"What would happen if I just left it alone?" I asked, still looking out the window. My mother was sitting in the chair next to me, trying to smile and seem positive. The doctor had several interns standing behind him—this was a teaching hospital—and I could see their reflection in the window. I had gotten used to the many changing faces over the years—young residents who followed Dr. Friedman around like he was the mother goose, hanging on his every word. They were always nice, and I never minded them; it was just that they represented a sea of anonymous faces that changed every time I came to the hospital, which was a few times a year. To them, I was something to study, but to Dr. Friedman, I was more. He had been following my progress since the age of two, and it was his opinion that mattered the most to me. None of this was true unless *he* said it was. They had all been talking quietly, consulting with each other over my file. My doctor glanced over at them, and they stopped talking immediately.

"Lisa," my mother said softly. I knew she wanted me to stop looking out the window. I told myself that as long as I didn't make eye contact with the doctor, none of this was really happening. Hearing her whisper my name, I knew I had to turn around. Something in the back of my mind told me that it was time to grow up—one of those small moments that seem insignificant at the time, but end up being something you remember forever.

I turned around and faced him.

"The degree of your spinal curve is severe, and it will only get worse. Unless we intervene, you will end up being disfigured. You will have a large hump on your back, and your internal organs could also be affected by the twisting of your spine." The doctor put his hands on my shoulders and bent down to look directly into my eyes. "You would be in constant pain for the rest of your life. You could even end up in a wheelchair."

I swallowed hard and just looked back at him. I had known this doctor for many years. He had watched me grow up. He wasn't smiling and teasing like he usually did. He was looking at me, waiting for an answer. I looked at my mother, and she asked me, "What do you want to do? The final decision is yours." We had talked about this at length for several days. My mother had read the pamphlets they had sent us, and explained to me the possible side effects, knowing that on our next visit, I would probably be faced with making this decision. I hadn't wanted to talk about it and had initially refused to read the pamphlets, but my mother knew me. She had left them out on the table in the kitchen, knowing I would read them when no one was around.

I looked at the doctor and answered him. "Okay. Let's do it."

My mother smiled at me, trying to hold back her tears. We looked at each other for a long moment. We had been traveling to this hospital for thirteen years in hopes that this day would never come, even though we both knew that it was probably inevitable. She sat up straighter and looked at the doctor. "When can you schedule it?"

It was these thoughts that weighed heavily on my mind when I would go to the church in the morning. Sometimes I felt like a liar, or a hypocrite, sitting in the back of the church secretly eating breakfast and escaping from either the cold, or the heat, depending on the season. I spent a lot of time feeling sorry for myself, too. There were not many places open that early in the morning, and I had ended up at the church only because the doors would be open for the 5:30 AM Mass. As time went on I started to think that maybe I enjoyed the smell of the incense and the peaceful quiet of the worship service, where only a handful of people were ever in attendance.

One morning as I sat there, lost in my thoughts, I heard a soft voice behind me. "You are such a pious young lady, here every morning. Perhaps one day you will be a nun?"

Startled, I looked up to see Miss Aggie smiling down at me. I guiltily pushed my cup of hot chocolate behind me. "Um, I'm not sure yet," I stammered. "I don't think I would be a very good nun, but thank you."

"Then there must be another reason you are here so often," she said, smiling at me. I noticed that even though she was hunched over and disabled, she always had a kind smile on her face, and her eyes were a sparkling sky blue. She was very friendly, and I found myself smiling back at her.

"I know what it is." She leaned in closer to me and whispered, "And it will all be better soon. It's a good thing. Think of it as a blessing." I looked up at her, not really understanding how all of this could be considered a blessing. As if she could read my thoughts, she lightly rested her hand on the back of my neck where you could easily feel the brace under my clothes. "An odd blessing, but a blessing all the same," she said gently. I smiled at her. I was beginning to think I understood what she meant. She had never been given the opportunity to stand up straight, but that opportunity was going to be given to me.

"How did you know?" I whispered, curious.

"We can recognize each other, can't we?" she said.

I nodded. Yes, we could. (Although I figured she might have found out about me from one of the older women who lived in my building, since I'd seen her chatting with some of them on occasion.)

"Don't spill your cocoa now," she said with a wink, and then turned and walked away.

It hadn't occurred to me until that day, meeting up with her again in her kitchen, that when I'd watched Miss Aggie walking around town during my childhood, she'd been watching me, too. If anyone would be able to recognize someone with scoliosis, it would be someone who'd had it themselves. After our chat in church, whenever I saw Miss Aggie walking around town, I thought about how hard it must have been for her, growing up without the medical intervention that was available now. I started to feel grateful, instead of filled with self-pity. In many ways, the thought of Miss Aggie made the pain easier to bear in the difficult months to come. I started to look at other things in my life in a more positive light. Sometimes it takes a life-changing event to do that, but for me, it was a quiet moment in a church that was responsible for my shift in attitude.

"Miss Aggie," I said, when I finally found my voice, "I am the girl you used to see in church. The one with the back brace— the scoliosis. Do you remember?" Miss Aggie looked at me, and I could see that her eyes, once so clear, were now hazy and confused. She looked from me to Mrs. Lucas, who now appeared entirely frustrated.

"You know my mom?" Mrs. Lucas asked, looking at me, a bit surprised. It wasn't too much of a coincidence. After all, in this town everyone knew Miss Aggie.

"Yes, she, um, really helped me when I was young. She talked to me in church one day, she made me feel so much better about having spine surgery . . . actually, she made me feel better about a lot of things."

Mrs. Lucas smiled wanly, I noticed that she had dark circles under her eyes. I had to stop talking and get some of these cats out of here. This was wearing her out.

"You had the twisted spine too?" she asked. I nodded my head.

"You can hardly tell now," Mrs. Lucas said. "There's so much they can do for that these days, not like in Mom's time."

"I know," I said while trying to control my emotions. "I'm really lucky."

Miss Aggie tilted her head to look up at me as best she could. She didn't remember. I could see it in her eyes. The only thing I saw there was confusion.

"Are you going to take my kitties?" she asked, with tears running down her cheeks.

Mrs. Lucas turned to me and said, "Every day is a new day for Mom. The only things she remembers consistently are five-thirty Mass and her cats."

Miss Aggie turned to Mrs. Lucas. "Margaret, where is John?" she asked. "He won't let you give away my kitties!"

Mrs. Lucas reached out for Miss Aggie's hand. "John is still at work, Mom. He'll be home soon." She looked at me, tears starting to form her in her own eyes now. She leaned over and whispered in my ear. "That is the other thing she never forgets. John, her son . . . he was my husband. He passed away three years ago, and she asks for him every day. I always tell her he will be home soon."

Miss Aggie turned and slowly ambled over to the counter. "It's time to feed my kitties." She turned to face both of us. "All *twenty-three* of them." She turned back to the counter, and soon we heard the sound of an electric can opener. It seemed to go on forever.

I looked at Mrs. Lucas. I expected her to be very upset, yet she was smiling. She began to chuckle softly. "She surprises me once in a while. Twenty-three kitties . . . she knows exactly how many there are! I miss her, you know. Before she began to forget everything, she was so witty and kind and . . ."

"Intuitive," I said, looking at Mrs. Lucas.

"Yes, exactly—very intuitive," she said. "Why don't we give this a week—can you come back then, and we'll try it again? It's no use now that she's up and opening cans. I'm a bit tired now, too."

"That's fine," I said. "Would you like me to leave a Havahart here, just in case?"

"No." Mrs. Lucas looked toward the kitchen and sighed. "But definitely next week. I have to do something about this soon."

"Call me at the station and let me know when it's a good time for you," I said. I picked up my clipboard and shelter book from the table. "I'll come right over and bring the traps."

I felt a bit pulled in both directions. One side of me was saying that this was my professional obligation; Mrs. Lucas was on the brink of exhaustion with all of these cats, still grieving for her husband, and taking care of someone she loved who sometimes didn't even remember who she was. The other side of me could only see Miss Aggie, looking at me and crying out, "Don't take my kitties!" I knew that even though there were so many cats—too many for one residence, according to municipal code—each one of those twenty-three cats was truly loved. They didn't have any close neighbors—just the Public Works depot on one side, and an overgrown empty lot on the other. This part of the city was rather desolate. The cats didn't roam. Maybe this could be done slowly, just one at a time, until the number was more manageable. I left that day thinking that even if I didn't hear from Mrs. Lucas next week, I'd still stop by and check on them.

When I got back to headquarters, I made a quick trip next door and left a message at the senior center about the possibility of getting Mrs. Lucas some help with Miss Aggie. Maybe I would bring them some coffee cake or something from the bakery next time I stopped by. As for the cats, we would take it one week at a time.

I didn't get a chance to go to the bakery. Only a few days after our meeting at her house, I heard the dispatcher send an ambulance out to Mrs. Lucas's address on Lower South Street. When I went out to the parking lot outside headquarters, I saw the ambulance slowly driving up the street toward the hospital. No lights. No sirens. This could only mean one thing.

Officer Angelo Leo came in later to fill out the paperwork, and I walked over to his desk. Angelo was a big guy. He had been involved in bodybuilding contests before he'd become a police officer. As tough as he looked, he was really a big teddy bear who was known for hugging people good-bye, even folks he'd just met. It was a rare day when Angelo didn't have a smile on his face. He looked up at me when I came over, and he wasn't smiling.

"Sorry about your friend down on South Street. I know how much you liked her. Died in her sleep. If you ask me, that's the best way to go."

"Thanks for telling me," I said, and started to walk away. I was sad, but I thought about how vibrant and alive she had been when I'd first met her. It was hard to think of her getting slowly more and more confused, when at some point she wouldn't even remember her kitties anymore. I would stop down and see Mrs. Lucas when everything quieted down. I had to find out where the wake would be.

"The problem we do have," Nick continued, while filling out his paperwork, "is what's going to happen with the old lady. There's no next of kin left alive, and I don't know how she could take care of herself, all hunched over like that."

I spun around to look at Angelo. I thought that maybe I hadn't heard him right. "Mrs. Lucas died? How? I don't understand . . ."

I was astonished. I couldn't get my mind around it. I had just spoken with her, and she was much younger than Miss Aggie. But then I started to remember how tired she had looked that day; how she'd seemed to move so slowly, even more slowly than Miss Aggie, who was in her nineties; how even reaching for a pen had seemed difficult for her.

"Cancer," Angelo said gently, looking up at me from his report. "She wanted a break from the chemo . . . that's what Doc said. Sometimes it happens very fast."

"Thanks," I whispered, and turned around to continue what I had been doing before I had heard the news—except that I couldn't remember what it was. I stood there in the middle of the dispatch room. It was busy and I was in the way, yet no one asked me to move. I looked around at all the activity, and for a moment I felt like I was watching it all from somewhere above myself. Mrs. Lucas had been alive yesterday, and today she wasn't. Would Miss Aggie even notice that she was gone? Who would take care of her now—and what about all of those cats?

I felt as though I had to do something, and do it immediately, although I had no idea what it might be. Before working at this job, I'd hardly given a thought to mortality. But lately it seemed that death was hiding behind every corner. I had been at headquarters recently when some really sad calls had come in: sudden infant death syndrome, fatal car accidents, and even a homicide. This was the first time that it was someone I'd known . . . someone I'd just spoken to. I had sat at Mrs. Lucas's kitchen table. I had made a promise to come back to help her, and now I didn't know what to do next.

"I have to go and get some of those cats," I said out loud, to no one in particular.

"No, you don't, girl—not right now." I looked up to see that everyone had left the dispatch room except for Guy, the dispatcher. It took me a second to realize that more than a few minutes had gone by while I'd been standing there.

"Why can't I go? Who's going to take care of them now if I don't? And besides, I made a promise to Mrs. Lucas . . ."

Guy put up his hand to stop me from continuing. I swallowed. My throat was dry. I needed a drink of water.

"What you need to do right now is sit a while on this. You're upset." Guy was looking at me carefully.

I nodded my head. Yes. I was really upset. I couldn't think clearly. I couldn't go down to get the cats now anyway. The Department of Social Services would be at the house right now, and I didn't even know if Doc had left yet.

"Have you ever known someone who died before?" Guy asked gently.

"Yes," I said. But then I thought about it a moment. My grandmother had died when I was very young, and I hadn't been allowed to see her for many years before that. My memories of her were distant and vague. There had been a teacher in junior high who'd had leukemia. He had left school to get treatment and had passed away over the summer. I had been sad, but I hadn't seen him for the entire year before he died. It hadn't seemed real at the time. I had talked myself into thinking that he had only left to go work somewhere else.

Mrs. Lucas's death felt different. I had been sitting at her table and talking with her just a few days ago. I hadn't expected this.

"You gotta take some time to feel things. You can't bottle it up and charge on ahead. That's no good for anybody. You see what I'm saying?" Guy looked at me, waiting for me to respond.

"I understand," I said.

"Good. I'm calling you out for lunch. You can go get a bite to eat, or go home and lie down . . . I don't care, but I'm not sending you on any calls for an hour."

I smiled at him. "Thanks, Guy."

"I'll bill you," he said, and waved me away. Guy was right. I had to follow up on Miss Aggie, but first I had to get a grip on my emotions. Tomorrow I would contact Social Services and find out how things stood with the house, the cats, and especially, Miss Aggie. She had been there for me when I needed her. She didn't remember me, and that didn't matter. Now it was my turn to help her.

After talking with Social Services, I learned that Miss Aggie had enough health insurance to pay for a home health aide to come in every day. She would be able to stay in her house. Eventually, two aides would stay with her, one overnight and one during the day. I occasionally saw her walking to church with her aide, now using a walker to get around. Eventually, I didn't see her around town anymore. I stopped by a few times to see how things were going, and the aide told me that Miss Aggie insisted on calling her Margaret, and seemed to think that it was sometime in the 1960s.

Miss Aggie would, however, go out on her back porch every day and count her kitties. She was still feeding them. The aides actually enjoyed the cats and helped to have several of them spayed and neutered. They took good care of them, and since there were no neighbors close by to notice or complain, everything seemed to be fine the way it was. As long as the situation stayed the same, I didn't see any reason to interfere.

I went to my files and pulled out the original complaint. Filling out the forms that would close the case and stapling them together, I wondered why things happened the way they did. As I pulled open the top drawer to file the report in my closed-case section, I thought about the fact that I didn't have to struggle to reach the top of this tall file cabinet. I could reach it easily, with no difficulty at all. Suddenly, I realized that I took a lot of things for granted. There were only a few people who could have understood how lucky I was to be able to do this, and one of them would never know how significant a role she had played in the process. In that moment, I knew I had a lot to be thankful for.

Miss Aggie and her cats were still alive when I finished my degree and left the police department. In time, my husband and son and I moved away, and I never saw her again—although I thought of her often, with gratitude. It's been quite a few years since then, but I like to think that somewhere, she is standing, straight and tall and beautiful, with her family beside her . . . and her kitties, too.

All twenty-three of them.

For Every Cat There Is a Reason

*T*hese were the worst kind of calls, the ones I had come to dread. As the animal control officer of a small city, hearing the police dispatcher over the radio saying the words *animal* and *car* in the same sentence was never good news. Sighing, I drove to the address I'd been given.

Pulling up to the scene, I saw several people out in front of the apartment building, huddled over an animal. She had been a beautiful cat, with gray stripes and white paws. She was already gone, which gave me some relief, as it always broke my heart to see them suffer. I wrapped her in a blanket I kept in the car for this purpose, and gently laid her down in the back of the wagon. I grabbed my clipboard and walked back to the small crowd that had gathered. The superintendent had his arms folded across his chest, shifting his weight from one foot to the other. He looked like a man who had many things to do, and taking the time to answer questions for my report wasn't one of them.

"No pets are allowed in this building—no dogs or cats—so I have no idea why this one was around." He looked pointedly from me to the elderly lady who was standing to the other side of me. Her eyes widened, and she quickly looked down at her feet.

"He's right. No pets in this building," she said in a low voice.

*Originally published in *Chicken Soup for the Cat Lover's Soul* © 2005.

I slid the clipboard under my arm and said, "I can write the rest of this myself." I wasn't in the mood to deal with yet another person who just didn't care. The super walked off in the opposite direction, obviously glad that this disruption to his schedule was over. As I walked to the car, pulling a pen out of my pocket, I felt a hand on my shoulder.

"Please wait," the voice said. "I want to show you something." It was the lady who had been standing with the super.

I looked at my watch. I was already twenty minutes late to my next call.

"I had to wait until he was gone," she said. She looked in the direction of the departing super. I was beginning to understand.

I walked with her around the back of the building and into the laundry room. The woman crouched down next to a dryer. "I knew the cat that died. I called her Misty because of her gray color, even though she would never come too close to me. I think she was one of those, what you call, um, feral cats. She didn't trust people, but I left her a can of food and fresh water every day."

When she paused, I heard a tiny mewing sound coming from behind the dryer. Reaching my hand in under the machine, I felt a warm fuzzy ball of fur. I carefully pulled out my hand to find a tiny, gray-and-white, spitting, growling, mewing kitten, a week old at most. She was looking at me with her one open eye (the other one not yet opened, as happens sometimes with newborn kittens). She seemed very frightened, although she was actively trying out all the new sounds she was capable of making.

"I couldn't say anything in front of the super. I've looked all around the building, and this is the only kitten. I didn't know Misty was expecting; like I said, I could never get that close." The lady struggled to stand up, gripping the dryer for help. "Isn't that strange, just one kitten in a litter?" she asked. "What's going to happen to her without her mother?"

I understood her concern. Kittens younger than five weeks old need a lot of care—nursing every four hours around the clock is only part of the challenge. The local animal shelter didn't have the manpower necessary to care for a kitten so young, but they would take her at six weeks, when she could eat solid food—which didn't help right now. I knew that the best place for this kitten would be with a mother cat that could nurse and clean her. The problem was, where could I find one that would accept this little orphan as her own?

"I'll figure something out," I said, and tucked the tiny kitten inside my coat. The day had started out with a tragedy, but I was determined not to let it end with another one.

It was easy enough to find the necessary equipment at the local pet store—tiny bottles and kitten formula—and even easier to find the time to stop and care for her during the day, given the nature of my job. It was a common sight to see me at my desk with a cat or a dog on my lap while I filed reports. In the hectic atmosphere of the police station, no one seemed to care, or even notice.

At night, I brought the kitten home with me, setting the alarm for feedings every three hours. Unfortunately, the kitten wanted to be fed every two hours, and soon the lack of sleep began to take its toll. I was also starting to worry; the tiny gray kitten didn't seem very strong, or to be growing as fast as I would have liked. I felt very alone—solely responsible for her survival, and at a loss about what to do next. To make matters worse, my new landlord had reached his limit regarding my pets, even the temporary ones. I'd moved to a larger apartment, tempted by the luxury of a separate bedroom and kitchen. It turned out to be a mistake. I missed my old landlords, and I even missed my garage. I'd found that sometimes moving up isn't what it's cracked up to be. Misty's kitten needed a home—and fast.

The next morning, the dispatcher told me to "Ten-Thirty-Three the lieutenant." This meant that I had to return to headquarters and speak with Lieutenant Harris. Lieutenaut Harris had been with the department longer than anyone else, and even the mention of his name was enough to make you stand up straighter. He commanded respect, and even a little fear. I knew that being summoned to his office meant it was probably something very serious, as he rarely had contact with the civilian employees.

I left the kitten in a carrier in my car and went inside to seek my fate, knocking quietly on the lieutenant's door.

"Come in," he barked. Slowly, I entered his office and stood in front of his desk. Lieutenant Harris didn't look up. I stood there awkwardly, scanning the numerous framed awards and commendations on the wall. He was busily writing on a legal pad.

"You can sit down now," he said, still not looking up.

I sat.

The lieutenant put his pen down, sighed, clasped his hands in front of him, and looked up at me for the first time, his eyes flinty.

"So, I understand that you have a very young kitten in your custody. Is this so?"

My heart sank. Now I was in for it! Flustered, I opened my mouth to tell him, yes, I did have this tiny kitten with me all of the time, but I hadn't let it interfere with my job. That I couldn't bring this kitten to the shelter because it was too young to survive there, and I was now worried that she wouldn't make it. That I was exhausted because I hadn't slept more than two hours at a time for a week, and that I felt like I was going to cry. I was going to say all of these things, but the only thing that came out of my mouth were the words "Yes, sir," in a hoarse whisper.

He looked at me sternly, and then his face broke into smile. "Can I see it?" he said.

Eager to comply, I rushed outside and brought in the carrier, a bottle, and some formula.

"Close the door," the lieutenant said, and gestured for me to give him the kitten.

"She has some long-haired breed in her," Lieutenant Harris said as he carefully scratched behind her ears. I handed him the bottle, and he started to feed the kitten. He looked happier than I had ever imagined he could look. I told him the story of how I had come to have the kitten.

When I finished, he said, "There's something very special about this little cat, surviving like that when the odds were against her. Yes, there's definitely a special reason for this little girl here.

Hey, that might be a good name for her—Reason!" He smiled at me and said, "Now let's put our heads together and figure out how we can help her."

By the end of the day there was a plan in place. It seemed as though everyone stopped what they were doing to consider how they could help. The assistant district attorney spoke to the youth officer who had a friend who bred Persian cats. The youth officer called her friend and learned that one of the Persians had just had a new litter and was nursing. The breeder said I could come over to her apartment to see if her cat would accept Reason and let her nurse with her own kittens.

When we got there, I put Reason down close to the mother cat and the other kittens. The youth officer and I stood there, waiting to see what would happen. The tiny gray-and-white kitten waddled over to the others and nosed her way into the crowd. As I stood there, holding my breath, the mother cat stretched out her paw and drew Reason to her. She started bathing her, licking her all over her head, as if she were saying, "Just where have you been? You're filthy!" The tiny gray-and-white kitten then took her place among the other five cream-colored Persian kittens to nurse.

Six weeks later, when she was weaned, Reason was adopted by a young woman who had come over initially to purchase a Persian kitten, but decided that she wanted Reason instead. Reason would be pampered and loved for the rest of her life.

I think the lieutenant was right. Reason *was* special—surviving against the odds and inspiring a whole police station to rally around her. So often in my line of work, endings were not the happy kind. Reason gave *me* a reason to believe in happy endings again, and taught me that sometimes, all you really have to do when you need help is to ask for it.

Of Moons and Minks

Strange things always seemed to happen during the last hour of my shift, on the last day of the week before a long holiday weekend. Some invisible radar went out all over the city, signaling the most eccentric of our residents to pick up their phones and call for the animal control officer. To make matters worse, the long weekend meant that the shelter would also be closed for three days, and it was up to me to find a place to keep the animal until then. While this really did happen every once in a while, it was guaranteed to happen when "Full Moon Murphy" was on the desk.

Sergeant Murphy was one of my favorite sergeants. He had a great sense of humor, and the entire department respected his leadership. He had that rare gift of being able to tell people things they didn't want to hear, and then having them thank him afterward. It was a useful talent to have in a profession like law enforcement. It wasn't unusual to walk in on him at headquarters talking to someone he'd just arrested like he'd invited the person over for coffee.

". . . and so, Mr. Davis, that appearance date on the ticket—yes, that one there—that's the date that we'll see you in court. Yes, of course. Well, that's perfect . . . I can wish you a happy birthday then too! Ha, ha . . . looking forward to it. You have a nice day now. Well, thank you, I definitely will too."

I don't think I ever saw anyone get upset with him; prisoners even waved good-bye to him when they boarded the van to go down to the county jail. Unfortunately, though, the oddest and strangest things would happen when Murphy was on the desk, giving him the well-earned nickname of "Full Moon Murphy." I think even he expected that almost anything could happen, and resigned himself to it. Sometimes, however, he would be the one responsible for the chaos.

One time he called me in off the road, insisting that someone had dropped off an animal that he couldn't identify. I followed him into the hallway outside the muster room, and there on the floor appeared to be several snakes sloshing around in a bucket. When I refused to open the bucket, insisting that my job description didn't include reptiles, and attempted to make my escape, he pried open the container, reached in, grabbed one, and flung it at me. It was rubber.

Then there was the time he sent me to the old empty high school on Washington Street, to listen for a barking dog possibly stuck inside. I spent over an hour in that abandoned (and very creepy) building, trying to find a dog that didn't exist. I never found out who was doing the barking, but I had a feeling he did.

He once thought it would be fun to "accidentally" lock me in the elevator that takes prisoners from the downstairs cells in the police department, upstairs to court.

"This is strange," Sgt. Murphy said, standing outside the locked elevator. "This key's always worked before. I have no idea what could have happened. I know, I'll have the locksmith come over and take a look at this, although that could be a while . . . Oh look, it's my lunch hour—would you like me to get you something?"

So when Sgt. Murphy called me on the radio to advise me that there was a woman who wanted to surrender a fur coat on Broad Street, I was prepared for another one of his practical jokes.

"There's a complainant at one-thirty-five Broad Street—said she wants to see you about a fur coat." I pulled into my driveway and went inside to use my phone, because I had no idea how to respond to that on the radio without offending the FCC.

"Sarge, it's me. Okay, very funny . . . What is it now?"

"No, really," he said, even though I could hear he was trying not to laugh. "This woman has called three times in the last ten minutes. She is raving about her mink, or minks—maybe she has more than one—but she wants you to come and pick it up or she's going to call the chief. She asked for the 'Controller of Beasts'—what do you think of that?"

"I think you're setting me up again," I said.

"No, honestly, it's no joke. I may be wrong, because I was having a hard time with her accent, but she's really angry, and"—he couldn't contain himself any longer, and I could hear him choke back what actually seemed to be a giggle—"waiting for you."

I drove over to the address. I had about fifteen minutes before my shift, and my week, was supposed to be over. Maybe it was all some type of misunderstanding, and she really didn't need to talk to me. At least I knew that this call wouldn't involve any animals, so I didn't have to start trying to make plans for finding shelter over the weekend. If this person wanted to give me a coat, well, why not? I'd drop it on Sgt. Murphy's desk and let him figure out what to do with it. I'd been on stranger calls.

I pulled up to the curb and parked. Grabbing my jacket off the front seat, I made sure to remove my badge from my shirt and put it on the lapel of my jacket. There'd been a memo out about that. Every time the seasons changed, it seemed that we had to be reminded about things like this: when to start wearing short-sleeved uniform shirts, or when to go back to long sleeves. You'd think it would be common sense—that when it was thirty degrees outside, you should probably go back to wearing your long-sleeved shirts—but it wasn't that easy. Everyone had to be the same; hence, the word *uniform*.

In some ways you were encouraged to think for yourself in the law enforcement business, to use your head. But in others, you were expected to follow orders and take direction, no questions asked. It still surprised me that it was sometimes the smallest things that could get me into trouble. Once, I had unintentionally insulted a close relative of the county executive on the phone when working the desk, which the lieutenant had found sort of amusing. No big deal. But—leaving your badge on your shirt and not putting it on your jacket when you met with a complainant? Now *that* was a big deal. I felt like a lot of the time, even after a year, I was still learning the ropes.

When I pulled up to the address, I found myself in front of a tall, old-fashioned row house. Most of them had been made into apartments years ago, but it looked to me like this one was still a single-family dwelling. I walked up some narrow stairs and knocked on the door. Opening the door in such a rush that I almost fell backward was a very tall, exotic-looking woman who seemed to be in her mid-forties. Her shiny black hair was pulled up into a very large bun at the top of her head. She had on a series of scarves in many different colors, and the smell of incense was overpowering. She looked at me carefully, like she was examining me for something. I noticed that she had on a lot of black eyeliner that extended way beyond the place where her eyelids would naturally end, and I was trying not to stare too hard. I opened my mouth to introduce myself, but before I could get a word out, she grabbed my hand.

"Good—you come take them. They lied to me about them. They are not the right kind!" She pulled me into the house, looking around as if to check for other people. Wouldn't she know who was in her own house? She was starting to make me a little uncomfortable. "I can't control them," she whispered. "Come in here quick and take them."

"Okay, hold on—let me get some of the paperwork ready." I looked at her, expecting that she would let go of my hand, but she held fast. I pulled my hand back, and she let go.

"Oh, I am sorry. I am so . . ." She started to wave her hands around her head. I pulled my pen out of my front pocket and started to write down some of the information for the complaint. She seemed to be getting more agitated by the minute, and the incense was starting to make me feel dizzy. *The faster I get this coat and get out of here, the better*, I thought. Only about five minutes remained until my shift ended, and I was anxious for this workweek to come to an end.

"Would you like to show me the, uh, problem?" I asked.

"They are in the basement. Come." She turned around, walking quickly down a narrow hallway to a door that led downstairs. I followed her, thinking that it made perfect sense to keep rogue, uncontrollable fur coats in the basement. "Of course—Full Moon Murphy! It makes sense," I said, not realizing I had spoken the words aloud.

She whipped around to face me as we were walking down the stairs, and one of her scarves hit me in the face. I had to claw at it so I could see.

"Is it because of the moon?" she asked.

I wasn't sure what she meant, but she looked at me wide-eyed, as though I had given her the answer she had been looking for. "No. I don't know. I'm sorry—if you could just show me where your, um, minks are." I couldn't imagine why she felt she had to give them to me, but perhaps since I was the animal control officer, and she claimed she could no longer "control" them, that somewhere within all of that, this made sense to her. I was starting to think that this was indeed a set up, perhaps the best practical joke the sarge had ever played on me. I was hoping that whatever was going on would end soon so I could leave and return to headquarters, where I could begin planning my retaliation against Sgt. Murphy.

We descended the stairway. She turned and looked at me intently in front of a door that had several chain locks on it. "They are here. The wrong minks are in here! They make too much noise so you take away!"

Noise? Fur coats didn't make noise, oh no, she couldn't mean . . . "Minks!" I exclaimed. "You have live minks in your basement?" All of the sudden I realized why Murphy had sent animal control to this call instead of a regular patrol officer. He knew these were animals she was talking about, but when he sent me here he left that part out. No doubt, intentionally. Were minks indigenous to the area? I didn't even know where you would usually find minks, although I knew they looked a little like ferrets. I should probably know more about them, but I hadn't ever come across a situation like this before. Dogs, cats, sometimes even raccoons and skunks, with the occasional possum thrown in there—but minks? I wasn't really supposed to be handling anything but domestic animals anyway. Was this lady some type of real-life Cruella De Vil?

"Yes, they said they are minks. I send money and more money . . . and I get this!" She unchained each lock and swung open the door. On the floor of the basement, in two wire cages, were four older kittens, all meowing and hissing as soon as they saw her. The unusual thing about these kittens, aside from the fact that they were locked up in a basement, was that they had no tails.

"You see this? These are not the right minks. These are not soft!"

I felt like I was going to start laughing. I didn't want to add *laughing at a complainant* to my growing list of mistakes. That wouldn't be a good idea. I bit the inside of my mouth, hoping the pain would distract me long enough to control myself. It didn't. I chuckled out loud. Maybe she would think it was funny too?

"These are Manx cats, not minks. Manx is a breed of cat with no tail."

She turned and glared at me. "First, you not come for a long time, and I call and call. Finally, you are here, and you tell me it is because of the moon. Now you are telling me these are minks with no tails?!"

"No, ma'am." I had to hold it together because it seemed like she was getting worked up again. "Manx. M-A-N-X. It's a breed of cat with—"

Before I could finish, she started to jog around the basement, flowing material spinning around her, making it look like she was performing some type of dance. "Cats! Cats! I can't have cats here. I didn't buy cats!" Her dislike of the cats seemed to be mutual. Every time she pranced closer to them, their hissing increased in volume.

The worst moment was telling her that I had no facilities for her cats until the long weekend was over. The shelter was already closed. Our outdoor holding area near Public Works was too cold to keep kittens, even older ones, in late February. I definitely couldn't take them home for the weekend because my landlord was still reminding me of the last time I did that, and there was absolutely no way I could bring them to headquarters. These cats would have to stay here, in the warm basement, but just for a few more days, three at most.

"I can't have them here, no!" She was very frustrated as I tried to explain my predicament. She was still reeling over the fact that she had spent a great deal of money on cats. She finally calmed down when she realized that I would indeed be taking them away, although not until Tuesday.

I decided I wanted to know what she had planned for the minks. Thinking the worst, I asked, "Why did you buy, or try to buy, minks?"

She looked at me like I was the crazy one.

"The lady I meet on the bus give me the phone number for mink *coats* at a good price. I thought maybe, for such a good price, I buy a few and sell some to my friends. But then they come to my house with these bad minks and no coats. I say take them back and they say 'no refund.' So I keep them for a while but then I see that they are not right, not soft. I think, now I have these bad minks." She looked sadly at the hissing kittens and sighed. "But I have no minks . . . just cats."

At least now I was starting to understand why she just didn't turn away the animals when she saw they weren't coats, but I still wasn't sure why she would have kept them if they had been "good" minks? I swallowed. I had to ask. "What were you planning on doing to these, um, animals? Make coats out of them?"

"No!" she yelled at me. I had insulted her somehow, again. "I never do such a thing!"

"Oh, okay," I said. Relief coursed through my veins. Standing in a basement with a crazy woman was bad enough, but the thought of standing alongside someone who had the capability—and the tools—to skin live animals for their fur was even worse.

"I sell them to man who make the coats for me. I no do that myself. I am not cruel woman!" I looked at her. I didn't know what else to say. *Oh, of course, having someone else make a coat out of them is so much more humane.* I had been starting to feel sorry for her, now I just wanted to get those cats out of there as quickly as possible. The bad news was that they would have to stay in her basement over the long weekend. The good news was that these cats were the "wrong" type of "minks" so their future didn't include becoming part of the new winter collection at a fashion show. I had to wind this up as it was already past the end of my shift. All I wanted was to go home and crawl under a blanket with a bag of chips and try to forget this day.

"I have cat food in the car. I will bring up enough food for the weekend and all you have to do is provide water, so there's no more expense to you. I will come and take them first thing Tuesday morning, bright and early, and I won't even charge you a surrender fee. What do you think?" I looked at her in what I hoped was an encouraging way, nodding my head and smiling.

She looked at me and then back to the cats and sighed. "Water?" she asked.

"Yes, yes . . . just feed and water them. They'll be fine, and I'll come and get them as soon as I'm back at work on Tuesday."

"Okay," she said, resigned to the fact that this was the only way she was going to get rid of these fake minks anytime soon.

"Water, right?" she asked again.

"Yes, just water. I'll give you the food." I ran upstairs and out the door, and then down some more stairs to my wagon. This was exhausting. I opened the hatch and took out several cans of cat food that I kept in a box in the back of the car. Too frequently, I had calls from apartment owners who found, sometimes several days later, that their former tenants had left behind more than just a mess. I'd lost track of how many dogs and cats people left behind without a thought to literally starve to death. I always kept food in the car for this purpose. Even though this day had been frustrating, it was nothing like that, for which I was grateful.

"Here you go," I said, handing her the cans and trying to catch my breath. "I promise I'll be here first thing Tuesday morning."

She looked at me warily, wringing the end of one of her scarves with her hands. I noticed she had rings on every finger.

"As long as you come back like you say." She seemed to begrudgingly accept this solution. I got into my car and put the key in the ignition. It was five o'clock, an hour past the end of my shift. I pulled away, thinking that the worst was over. Next week I would take the cats to the shelter where the staff would give them time to acclimate to humans before adopting them out. They would easily find homes. It wasn't even kitten season, and these were purebred Manx kittens. It was going to be just fine. It had to be.

As I walked into headquarters on Tuesday morning, I didn't get as far as the lobby before Rob, one of the night dispatchers, shouted over to me. "You gotta go over to one-thirty-five Broad Street right now. This crazy lady has been calling every few minutes, and insists on talking only to you, the 'Beast Controller.' She's driving me nuts!"

I turned and ran right out the door to my wagon and started it up. The sooner this was over, the better. Within a few minutes I was in front of 135 Broad Street. She was outside waiting for me as I pulled up.

"Why so long? You tell me you come back early. It is already past early!" She'd probably thought I would return at dawn, even though I had tried to explain to her last week that my shift started at 8:00 a.m. I knew that it didn't matter; there was some sort of communication breakdown, a language barrier of some sort. I smiled, trying to be pleasant. Perhaps there was someone at headquarters who could act as a translator. Why hadn't I thought of this before?

"You have a lovely accent. Do you mind if I ask you where you are from?"

She looked at me again, in a way that made me feel like she definitely thought I was missing some cards from my deck. "New York," she said, totally serious.

"Oh, me too," I said. I decided I'd give up on small talk in what now seemed to be a futile effort to encourage good public relations. Again, we traveled down the stairs, and there was the unchaining of locks.

"You tell me food and water, but now it is worse."

I couldn't imagine how giving these animals food and water would make it worse. I was really anxious to get those poor kittens away from this woman. She opened the door and waved her arm in the direction of the two wire cages. "Look!"

There sat the kittens, except it looked as though they had been swimming. They were drenched. They seemed fine and healthy—just incredibly wet.

"What happened?" I asked. "Was there a leak or something down here over the weekend?"

"No!" She turned to me. I could see that once again, I had said something to make her even more upset, although I still didn't know what it was. "You tell me when you leave to give food, so I do that. Then you tell me to water them, so I do that—and look at this mess!"

I looked at her, incredulous at this point. "What do you mean, water them? Did you *pour* water on them?"

"Yes, yes . . . just like you say. I water them with"—she looked around a moment and then picked up a watering can next to the step—"this . . . just like you tell me. Now look at this mess!"

First, she had thought she was buying coats; then, she'd thought she had minks; and then, the wrong type of minks with no tails. Finally, after realizing she had cats, she'd decided to water them like plants. Thinking back, I did remember saying that she should "feed and water them," so in some way, I was probably responsible for this. I looked at her and realized that she truly had no clue. I looked over to the wet kittens. They must have sensed the tension, because for the first time, they had stopped meowing. They were looking at me, blinking.

"Thank you. Thank you very much. I will take them now. Good job." I quickly strode over to pick up the cages. She finally seemed to loosen up a little, and she smiled back.

"Thank *you*," she said, moving aside so I could carry the dripping cages up the stairs. "You keep cages, too. I am out of the mink business."

She followed me out to the car and watched as I struggled to put both of the cages in the back. I started the car and turned up the heat so they would be warm, and hopefully dry, by the time we got to the shelter.

"Oh, you stay for some tea?" the woman asked, by this time more cheerful than I had seen her yet.

"Oh, no thanks," I said, smiling back at her, hoping she didn't notice my smile bordered on crazed. "I have to get these minks to the animal shelter!" and then chuckled, probably more out of near hysteria than anything else.

"Oh, no, no," she said as she wagged her finger at me. "You mean cats!" She laughed. I waved and laughed back.

I pulled away, watching her become smaller and smaller in the rearview mirror. Every time I looked back and saw the Manx kittens, now nearly dry and quite content, I found that I just couldn't stop laughing.

At a red light I had that strange feeling you get when you sense someone is looking at you. I glanced over at the car in the next lane and saw an elderly couple peering over at me in an odd way. For some reason that just made me laugh harder. As a matter of fact, I couldn't stop laughing for quite a while, until well after I was beyond the city limits and heading south on the highway toward the shelter.

Buster's Last Stand

During the four years I spent as an animal control officer, I learned that dogs are the first to know when spring has arrived. Dogs who typically never venture farther than their own backyard will somehow find themselves across town, following the scent of spring.

Buster was no exception. Each year Animal Control received several phone calls complaining about Buster—and always in the spring. Buster was an ancient, overweight, and often cranky bull terrier with a profound underbite that snored in the shade of his yard all summer and seemed content to stay behind his fence during the winter. But as soon as it started to thaw, Buster began to terrorize the city.

In actuality, Buster, at almost thirteen years old, was too old to terrorize anyone. His once tan-and-brindle coat was mixed with so much gray that he appeared to be even older, and I noticed the beginning of a limp that looked to be a sign of arthritic hips. He never chased anyone; I don't think he could have if he'd tried. Still, his appearance and his perpetual nasal congestion, combined with his bad attitude, made people uncomfortable when he got loose.

Sometimes he would get it in his head to sit outside the local deli and glare at the customers. First, the deli owners tried throwing roast beef at him, but he just sniffed at it, gobbled it up, growled, and

*Originally published in condensed form in *Chicken Soup for the Dog Lover's Soul* © 2005.

stayed right where he was. Then they tried shouting at him. That didn't work either. Most people just got out of his way when they saw him coming, and called Animal Control.

His owner, Tim, a thin, silent man who appeared ageless in that way men do who work outdoors most of their lives, usually showed up at the pound, apologized, asked someone to tell me to drop off his ticket, and took Buster home. He wrapped his thin arms around Buster's very large middle and heaved him into the back of his pickup truck. He never complained, never asked for a court date. He just apologized and paid his fines.

Tim didn't seem the kind of person who would be interested in having a pet, especially one as difficult as Buster. He lived alone in a large, dilapidated Victorian house in a perpetual state of renovation. He had never married, and no one really knew if he had any family. He didn't seem comfortable showing affection to anyone, least of all a fat, grumpy old bulldog, and Buster never let anyone touch him, except for Tim, and even then he didn't look too happy about it. Yet year after year, Tim spent a lot of time leaving work to come and drag his grouchy old dog home.

One spring, it seemed as though Buster had finally gone into retirement, merely growling at passersby from the comfort of his own yard. That was why I was a bit surprised when I got a call on a very warm mid-June day that a very ugly, old, fat, and wheezing bulldog was causing a problem up at the high school.

How did he get all the way up there? I thought to myself as I drove to the school. The route from Buster's home to the high school was all uphill. I had seen Buster recently, and he surely didn't look as if he could make a trip like that.

I pulled into the high school parking lot and saw the gymnasium doors open, probably for a cross breeze. Buster must have entered the school through the gym.

This should be fun. I grabbed a box of dog biscuits and the snare pole and threw a leash around my neck. No animal control officer had ever actually touched Buster. The equipment was going to be of no real use; he would likely never let me near him. I had to figure out a way to get him to *want* to leave. I hoped the biscuits would do the job.

Entering the hallway, I saw lines of teenagers standing in suspended animation along the walls. One called out to me, "Every time I even go to open my locker that dog growls at me. He's going to eat us!"

Sure enough, there was Buster—holding the entire hallway hostage. I could see him standing, bowlegged, wheezing like I had never heard him before, and growling at any sudden movement. *Uh-oh*, I thought to myself. Frightening the occasional neighbor was one thing, but growling at kids on school property—Buster was looking at some serious penalties, possibly even a dangerous dog action complaint, which was a rare occurrence, but one with dire consequences if he was found guilty.

"Buster," I called to him, and he managed to twist his pudgy body around to see who knew his name. He looked at me, wheezed some more, and growled loudly. I reached into the box of biscuits and threw one over to him. He limped over to it slowly, sniffed it, sneezed, and sat down, glaring at me. So much for Plan A. I was going to have to use the snare pole on him, and I wasn't looking forward to it.

Suddenly from behind me I heard, "Hey, ugly dog. Try this." A tall teenage boy put his hand into a baggie and threw a Froot Loop at Buster. Buster stared at the cereal, then up at the boy. He snuffled around it, picked it up, and swallowed it. I turned to the tall boy leaning against the wall.

"Hey, can I borrow those?"

"Sure." He handed me the baggie, and I threw a Froot Loop toward Buster. He waddled over to suck it up off the floor. *Hey*, I thought, *this just might work!* Hoping I would have enough to get Buster all the way to my car, I kept dropping them as I backed toward the open doors of the gym. Buster was in bad shape; his bowed legs seemed to have a hard time holding up his rotund little body. Every step seemed to cause him pain, and the wheezing was getting worse. I wanted to pick him up, but as I started to approach, he growled and backed up. So I continued to drop one Froot Loop at a time, inching my way toward the patrol car.

Finally Buster was at the car. He was wheezing so much I worried he would have a heart attack. I decided to just get him home and worry about the report later; Buster was fading fast.

I threw what was left of the Froot Loops into the backseat of the car. Buster waddled over and stuck his two front paws on the floor to finish them up. I swallowed hard and quickly pushed Buster's rear end into the backseat. He grumbled and growled, but was mostly concerned with chewing the last bit of cereal. I couldn't believe it; I had touched Buster and survived!

By the time I pulled up in front of Buster's house, Tim's truck was parked haphazardly in front. Tim ran out of the house, letting the door slam behind him. "Is Buster okay? I called the school, but you had already left. I'll pay the fine, whatever it is. Give me a couple of 'em. How did he get out of the house? I can't believe he made it all the way to the high school. He's so sick. How'd you get him in the car anyway?" Tim spoke more in that minute than I had ever heard him speak in the several years I had known him.

Before I could answer, Tim walked over to the patrol car and opened the door. Buster was snoring loudly, sound asleep on his back, covered in Froot Loop crumbs and looking very un-Buster-like. Tim put his arms around the old dog and with a lot of effort, pulled him out of the car, holding him as you would an infant. Buster never even woke up, just grumbled a bit in his sleep.

"I, um, used Froot Loops," I said. "He followed a trail of them into the car."

Tim lifted his eyes from the sleeping dog to look at me. "Froot Loops? I didn't know he liked Froot Loops."

The lines in Tim's pale face seemed deeper in the harsh sunlight. He looked tired, but something more. He looked worried. "I can't believe he got out. I had him locked in the house with the air conditioner on." Tim's voice dropped. "The vet says he has cancer and heart failure. They told me to take him home from the animal hospital for the weekend, you know, to say good-bye."

I looked at Tim holding his old, fat, gray bull terrier, and I understood, now, what I hadn't before. All those years that had etched the premature lines on Tim's sad face—Buster had been there to share them. They had each other, and for them, that had been enough.

"I'm so sorry, Tim," I said, and turned to get back into the car. "I'll talk to you when I see you."

"What about my tickets? I know I'm getting a few this time, right?"

I turned around to look at Tim. "Let me see what the sergeant says first, Tim. You just worry about Buster right now, okay?"

I started to go again, but then remembered there was something else I wanted to ask.

"Tim?" I called over to him as he was carrying his dog into the house. "Why do you think he went to the high school? I don't remember him going all the way up there before."

Tim smiled at me, another thing I had never seen him do. "Buster really loves kids. I used to bring him to the playground when he was a pup. Maybe he remembered that."

I nodded and waved to them, the thin, tired man with the gray flannel shirt carrying his thirteen-year-old puppy into the house, perhaps for the last time.

Buster died soon after that day. I never even wrote up a ticket for his caper at the high school. I figured Buster had just been revisiting his youth, saying good-bye in his own Buster way. You think you know people, and then you find out there is more to them than you could ever imagine.

Whether it's a quiet loner who keeps his feelings to himself, or a bulky, aging bulldog with an underbite—what you see on the outside rarely reveals the depth of what's below the surface. The face of love takes many forms, and all of them are beautiful.

His Master's Voice

$\mathcal{T}$here was an almost palpable sense of dread in the silence that followed the phone call. It was known as a "check on the welfare." Many of these types of calls ended up being routine. Someone accidentally pulled the phone line out of the wall, or had forgotten to turn the ringer back on after a nap. At least, that's what everyone hoped it was.

Sergeant Murphy, known for his sense of humor and penchant for practical jokes, was unusually grim. "I'm not sending the ACO up to that house yet." He glanced over at two police officers standing near the dispatch desk. "You go on up to Summit, and take Officer Romano with you. The niece said that the key is taped under the mailbox. Seems Mr. Carlson had . . ." Sgt. Murphy paused and took a breath. The only sound was the faint noise of the traffic outside. Clearing his throat, he corrected himself. ". . . *has* a tendency to be forgetful."

Mr. Carlson's niece had called from Long Island. She had been trying to get in touch with her uncle for days, and had finally decided to call the police. She was worried because he was in his eighties, and shared his large house with only his fourteen-year-old schnauzer, who in dog years was even older than Mr. Carlson.

"His dog's name is Harry, and he's not good with other people," the niece had warned Sgt. Murphy. "He's lived with my uncle his entire life and doesn't interact with other people or animals. He's antisocial. He'll probably try to bite anyone who comes into the house."

"Sarge, I can go too, if you want. I can handle it," I said, hoping I didn't sound as scared as I felt. If there was a situation that included a dog trapped in a house, and one that possibly hadn't been fed in a few days, then it was likely that the dog could be aggressive and would need to be handled with equipment. It wasn't the dog that scared me; it was discovering the reason why no one had been able to reach Mr. Carlson.

"No, Lisa, I'm not putting you through that. If we need you to pick up the dog, we'll call you on the radio and meet you." Sgt. Murphy stood up from the desk and put on his hat. Walking past me on his way out the door, he lightly yanked on my ponytail.

"You're okay, kid." Sometimes Sgt. Murphy treated me more like his daughter than one of his officers. I didn't mind, especially today.

About an hour later, I received a call over the radio to report up to Mr. Carlson's street. By the time I got up to Summit Place, there were flashing lights everywhere. The ambulance sat outside the house and the department's police doctor was already there. They had found Mr. Carlson lying in his bed, where he had apparently passed away in his sleep a few days before. When the police had entered the house, they had brought along my snare pole, just in case Mr. Carlson's dog tried to attack them.

"We didn't need it," Officer Phil Romano said as he strode over to my car and handed me the snare pole.

"It was the strangest thing, like something out of a story I read years ago. That dog didn't move or make a sound when we came in; he was just lying across his owner's chest, sort of like he was trying to protect him. It was real sad." Phil's eyes seemed watery. These were the hardest types of calls, and it seemed like everyone tried to be as businesslike as possible. It was sometimes the small things afterward, like finding a devoted pet lying next to its owner's body, that would break through the walls they had built to protect themselves.

"He came right to us when we called his name, like he knew there was nothing else for him to do, sort of like he was waiting for us," Officer Romano said. "He had those bowls that automatically refill with food and water, but he would've run out in another day."

"Where is he?" I asked. "Is he inside? Should I . . . ?" Before I could continue with my questions, Sgt. Murphy came walking across the lawn holding a black-and-gray medium-sized schnauzer. He didn't look like an antisocial dog to me. His sad eyes were partially obscured by cataracts, but he seemed to be able to see pretty well. His muzzle was entirely gray, and his whiskers made him look like an old man with a mustache.

"Hi, Harry," I said, surprised when his little stump of a tail started to wag in response to hearing his name.

"Sad situation, but if you have to go, that's the way to do it," Sgt. Murphy said as he handed Harry over to me. "The niece is already on her way up with her husband to make funeral arrangements. I asked them what they wanted to do with Harry here, and you're not going to like it. Hell, I don't like it."

"What did she say?" I couldn't imagine what anyone could say in a situation like this to make Sgt. Murphy mad. I didn't often see him this way.

"They said that he could never adjust to living with them. He only liked Mr. Carlson."

"So, she's surrendering him?" I asked, wondering two things at the same time: Why did Sergeant Murphy look so upset, and who could I find that would adopt a fourteen-year-old dog? Harry let out a sigh, like he knew what I was thinking, and rested his muzzle on my shoulder. How could anyone think this dog was antisocial?

"No." Sergeant Murphy looked uncomfortable. "She's not." He looked back over at the house.

"Rob," Doc called, gesturing for Sgt. Murphy to come over.

"I'm coming," he called over his shoulder, then looked back at me.

"They want to bury him with their uncle," Sgt. Murphy said in almost a whisper.

I thought that perhaps I hadn't heard him correctly. "They want to bury Harry with Mr. Carlson?" I asked, thinking that I definitely hadn't heard him right. The sergeant nodded his head yes.

"They can't do that. He's not dead."

"Yet." Sgt. Murphy spit out the word in anger. I didn't understand what he was getting at; then, all of the sudden I realized what they wanted to do.

"They can't do that. They absolutely *cannot* do that! There's nothing wrong with this dog. I don't think they have the right to make that kind of decision!" I was practically shouting by this point. Sgt. Murphy put his hand on my shoulder.

"I think they can, hon. Listen—hold on to Harry right now, and we'll see what we can do. They won't be up here for a while, since it's about a two-hour drive from Long Island. I have to attend to things here."

I nodded, my mouth still open. I couldn't believe what I had heard. Two people, who obviously didn't know anything about this dog, were planning to have Harry, who was still quite alive and seemingly healthy, put to sleep!

"Don't worry about anything, Harry," I whispered into his ear, wondering if he would understand what I was saying. "There's nothing to worry about." I placed him on the passenger seat in my car, knowing the entire time that the words weren't meant just for him.

I drove to the riverfront and parked the car. I sometimes went there when it wasn't crowded to fill out paperwork between calls. It had started off partly cloudy that morning, with the sun occasionally poking through the clouds, before finally settling on a light drizzle that seemed appropriate for the kind of day I was having. Harry sat up and stretched, and then gave a little snort.

"You probably have to go outside; what was I thinking?" That was usually the first thing I did when I had an animal in my custody. I had been so distracted by the situation surrounding Harry's fate that I hadn't been thinking clearly. "C'mon, Harry." I hooked a leash up to his faded red leather collar. His license and rabies tags were attached to it, and jingled when he moved. Even though he was in need of a bath, you could tell that he had been well taken care of. I noticed the most recent date on his tags was over three years old, and wondered if that had been the last time Mr. Carlson had had the energy to take Harry to the vet. Maybe he hadn't known that the senior center had volunteers to help with things like that. He could have called Animal Control. I would've brought Harry to the vet for him.

I walked him over to the water. The river looked as gray as the sky. The only other people around were the regulars who came every day to feed the geese and the ducks. They would sit on benches in nice weather and in their cars on days like this, reading the paper and sipping coffee. I was starting to feel jealous, wishing that coffee and the paper were the only things I had to worry about at the moment.

Harry walked slowly; however, he didn't limp or seem to have problems with his hips, which can often happen with older dogs. When he was done with his business, he led the way back to my car, where he jumped up on the door with his two front paws.

"You like the car?" His tail started to wag. This was a great dog. He seemed very adaptable, friendly, and well trained. In a way, I thought he understood that things had changed, but he was going to make the best of it. He hadn't chased any of the birds; he had let one of the women feeding the geese pet him; and he enjoyed riding in the car.

It occurred to me then, what I had to do. I had to prove Mr. Carlson's niece wrong. If I could show them enough evidence that Harry would easily adapt to another person, and that he still had life in him that he deserved to enjoy, perhaps then they would sign him over to me and I could find him a good home. Even better, maybe I could find him a home *first*; then they would have to admit that their decision made no sense. Burying a beloved dog with its owner did seem to be a poetic way to ensure they would be together forever, but only if both of them had died. What if it had been the other way around? What if Harry had died and Mr. Carlson was still alive? Maybe putting it that way would force them to see how ridiculous this was. I had to prove that Harry deserved to live. And I had a little less than two hours to do it.

I pulled files out of the file cabinet, put them back, and pulled out some more. There had to be someone I had dealt with who would take Harry in as their own. I was beginning to feel overwhelmed with the deadline looming over my head. I looked down at him, snoozing peacefully at my feet. I usually brought seized and surrendered animals directly to the shelter, although because of Harry's advanced age, it was unlikely that anyone would adopt him after the seven-day hold had expired. This was different, though; Harry was a purebred. Yes, he was an old purebred, but people are very loyal to their favorite breeds, and perhaps there was a rescue organization that dealt specifically with schnauzers.

I decided I would call Maureen at the shelter. She might give me a hard time, but there was something about Maureen; I knew she would help in this situation. She had a keen sense of justice. Killing a healthy and happy dog simply to make some dramatic statement at a funeral wouldn't make sense to her either. She would know what to do. She knew that when I "found" some pit bull puppies, I was really rescuing them from the drug dealer who bred them, and who had planned a life of dogfights and abuse for the dogs. Sometimes Maureen would look at you with her piercing gaze, and you would find yourself admitting to all sorts of things. Some days it seemed as though she was angrier than usual, and I would turn around and leave to come back the next day, just to avoid her wrath. But regardless of any conflicts we'd had with each other from time to time, we liked each other and shared the same goal. She wanted the animals she came into contact with to be treated humanely, as did I. I picked up the phone and called the shelter.

"You want a favor? Yes, I see; you think that I have all the time in the world to stop everything and do you a favor?" This wasn't that bad. She seemed to be in a regular type of mood. I could handle that.

"Maureen, you have to help me; it's literally a matter of life and death." As dramatic as I sounded, I knew that it was true. Maureen seemed to hear something in my voice that made her stop harassing me. I explained Harry's situation to her—how his owner had died, and how he had stood vigil over Mr. Carlson until someone had finally come to take him away. When I told her about what Mr. Carlson's niece had decided to do, she sounded upset.

"I've actually seen that happen before," she said softly, in a very non-Maureen voice. "Not often, but it has happened. Since the niece is the only next of kin, then legally, she has the right to make all the decisions about his belongings, and that includes his pets."

"But a dog is not a belonging; it's a living thing!" I couldn't believe what I was hearing. Sgt. Murphy had been right. They really could do this.

"Now, if they took charge of the dog and didn't care for it correctly, you could cite them with animal cruelty. But if they choose to have this dog euthanized, well, unless there is some provision made for the dog in a will, they're allowed to do this."

I didn't know what to say. I felt like all the wind had been knocked out of me. I looked down at Harry, happily chewing on the rest of my ham sandwich. (I hadn't felt all that hungry.)

There was silence on the phone; neither of us said anything. Finally Maureen spoke. "I think I know of a schnauzer rescue group around here. Let me see if I can find the number and give them a call. Legally, you're going to have to bring him down here, but we'll take good care of him. We'll keep him in the cat building where he won't have to share a pen. He'll be warm and comfortable, and we'll hold him for as long as you want. That will give you some time to work on this."

"Thanks, Maureen; I appreciate it." She was doing everything she possibly could. With the shelter as overcrowded as it was, offering to hold Harry indefinitely was a huge favor. The cat building was warm and inviting, and Harry would have a soft pillow to sleep on and lots of attention. Now all we had to do was to find a home for him, in less than an hour.

"The only thing I can't do is disregard the law," said Maureen. "If the niece calls and directs me to, you know . . . I'll have no choice. You should contact her as soon as you can and talk to her about options."

"I know, Maureen. Thanks for helping me. I have to convince her—that's my job today." I knew that the clock was ticking, but there was still hope.

"Good luck," Maureen said, and then hung up. I knew that no matter how busy Maureen was, even if there was a line of ten people waiting at the counter, she would look for that schnauzer rescue number before dealing with anything else.

I looked at Harry, who had gone back to sleep on my shoes, and then at the ceiling, hoping that an answer would drop out of the sky or something. I heard the squeak of someone's shoes, and I turned around.

"What do you have there? Is that a schnauzer?" It was Sergeant Kale, the in-house computer expert. We had just started to computerize the department, and he was the only one who could make sense out of it. He was the one everyone went to when the communications system acted up. If it was electronic, he could fix it. He wore his hair the way men did in the early 1960s. I had seen photographs of him when he started as a police officer. He looked pretty much the same, except for the silver coming in around his sideburns.

"Yes, this is Mr. Carlson's dog, the one—"

"Yup, I know—the DOA." Sgt. Kale bent down to pet Harry, scratching him behind the ears and leaning in to get better access.

"This is a standard schnauzer, looks like a salt-and-pepper. He was probably less gray when he was younger." Sgt. Kale was now giving Harry a good rubdown, and the dog was enjoying it.

"You know about schnauzers?" I asked. I was always carrying dogs of all types around the department, and Sgt. Kale had never seemed to notice. I hadn't thought of him as a dog lover.

"You've never seen Boo?" he asked, peering at me over his rimless glasses. I thought about it for a moment and then realized that I had seen his daughter walking a black schnauzer around my neighborhood. "Yes, I guess I have seen Beth walking a dog."

"You bet. That's my Boo. He's a standard schnauzer, too. They come in three sizes: miniature, standard, and giant. We had a giant schnauzer when I was a boy. Great dogs." It seemed to me that my answer hadn't dropped out of the ceiling. It had walked out of the back office.

"Sarge, I have a problem. Maybe you could help me with it?"

"Shoot," he said simply, giving me his full attention.

I explained the fate that was in store for Harry, how I was trying to find a way to keep him alive, and that time was running out. I told him how Mr. Carlson's niece had misjudged Harry, and that everything she had said about his temperament had been absolutely wrong. Sgt. Kale never stopped petting Harry the entire time I was talking.

"I'll take him," he said. "He's an old man, but he deserves to spend all the time he's got left with someone who knows schnauzers. Boo loves other dogs; it would be good for him." I heard a cracking sound when Sgt. Kale got up from petting Harry on the floor. He put his hand on his back and stretched, pivoting one way and then the other.

"None of us are as young as we used to be," he said, smiling. "I just have to call the wife and see if this is okay with her. She's on the road today, running errands. I'll keep trying until I get her."

I smiled back at him. I wanted to tell him he was an answer to a prayer, but I couldn't get the words out due to the lump in my throat. Everything was going to work out.

"ACO Duffy, phone call," Guy yelled over to me from the dispatch desk. "Pick it up on 8004." The red light on the nearest desk phone started to blink. I picked it up.

"Hi, Lisa, it's Rob." It was Sgt. Murphy. (That was another thing I liked about him: He only wanted to be called "Sergeant" when he was in public. On the phone, he was Rob.)

"The niece is here, and she wants you to notify the shelter that he is to be euthanized. She says she can't finalize the funeral arrangements until that's done." Sgt. Murphy sounded like he was talking louder than usual. I could imagine that he had an audience.

"Sarge, it's okay. I found him a home. Sgt. Kale is going to ask his wife if they can keep Harry. It's almost a done deal. He's a great dog, not the least bit antisocial. He likes people, he's affectionate, he's happy . . . Sure, he's old, but—"

"You're preaching to the choir, Lisa. I know all that. Phil told me how you've spent the day. Unfortunately, the niece is pretty set on it, and legally, she's the one that's in control of what happens to the dog. I don't know if I can sway her."

"Sarge, is there a will? Maybe there's something in there about Harry?"

"Thought about that already. Nope."

"What if I brought him to see her? Maybe if she saw him in person . . ."

"Tried that . . . not amenable to it . . . not at all."

"Can I talk to her?" I asked, not really wanting to confront this woman. I felt that if she didn't want to let this dog live because she had some strange storybook idea about burying the dog with her uncle, I would become angry and say something that would get me in trouble. I had become too emotional about this case, and that was the problem. Actually, I'd become emotional about a lot of calls lately. It was starting to exhaust me.

"She doesn't want to talk to anyone else; I tried that too. I thought you could work your magic on her, but she's as hard as nails." He whispered into the phone. "Let me try and talk to her again and tell her about one of our officers giving Harry a home. I'll call you back, but for now, you've got to bring that dog down to the shelter, because otherwise, she could say we are trying to steal her property. She's already counting the silverware in that house. If Harry's in the shelter, he'll be safe until we get this all ironed out." Sgt. Murphy sounded like he was exhausted, too. I knew he was right.

If only Sgt. Kale's wife would answer her phone! That could change everything.

"Yes, Sarge, I'll bring him down now." I hung up the phone and looked down at Harry, who opened one eye to look at me and wagged his tail a few times. There was still hope.

I drove Harry down to the shelter, taking great care to abide by the speed limit, something I did not have a reputation for doing. When I walked into the reception area, Maureen was already out from behind the counter. She quickly came over to Harry. When Maureen was behind the counter, you couldn't tell that she barely reached five feet tall. (The floor behind the counter was a foot higher than the reception area floor, and I'd always suspected that Maureen had demanded they build it that way.)

"This is an old dog," she said as she walked around him. Harry followed her with his eyes until she was out of his field of vision, and then he started turning around so he could keep looking at her. "Old, but smart. There's nothing wrong with this dog that a good bath can't fix." Maureen folded her arms and looked at me, then back to Harry, and then back at me again.

"I'll do everything I can. I can stall the niece. She called here about ten minutes ago, and she's a tough cookie. You may not know it, but I'm a tough cookie too."

"Oh, I know it," I said, smiling. Everyone knew it. Maureen raised one eyebrow, contemplating whether or not my statement had been a compliment or an insult. It was neither. It was a fact.

She put her hand out to me, and I placed the leash in it. She nodded, which was Maureen's signal for me to leave. I turned and walked out to my car, got in, and started it. I wondered if Mrs. Kale had come home yet. I wished I could just keep him myself, but then, I felt this way all the time. If my landlord would've allowed it, I would've been living in a zoo.

It seemed to have stopped raining suddenly; maybe that was some sort of sign. I was startled when I heard a knock on the driver's-side window. I must have jumped quite a bit, because when I looked out of the window, I saw Maureen standing there, shaking her head. I rolled the window down.

"Lay off the caffeine, girl." I hadn't had any caffeine since early that morning, but I knew the best thing to do with Maureen was to agree. "Okay," I said.

"I just wanted to tell you that I left a message with that schnauzer rescue league. As soon as I hear something, I'll give you a call." With that, she turned on her heel and briskly marched back inside. As soon as the door closed, it started to rain again. It made sense. Even the rain was intimidated by Maureen.

On the way back to the department, I drove past Sgt. Kale's house to see if there were any cars in the driveway. I was surprised when I saw Sgt. Kale himself jogging across his lawn to flag me down. I stopped the car and backed it up in front of his house.

"It's a go!" he said. "The dog's name is Harry, right?"

I nodded. I had been hoping for this solution so much that I was speechless.

"Call the shelter. Let's go get him and bring him home," said Sgt. Kale, who seemed very excited. He reminded me of a boy who had just found out he was going to get a puppy. At that moment I wanted to give him a hug, but I didn't. I smiled instead.

"I'll meet you back at headquarters," I said. "I'll call from there, and I can go pick him up." It was almost four o'clock, the end of my shift. I didn't care; I wouldn't even put in for overtime.

I rushed into the lobby, anxious to have Sgt. Murphy call Mr. Carlson's niece back and let her know that there was no need to put Harry to sleep. He would have a great home with another schnauzer to keep him company. He would be taken care of and treated like a king. Who could turn that down? I walked over to the desk to tell him the good news.

Sgt. Murphy was rubbing his temples like he was trying to relieve a headache. He looked up at me, and I knew.

"She agreed to it to my face—said that she would discuss it with her husband and consider it. She said she wouldn't make any decision until she spoke to me again." He shook his head and looked down at some invisible spot on his desk. "But she called the shelter anyway and told them to put Harry to sleep so she could bury him with her uncle. She never had any intention of doing anything else."

"Let me call the shelter," I said. "It's not too late!" I reached for the phone on his desk, but Sgt. Murphy put his hand on top of mine to stop me.

"She has a lawyer. She threatened to sue the shelter unless they followed her directive. She has a right to do this, as stupid as it is. It's her right."

I could feel my heart pounding in my chest. I couldn't think of anything else to say. There were so many reasons why this dog deserved to live, so many reasons why he shouldn't die. I kept staring at the phone.

"We all explained it to her. We told her how well he got along with people, and that he wasn't the dog she thought he was. But in the end, it didn't matter. She wasn't concerned about his temperament. I don't think she even met the dog more than once or twice. All she wanted was to bury that dog with John Carlson, and it didn't matter that only one of them was dead. Your friend at the shelter—what's her name, Francine?"

"Maureen," I said quietly.

"Yes, Maureen . . . Well, she gave Carlson's niece a run for her money. Gave her a hard time, but you can't argue with the law. Maureen met her match with that woman."

"I guess." I was too angry to say anything else. None of this made sense.

"She called here, you know . . . Maureen."

"What did she say?" I asked, still looking at my shoes. If I looked anywhere else, I knew I'd lose it.

"She told me to keep an eye on you—that you would be upset."

I looked up at Sgt. Murphy. I was surprised.

"I'm sorry. This has been a rough day for you. Why don't you go home and get some rest, eat something." Sgt. Murphy's eyes were rimmed with red. This day had been hard on everyone.

Several days later I received a copy of a letter in my mailbox. When citizens are appreciative of something, they sometimes write letters of commendation. In the law enforcement world, they are some-times referred to as "Atta boys." They are very sought after—a great thing to have in your file, and taken very seriously by the chief and lieutenant at your annual review. I opened the envelope and read.

Dear Miss Duffy,

Thank you for helping our family when my Uncle John passed away last week. We appreciate all of your efforts in regards to his pet dog. Your hard work and diligence should be noted by your superiors. Unfortunately, as you know, we decided to put him to sleep. He was not the type of animal that could easily adapt to a different owner due to his aggressive temperament, advanced age, and weak condition. I would like you to know that we buried our uncle with his beloved Harry. It was a lovely ceremony, and everyone said how touching it was that they could still be together. It was something he would have wanted. Thanks again.

Sincerely,
The Carlson-Perry family

They'd never had any intention of listening to any of us. They thought they knew Harry better than any of us could, when in reality, they hadn't known him at all. And even though I had never met Mr. Carlson, I knew that I had known him better than they did too. He had loved that dog. It was apparent that Harry had been raised with a lot of love and care. Mr. Carlson wouldn't have wanted this.

I took the letter and folded it back up. I tore it down the middle and folded it again. I tore it again and again, until it was in shreds. Carlos, the desk officer of the day, watched me walk over and drop it in the trash.

"Wasn't that an 'Atta boy'?" he asked, looking at me like I'd lost my mind.

"Yeah," I answered. I picked up my clipboard and my car keys and started to walk toward the lobby.

"Why would you throw that away? That doesn't make any sense," he called over to me as I walked away.

I stopped and looked at him for moment. "I know," I said, and pushed open the door to go back to whatever my job would entail for the day.

It made no sense at all.

The Protest March

The call came in at a really inopportune time.

"Two Five Two to ACO." I reached for the radio on my hip while trying to hold on to the leash with the other. This dog was enormous. I couldn't tell what type of dog he was because he looked like a potpourri of breeds. Maybe some Airedale, a little Great Dane . . . there were spots, so perhaps a touch of Dalmatian? Whatever it was, it was an unfortunate combination. As sweet as he was, this was one dog that would never end up on the cover of a magazine. Even the texture of his coat was a variety show. The only thing I could tell for sure was that he was really big and really strong. He was pulling as hard as he could to get closer to Abby, a Wheaton terrier, who knew the back of my car so well that she remembered where I kept the biscuits.

"No, Abby . . . too much . . . *Stop!*" I was shouting at her so that she would stop ripping the box open. "I'll give you one in a minute." I dropped the radio on the floor and grabbed the dog biscuits before she ate the entire box. She'd done this before. I should've remembered to hide them better. Meanwhile, the large dog of indeterminable ancestry pulled harder. "Hey, you stop too!"

Now I was sprawled across the backseat of the car holding on to a leash with one hand and a box of dog biscuits with the other. I stretched as far as I could and finally managed to hook the big dog's leash up to the grill, far enough away from Abby so nothing risqué could go on. I was breathing pretty hard.

My radio! I hadn't answered it yet. Where was it? Abby and I spotted it at the same time, lying on the floor of the car. We dove for it. I grabbed it a half-second before she could. She was looking up at me, her tail wagging furiously. She thought it was a game. "I win!" I said. Abby could be infuriating, but she was really cute.

"Repeat?" I spoke into the radio again. I couldn't remember who had called me. It wasn't coming from headquarters, so it had to be someone out on the road.

"ACO?" they asked again. I pressed the button to respond, but before I could get a word out, Big Dog decided to put in his two cents. "WOOF, WOOF, WOOF!" His bark was as big as his body. The entire car vibrated with each bark. I pressed the button again. I had to yell over Big Dog's barking. "*Affirmative!*" I responded. I got out of the car and shut the door. I walked around to the other side and reached in through the window to scratch him behind the ears. There, that was better. Maybe he just wanted some attention.

I got in on the driver's side and flopped down on the seat. It was November, yet I was sweating.

"Are you okay?" I recognized the voice. It was Gus, one of the park rangers. I knew things must have sounded very strange on the other end of this conversation, if it could even be called that. At this point it was more like a game of Marco Polo.

I pressed the transmit button and answered, "Affirmative."

There was no possible way that I could explain over the radio what had just transpired. I looked in the rearview mirror and saw that Abby had found the box of dog biscuits again. I must have put them down when I picked up the radio. "Oh, c'mon, Abby—*no!*"

She had her face stuffed so deep into the box that when I yelled at her, she swung her head around to look at me with the box still stuck on her snout. She shook her head a few times and then figured out that she had to use her paws to pull it off. When she got it off, she looked at me as if to say "You called me?" At that point I was laughing too hard to admonish her any further.

Abby was a frequent flyer. No matter what her owners did, she escaped. At first I had thought they were making excuses. "She opened the window." "She was in the house when we left in the morning." "She ripped a hole in the fence. Yes, it is a chain-link fence; that's what makes this so frustrating!"

Her owners were a nice middle-aged couple. They both commuted to the city for work, so when I did pick up Abby running loose, I would either have to keep her all day long, which presented its own challenges, or bring her down to the shelter where they'd have to pick her up later. I had written these people so many tickets, it had come to the point where I was doubling the fines. As nice as they were, I still had to do my job.

I felt bad about it. They weren't bad dog owners; they took good care of Abby. She was always clean and looked healthy, and her shots were always up-to-date. But when Abby ran loose, she didn't do it like any other dog. She took it to the next level.

I found Abby all over the place. She didn't limit her travels to her neighborhood; no, that wouldn't have been as much fun. Several times I had found Abby trotting up the side of the highway on her way out of the city. I had found Abby playing "beat the train" at the railroad crossing. I found Abby on the bridge and under the overpass. Once, she had even snuck in a door in the back of the movie theater; when I came to pick her up, she was happily sitting in the aisle, waiting for the show and crunching on some old popcorn someone had left behind. Everyone at the department eventually came to know who she was.

"Police Department, Dispatcher Wells. Yes . . . hmmm . . . Okay, I'll send someone right out." Guy hung up the phone and picked it up again on the next ring.

"Police Department, Dispatcher Wells. Yes, we've already received calls about it. Yes, of course, a dog blocking traffic is a problem. Backed up how far? Yes, we have someone responding. Thank you.

"Lisa!" Guy shouted across the room at me while I was on my way out. "Go get Abby. She's blocking traffic on Route 9 near the bridge."

In a city of over twenty thousand people and probably thousands of dogs, I didn't have to ask how he knew what dog it was. If it was a bridge, and it was rush hour, and there was a lot of chaos, it was Abby.

On this day, I had already picked up Abby down at the riverfront blocking the morning rush hour traffic of people trying to catch the train. She actually seemed relieved to see me, what with all the people yelling out their car windows at her. She had basically jumped into my car when I opened the back door. She hadn't yet learned that it's not a good idea to mess with commuters, especially in the morning. Big Dog had stuck out like a sore thumb sitting down smack in the middle of Division Street. He was obviously clueless about traffic. It had been a simple process to get him in the car as well. That was when all the easiness ended. Now that they were both in my car, they were driving me a little crazy. Gus continued his radio transmission, saying, "Meet me at twelve-hundred Stewart Lane, and, uh . . . bring . . . uh . . ." Gus didn't finish; he must have been cut off. He wanted me to meet him at Stewart Lane? Nothing ever happened out there. It was the most rural area in the city. There was a small farm that sold eggs, a few houses, and a lot of open space. If you walked back far enough, you would end up at the reservoir for the city's water supply.

"Ten-four." I hadn't heard what Gus had told me to bring, but figured I should get over there. I drove out of the parking lot and headed toward the entrance ramp to the highway. Stewart Lane was at the opposite end of the city, and this would be a faster route.

Big Dog started crying. He was watching Abby make her way through the dog biscuits that were now out of the box and strewn all over the back of the car. They were just out of Big Dog's reach. I had no doubt that Abby had planned it that way.

A few minutes later, I pulled up behind Gus's car. I didn't need to ask him why he'd called. The reason was marching downhill toward me. There must have been at least fifteen to twenty turkeys walking in formation, heading right toward the main road. If they didn't stop soon, they were going to march straight into the busy morning traffic. Gus was standing in the middle of the road, waving his arms at them. I started to laugh, but then stopped. I was usually the one in the middle of a mess like this, and I knew how it felt when your colleagues started laughing at you. Although I had to admit that from this vantage point, it really was quite funny.

As they got closer, I could hear them. I had never heard turkeys before. They sounded nothing like that *gobble, gobble* sound I'd heard in cartoons. Not to say they weren't loud; it was just different from what I had expected. Beside the little clucks, they were also making yelping noises that reminded me of puppies. Thinking of puppies, I turned around to see how Abby and Big Dog were doing. I could see Big Dog's head hanging out the window, panting at me. I didn't think I had opened the window that much. He looked fine, however, and seemed to be enjoying the entertainment.

I walked up to Gus. The turkeys were still coming toward him. None of his shouting had seemed to deter them. He stopped momentarily from his frantic gesturing to yell over to me. "They're not gonna stop! They're going to walk right into the middle of the road and either get hit or cause an accident."

"What do we do?" I asked him.

"I don't know . . . that's why I called you! This is your area of expertise!" He seemed really frustrated. Animal calls were not Gus's favorite.

"Where are they going?" I was thinking out loud, not really expecting an answer.

Gus had started to back up. The turkeys kept coming. "Can't you see!" Gus yelled over to me. "They're heading straight for the road! That's why I called you!" Gus was a bit snippy.

"I deal with dogs and cats, Gus. I'm not the turkey control officer! I know as much about turkeys as you do." I could get snippy, too.

At this point the turkeys had reached us. Without giving us a second glance, they continued to march on by, the clucking now in full surround sound.

Gus turned to look at me. "I think I know what they're doing!"

"Oh, so now you have all the answers," I said, as I tried to step out of their way. I was in the middle of them now.

"I'm sorry, okay? I just hate this stuff!" Gus said, raising his voice above the omnipresent clucking.

"Okay. It's all right." I could never hold a grudge. I looked back toward my car. Big Dog was watching the turkeys approach. He started barking, really putting his all into it.

"What's tomorrow?" he shouted over the turkeys, and now the dog.

"Thursday," I said. I was still looking over at the car. I didn't see Abby. Maybe she was lying down?

"Use your head! What is tomorrow?" Gus was shaking his head at me.

"Thanksgiving?" What did that have to do with this batch of turkeys? Obviously they didn't know that, and if they did, well, they'd had a reprieve.

"Exactly. They're angry or something." Gus started to walk down the hill, following the turkeys.

I followed him. As much as I believe that animals know a lot more than humans give them credit for, I didn't think that these turkeys were conducting some type of protest march, showing their solidarity for those of their brethren that hadn't been as fortunate. As far as I knew, this had never happened before—at least, not since I had been the animal control officer. Gus had been at the department twice as long as I had.

"Have you ever had a call here before, near the farm?" I asked.

"Once their horse walked off and tried to cross the highway, but he gave up and went back home. Other than that, no . . . I don't think so."

"Did you go up to the farm yet?" I hoped he had. That should have been his first step, since the farmers would certainly know their turkeys better than we did.

"Yes, of course I did. Nobody was there. All closed up."

The turkeys had reached the part of the hill that started to slope drastically toward the main road. To call it steep would have been an understatement. I thought that maybe this would stop them. It didn't.

"This is going to get ugly." Gus shouted over to me while he began to jog down the hill trying to catch up with the turkeys. Gus was right. On the one hand, this was funny, but the thought of all of these turkeys marching across a road in a city where people were not used to stopping for this sort of thing could prove to be dangerous.

It was one thing to find a bunch of turkeys taking a walk—albeit, an unusual organized type of walk—but it was another situation entirely if they were in danger of getting hurt or causing someone else to get hurt, especially the day before Thanksgiving. The newspaper would love a story like that. We had been advised to avoid talking to the press at all costs ever since one of our sergeants had been misquoted to the point where the article had explicitly stated that aliens had possibly landed in Annesville. All discussion with the media now went through the chief's office.

We looked at each other and started to run down the hill. We had to stop them before they got to the road. It was difficult to run down a hill this steep without falling, but we had to overtake those turkeys. We caught up to them and passed them. I sped up and passed Gus as I continued hurtling toward the main road. I didn't know why I'd thought we'd be able to stop them at the bottom of the hill if they hadn't found us intimidating enough before, but I didn't know what else to do. My shoes were skidding on the gravel. I didn't know if I would be able to stop. I could see the traffic whizzing by as I headed directly toward it, like I'd been shot out of a cannon. This was too much. I wasn't about to sacrifice myself for turkeys. I didn't want to be remembered this way.

"*Slow down!*" Gus was yelling from behind me. He was slipping on the gravel, too. I wanted to slow down, but I couldn't. At this point, what I was doing could no longer be described as running. Stumbling, tripping, sliding, skidding—that would be more like it.

I was rapidly approaching the bottom of the hill. I tried to push my heels into the ground. I had to stop. But this didn't work either. Gus was above me, yelling in my direction. I couldn't hear him that well. My ears were filled with the sound of my heart thumping. He kept yelling something. Was he cursing at me?

"Sit . . . *Sit!* YOU HAVE TO SIT DOWN!"

I sat.

After continuing to skid down the hill on the seat of my pants for what seemed like ten minutes (but was probably more like three seconds), I finally stopped. I was sitting at the foot of the hill, just inches away from the road. A car drove by and the woman inside beeped and waved. I waved back. I wondered if I knew who she was.

"Here." Gus was standing next to me. He took my hand and helped me up. "Are you okay?"

I stood up and brushed myself off. "Yeah," I said. That was as good an answer as any. I figured the internal injuries wouldn't show up until later anyway. I turned around to face the turkeys. After all of this, I wasn't going to let them get past me. I would make them stop. I saw them, but they weren't coming at me. I saw the backs of them as they were trotting back up the hill. They had decided on their own to turn around and go home.

"What was that about?" Gus asked me, watching the flock of turkeys making their way back up the hill. I looked at him. I had no answers. It occurred to me that I should check the back of my pants. Gus seemed to know what I was thinking.

"Turn around," he said. I stared at him.

"Geez, just turn around, will you, and I'll tell you if you ripped them." I slowly turned around. This was beyond embarrassing.

"You're fine. It's just dirt, but you'll probably want to go home and change."

We started walking back up the hill. My legs were aching. I thought that I should probably get more consistent exercise between the long periods of sitting in a car interrupted by running down hills chasing turkeys at breakneck speed.

"I'll head back up to the farm, see if anybody's there yet." Gus took his keys out of his pocket. "You have enough to do with that pony you have in the back of your car."

"I know," I said. "He's enormous, isn't he? I have to bring both of them down to the shelter."

I started fishing around in my pocket for my car keys. I hoped I hadn't dropped them somewhere along the way on my trip down the hill.

"Both what?" Gus asked.

There they were. I had put them in my shirt pocket. That was probably a good idea considering what had happened. I looked up at Gus. "Both of them. The dogs. I have the big dog and Abby in the backseat."

Gus was looking at my car. "I don't see two dogs."

"Yeah, she's in there. This time she was blocking commuter traffic at the train station. You know Abby; the more danger involved, the more fun she thinks it is." I walked over to the car. Big Dog was unusually quiet. His head was leaning on the window, watching us patiently. He was chewing.

"Abby," I called, expecting her to pop up from the backseat. The leash she was hooked up to was long enough so that she could lie down if she wanted. "Abby!" I called again. Big Dog started wagging his tail, crunching loudly on something in his mouth.

The leash was still hooked up to the grill, but there was no Abby on the other end. The window was opened almost all the way. I knew I hadn't left it like that; I'd only cracked it about five inches so that they could have fresh air without it getting too cold for them.

Somehow, Abby had been able to get out of the leash, roll down the manual window, and escape—but not before giving Big Dog the rest of the biscuits. It appeared that she had tried to break him out, too, but when he was too big to fit through the window; she gave him the biscuits as a consolation gift.

"That is a very smart dog." Gus was laughing. He walked over to his car and opened the door. "Lisa," he called over to me.

I had been leaning over the seat trying to see if Abby had chewed her way out of the leash. Nope. Of course not. She had somehow managed to unhook the leash from her collar. Damn Houdini dog!

"What?" I turned around to see what Gus wanted, but banged my head on the side of the rearview mirror. "WHAT?!" I yelled over to him again, rubbing my head with one hand and trying once again to locate my car keys with the other.

"Uh, nothing. Never mind. See you later." Gus gave me a two-finger salute and drove away.

I decided that I would stop at home and change, and then take that time to get Big Dog a drink to wash down those biscuits. I had to get down to the shelter soon, so I didn't have the time to search for Abby. There would always be time for that. It wouldn't be long before I got a call that a dog was chasing the trains or trotting up the highway. She may have been a very smart dog, but she was also predictable.

My radio went off as soon as I pulled into my driveway. "Eight Forty-Four to Three Oh Six, Ten-Five Park Ranger Santos."

Ten-Five meant to call by phone. I got out of the car to go inside. "I'll be back, Big Dog," I said, rubbing his head. I grabbed the metal bowl from the back of the car, planning to fill it up inside and bring it back out to him. Then we would have time for a short walk before I took him down to the shelter.

I picked up the phone once I was inside and called headquarters. "Hi, it's me. Can you transfer me to Gus?" The dispatcher put me on hold for a second, and then there was a click.

"Park Ranger Santos."

"Hey, Gus, it's me. What's up?" I started running the water for Big Dog's drink. My cat was trying to get her head under the faucet. This was her new way of getting a drink. "Wait a minute," I told her.

"Wait for what?"

"Sorry, Gus, I wasn't talking to you. What is it?"

"Two things," he said. "The first thing is that the woman who owns that gigantic dog is here to pick him up. I told her to wait for you in the lobby."

"Thanks," I said. This would save me a trip down-county, but the best part was that I wouldn't have to worry about what would happen to Big Dog once he was at the shelter. I wasn't sure how he'd make out with the other dogs there. As big as he was, he didn't seem too worldly.

"Now, the second thing: I went up to the farm and talked to the owner. He says that those turkeys just do that once in a while and they always come back. He doesn't sell them for food or anything. They're like his pets."

"I'm glad to hear that. Did you tell him to try to keep them out of the road in the future?" I was balancing the phone on my shoulder and trying to carry the water bowl over to the table without spilling any.

"What do you think? Of course I did. Oh, and the third thing."

"You said there were two things. What's the third?" The sooner he let me get off the phone, the sooner I could get this dog back to headquarters. As it was, it looked like I wasn't going to get a lunch break today.

"Did you change your pants yet?" Gus asked.

"No, not yet. Why?" I'd been thinking that since I had to go right back out and deliver Big Dog to his owner, and then decide whether this was going to be a ticket or a first warning, it really didn't make sense to change my clothes. It would be time for me to go home, and there was no sense making more laundry for myself. It wasn't like folks weren't used to seeing me like this anyway. This was hardly a desk job.

"The third thing is . . ." Gus sounded like he was trying not to laugh.

"What? What is the third thing?" I was on the verge of hanging up. Big Dog had spotted me in the window and was barking. The entire car really did shake when he barked.

"Your pants . . . well, you see, there's a pretty big hole in the back."

"*Gus!* Why did you lie to me about that?" I was twisting around to try and see where they were ripped. I hadn't felt anything.

"You seemed embarrassed enough. I was going to tell you when you got in the car, but then your dog had escaped on you, and, I don't know . . . At least I'm telling you now."

"Okay. Thanks, I guess. Bye." I hung up. I would have shown more gratitude if I hadn't known that he would be laughing it up at headquarters about this as soon as he got off the phone. I hung up and went over to my closet to pull out a pair of uniform pants.

When I brought Big Dog into the lobby, at first I thought his owner was a little girl. When I got closer I realized that she was a grown woman—just a very petite one. Big Dog spotted her and began pulling in her direction, dragging me with him.

"Alvin—there you are!" The woman came running up to Big Dog, and he sprang up in the air toward her. Before I could pull back on his leash he landed on her. Instead of collapsing on the floor, she held him in her arms like he was a miniature poodle.

"Wow," I said. That was impressive. I really did have to get more exercise, maybe lift some weights.

"I was really worried about him. I'm so happy that he's okay. Isn't he just the cutest dog you've ever seen?"

I remembered something my mother had told me once, something like "Every baby is beautiful to his mother."

"Yes, he really is," I said. "What is he? I mean, I can't quite place the breed."

"From what the vet says, he's part Irish wolfhound, with a touch of English mastiff. We think there's some Dalmatian in there somewhere too."

Well, there you go—first thing I'd gotten right all day.

Big Dog, or Alvin, didn't live within the city limits. I knew that I had never seen him before. You didn't forget an animal that looked like that. He had gotten loose from a neighboring town that was a lot more rural than Annesville. It seemed that once he had found himself on busy streets with cars and lots of people, he had panicked and forgotten how to get home. I was glad for the happy ending, and since this was a situation where Alvin had never been loose before and had lost his way, there was definitely no reason to write a ticket. Besides, I wanted to get home so I could make the baked yams I was bringing to my aunt's house for Thanksgiving dinner the next day.

I still hadn't decided if I was going to eat any turkey.

The Bonds of Earth

"Why don't we just hire school crossing guards for the spring and fall? Why do we even bother assuming they'll work when it's below thirty-five degrees?" Sergeant Pierce was frustrated. He had every reason to be. With the amount of staff out sick with the flu this week, and the day-to-day responsibilities of running a police department when the phones were ringing off the hook, the last thing he needed was to staff all of the city's school crossings with both civilian and non-civilian employees who would be better off performing those jobs necessary to keep the city functioning.

The mornings from 8:00 to 9:00 a.m. were pretty much set in stone. The afternoons usually ran from 2:00 to 3:30 p.m., and there were still a few places that required a crossing guard between 11:00 a.m. and 1:00 p.m., even though they were rarely used anymore.

The 11:00 to 1:00 crossings used to be popular when there was half-day kindergarten, or when students would walk home for lunch in the middle of the day. But times had changed, and it was rare that any children crossed the streets in the middle of a school day. With full-day kindergarten and only the upper grades allowing students to leave campus for lunch, the 11:00 to 1:00 school crossing was eventually going to be discontinued. But, as is the way with city and town government, it sometimes takes years to make even small changes.

While most everybody grumbled about having to cover school crossings, I never did. I didn't mind for a few reasons. One reason was that I was one of the lucky civilian employees who had their own patrol car. This way I could keep the heat running and occasionally run back to the car to warm up during a lull. It wasn't because I had any type of status that allowed me this privilege; it was because my car was used for the primary purpose of transporting animals. Since animals shed and are not immune to car sickness (these being the least noxious issues associated with my job), I rarely had to worry about anyone pulling rank to use my car on even the coldest days.

Another reason I didn't mind the school crossings as much as everyone else was because I really needed them. If I was lucky enough to be posted at an 11:00 to 1:00 crossing, I could get a lot of my work done for college. Actually, most of my research papers had been written at school crossings. With an hour for lunch, a day full of school crossings was, although monotonous, one of the easiest schedules. With the unpredictable and often insane pace of most of my days, doing school crossings during these cold weeks in the middle of the winter was a welcome break—at least, when I wasn't sent to Joan's crossing.

Some of the busiest intersections required two crossing guards. One crossing in particular was in the middle of two busy main roads outside of town that intersected with both on- and off-ramps onto the highway. With trucks barreling off the highway, commuter traffic rushing to get on the highway, and all the regular traffic trying to navigate the complexities of this labyrinth, the Bear Mountain Extension crossing was the Super Bowl of school crossings. Standing in the middle of the road here was not a job for just anyone. The meek may inherit the earth, but they definitely wouldn't be hired to cover this school crossing. There was only one person who could do it right, which she would tell you if you asked (and even if you didn't).

Joan Conklin had worked at this crossing for years, and was one of the few crossing guards that took her job seriously. Very seriously. Whether or not it was pouring rain or sleet or 20 degrees below zero, Joan was always at her post. It was difficult finding someone to work with her on a regular basis. This was because not only was it nearly impossible to find school crossing guards willing to stand out in the cold, but it was also such a busy intersection that there was never any opportunity to sit in your car to warm up, even for a minute. These factors, on top of the fact that Joan was the self-appointed commanding officer in the school crossing guard pecking order, led to frequent turnover, and meant that a department employee was dispatched to this area during much of the school year.

"Don't stop trucks coming up the hill," she advised me after taking a deep drag on her ever-present cigarette.

"Okay . . . Why?" I asked. She seemed intent on stopping everything else, including police cars, so I wondered why she had a soft spot for trucks. Joan looked at me like I'd had a frontal lobotomy and blew out a cloud of smoke.

"Trucks take longer to stop than cars. Some of them are hauling loads that weigh, like, over thirty tons. Don't you know how much distance it takes to stop a truck hauling a heavy load?" Joan glared down at me, waiting for her answer. She was quite an intimidating figure, with her spiky bleached platinum hair and cigarette hanging out of her mouth. She had spent her youth soaking up the sun, and now that she was in what appeared to be her late forties or early fifties, she looked, well . . . *leathery* would be an understatement. Joan didn't smile much. She was too busy to smile, working three jobs to help support her grandchildren, who seemed to spend a lot of time at her house. She spoke about them sometimes. She also liked to talk about how attractive some of the police officers were. These would be the rare moments when you could catch her smiling.

"I don't know, Joan, maybe, like, um, ten or twenty feet?" Joan was always asking me questions like that. I knew that she wondered what I was learning in "those useless books" I was always reading. Sometimes, especially when I was around Joan, I wondered that too.

"Ten feet?" She rolled her eyes, shook her head, and took another pull on her cigarette. The ash was getting longer, and I watched her hand while she gestured in my direction. I sensed that she didn't like my answer. "Sometimes it can take up to the length of a football field. That's a helluva lot longer than ten or twenty feet, kid," she said, shaking her cigarette, with the even longer glowing ash, at me.

"Wow. That's quite a distance," I said, still watching her hand holding the cigarette.

"Damn right!" she said, and finally flicked the ash in the opposite direction. I had the feeling she was disappointed that I had been the one who was sent to help her with the school crossing.

"Eight Forty-Four to Three Oh Six," squawked the radio from my hip. I pulled it out to answer, thinking that I would probably be sent to a call after 3:00 p.m. It wasn't even 11:30, and they wouldn't pull a police officer off the road to take me off a school crossing unless it was absolutely necessary.

"Nine-Forty Constant Avenue, see complainant. She'll be waiting for you. Officer Nash is en route to cover your crossing."

"Ten-four," I answered, sliding the radio back into its clip on my belt. I knew that Helen Mueller lived here. She was an elderly woman I had come to know quite well due to her habit of taking in old and sick cats and nursing them back to health. I was surprised that they would pull me off a crossing for her unless it was something that couldn't wait.

"Pretty Bobby Nash?" Joan brightened at the prospect of Officer Nash replacing me. "We were in the same class back in high school."

"Yeah, Pretty Bobby." I smiled at her while I got into my car, thinking that I could have some fun with that later. "I bet he knows more about trucks than I do."

Joan gave what sounded like a cross between a laugh and a snort. "He knows a lot more about a lot of things, kid." She ran her fingers through her short hair to fluff it up and winked at me as I pulled away. Before I turned around to head toward Constant Avenue, I saw Officer Nash's patrol car pulling up to park on the side of the road. He was looking straight ahead with a scowl on his face. I definitely thought that Joan's admiration for Officer Nash was a one-way street.

Mrs. Mueller was waiting for me on the porch of her tiny two-story house. The house needed a good coat of paint, and the porch creaked a little bit too loudly under my feet. She had been alone since Mr. Mueller died, probably more than ten years ago. They had never had any children, although she had a nephew who would come over to check on her and take her shopping once in a while. He helped her out a bit financially, probably intending that the money go toward groceries or utilities. However, much of it went toward veterinarian bills.

"Hi, Mrs. Mueller," I said. "What can I do for you?"

"It's Rose. She's very lethargic, and I wanted you to take a look at her. Would you like some tea? It's almost lunchtime and I have tuna fish for sandwiches. You take your tea with no milk, just a bit of sugar, right?"

Mrs. Mueller and I had lunch together every once in a while. Most of the time I brought something, but I hadn't expected to stop by today. With it being so cold outside, the thought of staying in the warm house and having lunch rather than going out in the cold to pick up an animal seemed like a wonderful idea. It was just a bit past 11:30, and I hadn't planned on taking a break yet, but it seemed as though she really wanted to talk. I would call in for lunch and spend it with Mrs. Mueller.

"Thanks, Mrs. Mueller, I would love some. Where's Rose?"

"She's upstairs on the window seat—you know where to go. I just want you to take a look at her before I call the vet."

Mrs. Mueller often called me to take a look at her cats. I had no veterinary training, but I could usually tell if it was something that needed immediate attention. I also had a friend at the animal hospital I could call who would tell me if he thought we needed to bring the cat in. This way Mrs. Mueller didn't incur any more expenses than she had to.

I had really grown to care about Mrs. Mueller, and felt concerned because she was starting to lose her sense of reality. I had a feeling that the reason I had been called off the school crossing wasn't so much an animal call, but a "check on the welfare" for Mrs.

Mueller. She could sometimes be cantankerous with the male officers when they would come by to check on her after her nephew had
been unable to reach her by phone. She would get angry if anyone
interrupted her "shows." The TV was always on in her house, probably to keep her company more than anything else, but the sound
was so loud that sometimes she couldn't hear the phone—or at least
that's what she said.

I could hear Mrs. Mueller filling the teakettle and opening and
closing cabinet doors as I walked upstairs to her bedroom. Sleeping
on her neatly made bed were two older cats, one of whom was snoring and didn't move when I came in. The other one, a chubby calico
named Samson, opened his one eye to take a look at me; he'd lost
the other one in some long-ago battle in his youth. Deciding that I
posed no threat, he went back to sleep. I figured she had chosen this
name because of Samson and Goliath, although I couldn't remember who had slain whom. (No, wait . . . that would be David and
Goliath; I could never keep my biblical stories straight.)

I went over to the window seat to take a look at Rose, who
had to be the oldest cat I had ever seen. Mrs. Mueller insisted she
was twenty-five years old, and even though there were no records
to prove it, I had the feeling she wasn't far off. Rose was missing a
lot of her teeth, and the ones she did have were in pretty bad shape.
This didn't stop Rose from eating well, as she probably weighed in
at more than twenty pounds. Even though she was a senior citizen,
Rose was always alert and on guard. She could sense anyone entering the house, coming up the stairs, and especially coming into the
bedroom. This was why I was a bit concerned when Rose didn't even
look in my direction when I walked up to her on the window seat.
She had a white face, and her ears looked like they had been dipped
in gray paint. Her amber eyes were as clear and observant as a kitten's, despite her advanced age. On this day, however, she didn't even
turn toward me as I said her name.

"Rose . . . *pssst* . . . *pssst* . . . Rose," I called. And then louder,
"*Rose!*" She just kept staring out the window. I walked around in
front of her so I would be in her field of vision. I didn't want to

startle her, but I was concerned that maybe Mrs. Mueller was right; maybe there was something wrong with Rose. Finally, she turned from the window and gave me a soft meow. She got up, stretched, and walked over to me, where I began scratching the top of her head and behind her ears the way she liked. I noticed that after I stopped scratching, she kept her head cocked sideways as she looked at me.

"*Oh no! Oh my God!*" Mrs. Mueller screamed from downstairs. I heard a clatter of dishes hitting the floor, and I turned to run downstairs, but not before I noticed that Rose hadn't moved a muscle in reaction to Mrs. Mueller's screams.

Mrs. Mueller was sitting on a kitchen chair staring at the television. A broken cup was on the floor and the teakettle was whistling on the stove.

"Mrs. Mueller, are you okay? What's wrong? Are you hurt?" I put my hand on my radio, ready to call for medical help.

"No, no . . . oh, honey, no—it's not me. It's . . . it's all those astronauts and that teacher on the shuttle . . . they . . ." Not able to continue, she pointed to the television where a plume of what looked like smoke had exploded into the sky in the odd shape of a y. The next shot showed a group of people and family members watching the *Challenger* take off, clapping and cheering as they watched it blast off into the sky. Then slowly their faces changed to confusion, and then a few started to cry.

I went over to the stove and turned off the teakettle. Mrs. Mueller began to cry, too, so I sat down in the chair next to her, watching shot after shot of the explosion, and the hideous plume of smoke that stood out against the crisp blue sky.

The newscaster's voice was playing over the footage: "The American space shuttle, the *Challenger*, has exploded, killing all seven astronauts on board. The five men and two women, including the first teacher in space, were just over a minute into their flight from Cape Canaveral in Florida when the *Challenger* blew up."

Mrs. Mueller and I watched in silence. I had been following the story about the shuttle on the news. It had been scheduled to take off days before, but had been delayed because of cold weather.

I struggled to grasp what had just happened. We had actually watched seven people die on live TV. The schools . . . the schools were probably holding assemblies for the kids to watch the *Challenger* take off because of Christa McAuliffe, the high school teacher who had been selected out of thousands of applicants to be the first teacher in space. All of those children were witnesses to this disaster, too.

I picked up the broken cup and put the pieces on a towel on the counter. I poured Mrs. Mueller a fresh cup of tea and walked over to the TV and turned the sound down. I couldn't stand listening to the commentators anymore, making projections about how long the astronauts might have survived inside the shuttle.

She looked over at me, tears streaming down her face. "Do you want a sandwich? I promised you a sandwich."

"No thanks, Mrs. Mueller," I said. "I'm not really hungry anymore. Would you like one? I could make it for you."

She smiled weakly at me. "No, honey, that's okay. I'm not hungry anymore either." She grabbed the sides of the chair, using her arms to help push herself up. "My babies are probably hungry, though; they must be ready for lunch." She walked into the kitchen and started opening cans of cat food and organizing water bowls. Suddenly she turned as she remembered why she had asked me to come over in the first place.

"Rose. What do you think is wrong with Rose? I couldn't handle it if something happened to her right now; I've had her the longest of all. I don't want to think of anything happening to her . . . especially today, after . . ." She looked in the direction of the television, still replaying scenes of the tragedy, but without sound.

"Well, Mrs. Mueller, I'll call my friend, but I think I have an idea of what's happened to Rose. While I think you should consult a vet, she'll probably be okay." I worried that what I was going to say next would upset her. "I think she's deaf."

"Deaf?" Mrs. Mueller stopped opening cans and looked at me. "I'm not surprised, at her age. That makes sense now. When I call her, she doesn't come, but if she sees me she comes right over." She wiped her hands on the dishtowel she had hanging over her shoulder. "I'm a little relieved. As long as she's not in pain, that's the only thing I worry about." She turned to look back at the television, still playing shots of the shuttle explosion.

"I'll leave a message for the vet tonight, and describe everything," I said as I picked up my coat off the back of the sofa. "I think the way she tilts her head may be related to it, too. If you have to take her to the vet, I can pick her up, like last time. I'll let you know tomorrow. I should probably go now, though."

There was a lot of autonomy in my job. As long as I responded to calls quickly and took care of my regular duties, nobody had a problem with me. I had taken more than a few dogs and cats to the vet's office for people who didn't drive, most often senior citizens. It wasn't out of my way, and I had to patrol the entire city anyway. I wasn't assigned to a certain sector each day like the police officers were.

"I have a question for you, dear, unless you have to leave right now?" Mrs. Mueller was holding a dishrag in her hands, and she was twisting it pretty hard. The shuttle accident had upset her more than I realized.

I knew that I might have to cover a school crossing, but I still had about fifteen minutes until then. "No, of course I have time. What is it?"

"I've been thinking a lot lately about them—Rose and Samson . . . and Prudence. I don't think that Donny—he's my nephew, you know?" I nodded. I had met him once and spoken to him on the phone a few times. He seemed concerned about his aunt, if a bit businesslike.

"If something happens to me, I don't think Donny would take care of them. He doesn't like cats, although I don't know why . . . he was raised with pets. Never mind that. I just wanted to ask you, and if it's too much of a burden, just say no—Could you make sure they don't get . . . you know?" Mrs. Mueller couldn't even say the word. I didn't blame her. I couldn't imagine saying that word in reference to my own cat.

"I'll do everything I can, Mrs. Mueller. I promise," I said, wondering as the words were coming out of my mouth how I was going to find homes for these cats. Two of them were over twenty years old, and one of them had only the one eye. They *were* lovable, I'd give her that. I would do everything I could, and besides, I didn't have to come up with a plan right now; all of them were still very much alive. Slower, a little confused sometimes, but there was nothing wrong with that. I was young and I was often confused, too. I wouldn't worry about this until I had to.

"Thank you, honey. I appreciate this, I really do." Mrs. Mueller was tearing up again, and now I was too. I had developed a deep affection for her. I had only known one grandmother in my life, but she had passed away when I was very young, leaving me with only vague memories. Maybe this was why I worried about Mrs. Mueller so much.

She came over to me and gave me a tight hug. "Say a prayer for those astronauts and their families, honey."

"I will," I said as I hugged her back.

I called headquarters on my radio and got no response from Dispatch. As I drove across town, I figured I better find out whether I was needed at the school crossing at 2:00 p.m. I walked into headquarters and whistled to have them unlock the door in the lobby. I pushed when I heard the click and walked in. Any other day the hallways would have been bustling with people running around, filling out paperwork, talking and joking; but today, it was silent except for the ringing of the phones and the TV set outside the dispatch room, which featured shots of the *Challenger* exploding accompanied by running commentary.

Sgt. Pierce walked into the dispatch room. "You know, right?" he said.

I nodded my head.

"Figured you'd hear about it, since Helen Mueller keeps that TV on all day and night. Is she okay? Her nephew called and was concerned over the way she was going on about one of her cats."

"She's fine. It's her oldest cat, and I think she's deaf. She might have an inner ear problem, or possibly she's had a small stroke. I'm going to call Dr. Sadler and see what he thinks, but I have a feeling she'll be okay."

"That's good." Sgt. Pierce looked over at the TV again. "Thanks for going over there. She likes you . . . makes it easier, you know."

"You're welcome. I like her too," I said. "Should I go back to Joan's crossing?"

"No, we sent Sam over there for the afternoon. He's pretty deaf, too." Sgt. Pierce smiled. "He won't be able to hear Joan talking! You go cover Union and Washington."

"Yes, Sarge." I zipped up my jacket, put my gloves back on, and went out to my car. Driving up to Union Avenue, I noticed that it seemed as though the city was in slow motion. People were walking around expressionless, going about their business without enthusiasm.

I enjoyed the school crossing at Union Avenue. I had come to know most of the kids, and we would do something different depending on which day of the week it was. Skipping on Monday, marching on Tuesday. Their favorite was "walking-across-the-street-backwards Friday." The kids seemed to look forward to it, and I did it with them which made them cross the street and get out of the main road without fooling around and hitting each other with their backpacks. Today, as I walked out to the crosswalk and stopped the car in front of me, a line of some of the students began to walk slowly across the street, most of them with their heads down. I figured they must have been among the many students in the nation had watched the shuttle launch on television as part of the school day. To see the first teacher in space . . . There was no giggling or talking with each other today. It wasn't like they were coming home from school, but from a funeral.

In a way, they were.

As soon as I walked in the door at headquarters, I called Dr. Sadler's office. They told me they would give him the message, as he was out on an emergency—and "Could I believe this horrible tragedy had happened on live television?"

When I finally got home, as much as I tried not to, I couldn't take my eyes off the television. I couldn't get over the thought that you could wake up one day and everything was fine, even monotonous, and then, in an instant, it could turn into one of those days you would never forget. I sat down in front of the television to watch the President speak to the nation. The weather forecast said that tomorrow would be just as cold as it was today. It probably meant another day of covering school crossings. A day just like today.

Except that everything had changed.

Sentenced by Man

"It's the Hermans again. She's claiming that the dog bit the kid, but they didn't want me to send an ambulance. It can't be too bad, so I'm just sending you." Sergeant Freeman stopped rustling through his desk when he got a glimpse of me standing there. Squinting, he looked me over. "What happened to you? Looks like you're molting."

"Sunburn," I said. Again.

He must have been the tenth person that day to say something to me about it. It wasn't like I didn't know that my skin was peeling. I'd spent half the night trying to figure out how to make it stop. I had probably used up an entire jar of Noxzema and another tube of lotion trying to make myself appear somewhat presentable. That was the downside of working with mostly men—or maybe it was just cops. They were brutal. Nothing was sacred. They would make comments about everything, no holds barred.

"You know, you don't have the type of skin for sunbathing; you should watch that."

"Thanks." I said. Again. That was probably *at least* the fifth time today someone had told me that fair-skinned, freckled people should never fall asleep in the sun. At least Sgt. Freeman had been more diplomatic about it. Lois, the midnight to 8:00 a.m. dispatcher, had really scolded me when I'd come in that morning (when she wasn't comparing me to a snake shedding its skin). She was a real stickler when it came to taking care of your skin. I told her that it hadn't been intentional. I wouldn't do it again. Point taken.

"Might want to put some Vaseline on that. I know that sounds, well, sort of disgusting, but it worked for my sister when she had a bad burn."

Vaseline? I would try it, but not until I got off work. There was no way I was going to drive around town with Vaseline all over my face and arms (although I would rather go out into the city like that than walk back into headquarters—it was a jungle in here).

I drove down to Smith Street. I didn't need Sgt. Freeman to tell me where to go; I knew all too well. I had been to this house on several occasions, as had the animal control officer who'd preceded me. The Hermans collected animals like stamps, except stamp collectors hold on to their collections; not so the Hermans. Sometimes people like this are referred to as "hoarders." They would bring home cats, puppies, ferrets, guinea pigs, and even the occasional bird. There should have been WANTED posters at the pet store warning employees not to sell any more animals to these people. As it was, the shelter refused to let them adopt any more dogs or cats. That meant a lot. With the shelter as overcrowded as it was, they were usually anxious to find homes for as many animals as possible. The simple fact that they refused to deal with anyone from this family spoke volumes.

I could hear them before I even got out of the car. There was some type of argument going on inside. I banged on the door, probably harder than I had to.

"She's here, she's here—get the door!" I heard them struggling to unlock it. There must have been more than a few locks from the sound of it. I wondered *why so many?* This was a pretty good neighborhood, but then again, if the Hermans had the kind of interaction with their neighbors that they had with their pets, the locks were probably a good idea.

"You're here—finally! I called a long time ago. What took you so long?" Mr. Herman didn't seem too happy at the moment, but I'd never seen him any other way. I had expected this.

"I came as soon as I got the call, sir. I apologize if you had to wait." I had learned that in this job, I had to often control the things I wanted to say. It was a good education for me. As a civil servant it was imperative I remember that the people I dealt with on a daily basis were the ones who, albeit indirectly, paid my salary. Most people were wonderful, and I considered it a privilege to serve their needs; however, once in a while you would come across some who were a little abrasive. They were usually the ones that would remind me that they paid my salary. I wondered sometimes if I should ask them for a raise; I could sure use it.

"Yeah, well, come on in. Damn dog bit my boy. It ain't worth keeping this dog anymore if I can't trust him."

I walked into the house and could tell, from using more than one of my senses, that they had quite a few pets at the moment. Add to that the fact that it was really hot in there. They had a large fan blowing from the window, but it seemed to only be blowing more hot air into the house. I thought of suggesting to them that they face the fan in the other direction and open another window across the room, then thought better of it. The quicker I could get out of there, the better.

I had been to their home recently to pick up a ferret, an animal I'd spent a long time trying to warn them about on an earlier visit. "She has to be spayed; unspayed ferrets can develop all sorts of health problems," I'd said. "You really ought to consider having her spayed." If ferrets were not spayed or neutered, they also emitted an overpowering odor. Even afterward, they still had a distinct aroma. It wasn't that bad if they were taken care of properly, but people who weren't prepared for this were taking on a larger responsibility than they imagined. These animals had become very popular as of late, and it seemed like I was going to a call that involved removing a ferret from a household at least once a week.

Before I was inevitably called to pick up the ferret, I was called to pick up their cat, Misty. Mrs. Herman had been very excited about the ferret. From the moment I entered the house, I could immediately tell that she hadn't had her spayed. The ferret was running loose, scampering all over the living room while one of her children, a toddler, napped on a blanket on the floor. I didn't know if that was a good idea, for many reasons.

"We want to mate her. We're going to get another ferret and then we can sell the babies. That's why we can't have Misty anymore. She doesn't like ferrets."

While I was taking the carrier with the Herman's cat in it out to my car, I realized that Misty seemed fine with the ferret. She'd been sitting on a chair giving herself a bath while it scampered around her. She hadn't given it any attention at all. It seemed to me, that in this case, the Hermans felt that the ferret had commercial potential, and the cat did not.

It never ceased to amaze me how some people could so easily give up pets they had had for years, simply to replace them with younger, or, in this case, more unique pets. This often happened during the month after Easter as well. The baby chicks someone had thought would be an adorable addition to the Easter basket had started to turn into less-than-cute chickens that weren't adaptable to living inside of a house.

About two months later I was called to the Hermans' house once again. This time to take the ferret away, as well, but not until I'd received several panicky calls about the ferret getting "stuck" behind the refrigerator, and sometimes the stove. I had a feeling that the ferret wasn't stuck. She was hiding. Today's call, however, was different. It involved Prince, a dog they had owned for quite a while, since he was a puppy. I remembered this because he was one of the largest German shepherds I had ever seen, and probably the most strikingly beautiful. I used to wish that they would let him run loose so I could seize him and find some sort of reason to get him out of there. That was no longer an option. A dog that bites a child, especially if it is not the first time, is not adoptable. It is labeled a "dangerous dog" and is put down, regardless of the reasons for the bite. Since this was not the first bite report I'd completed for Prince, I knew I would finally be able to get him out of there—but not in the way I had hoped.

"Who did he bite—which one of your children?" I had a feeling I knew who it was. This particular child was about nine or ten years old, old enough to know that you don't tease your dog on a hot day—actually, that you shouldn't tease any dog on any day. There was a difference between playing and teasing. Playing meant you were *both* having fun.

"Petey!" he yelled. "Come on out here and show the dog lady where you got bit." Yes. It was who I thought it was. I was always concerned about children who were cruel to animals. The youth officer, Nathan, had warned me about this very fact.

"We keep an eye on the kids who are hurting animals. If they're doing that at five or six years old, I know that in a few years we're going to have even more problems with them, so we create a file and keep track. It's a bad sign . . . a real bad sign."

Nathan had been proven right on almost every single occasion. He had been there for many years, long enough to see many of the kids he'd come in contact with when they were younger grow up into adults who most often turned out just fine. Not the ones who tortured animals, though; that was an entirely different situation altogether.

I looked at Petey. He had what looked to be an abrasion on his cheek. Great—a bite on the face. There was no way I could approach this now to try and have it end any differently. I had seen these types of bites before. Usually the child involved was trying to give the dog a hug around the neck. When the dog tried to get himself out of the embrace, because he couldn't breathe, the last choice he had was to bite the person preventing him from breathing. I knew there were indeed cases where aggressive and dangerous dogs had hurt and killed people with no provocation, but I had been lucky enough to never come across something like that; I hoped I never did. The laws were there for a good reason, but even if there was a large gray area, such as the situation I was looking at today, it didn't matter. Life can be gray, but laws are just black and white.

"I was just playing with him. He's mean," Petey told me while his mother went to get some antibiotic ointment and gauze to attend to his face. I wondered why she had waited to do this until I arrived, but I figured she wanted me to see the bite. She would have been better off bandaging it up before I arrived so I never would have known just how benign it was. Still, she was a mother, and he was her child. If a dog bit my child someday, I knew I would feel terrible, but I also knew that it wouldn't be caused by something like this, especially by a ten-year-old who was old enough to know better.

Prince had bitten before. The last time it had happened when a few of the kids had been rolling around the floor, wrestling, in what the Hermans had told me was "only a game." Prince had thought they were hurting each other and had tried to break it up. It had only been a nip, but I'd had to file a bite report about it. This would make two. There would be no more.

"I have to fill out a bite report for the state again. The Department of Health requires that I do this. Have you taken Petey to see your pediatrician?" I knew they hadn't, as apparently it had just happened, but I had to ask. The doctor would also have to complete a bite report. The paper trail had begun. There was no way this was going to be simply a case of a dog being teased on a hot day. I had no control over anything in this situation. If they had not wanted to file a complaint and the dog had bitten someone else's child, I would have had to file a dangerous dog action. That was a very involved process and included a deadline of ten days to have everything processed before a court appearance. I had only been involved in one case that had actually gone to court; the others had usually been dealt with by the owners agreeing to permanently secure their dog for the rest of its life. If they didn't, the dog's life span would be decided by the court.

"I just want to advise you that by filling out this complaint and surrendering Prince, he will be euthanized . . . put to sleep." I reiterated this just in case it wasn't clear to them. "Once I bring him down to the animal shelter, that's how this works." I wanted to make sure they understood the implications of their decision. There was still a chance that this could go another way, but that would involve Prince staying here with them, and I had mixed feelings about that to begin with. Quality of life versus euthanasia? I hated this. This shouldn't be something that ended up on my shoulders, but that's the way it was going to be.

I could see Prince lying in the hallway, panting. Mr. Herman got up and went over to grab him by the collar. Prince growled. It seemed that Prince was going to be the one to make the decision. "See how he gets?" said Mr. Herman. "He doesn't like men. He's started growling at the mailman now. Nobody can come near the house without him going nuts."

I wondered if that wasn't the reason they'd gotten a German shepherd in the first place; they were known for being protective of their owners and were excellent guard dogs. If that was the case, I wondered why I hadn't heard any barking or growling when I had knocked on the door?

Trying to decide whether or not I should get the snare pole, I slowly approached Prince lying on the floor. He looked up at me suspiciously.

"Hi, Prince," I said softly. What else could I say to him? *I'm going to take you away to die today.* My stomach started to hurt. He just looked up at me, and his tail thumped twice. Mr. Herman had to raise his voice to speak over the fan.

"You're not male. That's most of the problem—he hates males. He knows you, too, that's why he's calm right now; plus he got quite a smack before you got here."

I noticed a box sitting against the wall that seemed to be jiggling. I heard some rustling from inside. I looked down into the box to find a small puppy, his feet moving in his sleep. Probably a dream about running somewhere. I wished he could have run away from here. Now I had a better idea about why the Hermans weren't that upset about Prince's fate. They had already replaced him.

"Isn't he cute?" Mrs. Herman asked as she scooped him up out of the box. He looked like a little brown hound mix, with floppy ears and a sad little face. This was breaking my heart.

"Yes," I said. "He's really cute."

Using the snare pole just to be on the safe side, I guided Prince over to my station wagon, and he jumped into the backseat willingly. I slid the snare back over his head and swapped it with a leash that I would use to clip to the steel grill in the car. He sat there patiently, panting, while I did all of this. The first thing I was going to do was turn on the air-conditioning. I had to fill out the rest of the reports, but I didn't want to do this sitting in front of the Hermans' house. They hadn't even said good-bye to Prince as I led him out of the house, nor did I notice them watching from the window. As I pulled away I wondered if they had forgotten about him already.

I spent the rest of the day finding any reason I could to avoid going down-county to the shelter. The entire process would take about an hour, including the travel both ways. I still had time. Procrastinating wasn't doing anyone any good, but I still couldn't find any reason why I had to do this right now. I took a few calls, mostly just complaints that ended up requiring no paperwork. I thought that I would get some food from the department and feed him somewhere privately. He seemed so sad and peaceful, just looking out the window while I went about my duties. Occasionally he would wag his tail a little when I talked to him. I found myself talking to him more and more throughout the day, narrating what I was doing like I was telling him a story. He seemed to be eating it up.

On the way out of the department, trying to balance a bag of food and an old milk jug I had filled with water, I saw two of our officers standing over by my car. The barking was loud, and frightening. I tried to run over to my car, but it was difficult with everything I was carrying in my arms. I had left one of the windows open a few inches, even though the air-conditioning was on, and I couldn't believe it could be this loud with only that much space to hear through.

"Holy smokes!" said Kevin, one of our officers who actually volunteered to accompany me on calls because he loved dogs so much. He was standing there, horrified. It looked as though the blood had completely run out of his face. "What is up with this dog? I just came over to say hi. He's beautiful, but oh my God! Look what he did!" Before I could pull Kevin out of Prince's field of vision, I looked into my car to see that Prince had literally ripped the armrest off the door. Not just the upholstery, but the entire thing; it had been torn off, exposing the frame of the door. When I went to grab Kevin's arm to get him away from the car, Prince started throwing himself at the door, snarling and biting the glass with his teeth.

"He thinks you're hurting me or something; he's not usually like this," I said.

Kevin jumped back a few feet, and the barking started to subside.

"How can you drive a dog like that around? Aren't you scared?" Kevin was still looking over at the car. I felt bad for him. He loved dogs and had just wanted a better look. He did this a lot, but he'd never gotten a reaction like this.

"He's the dog-bite case, but he's not like this with me. He's just been abused so much that he doesn't trust everyone." I knew that dogs sometimes responded to women better than to men, but this was the most extreme example of that I had ever seen.

"Well, good luck," said Kevin. He went to give me a little pat on the shoulder, but thought better of it. "Are you allergic to that dog?"

"No more than I am to any other dog—why?" I asked, wondering if I should go look in the mirror.

"Well, it looks like you're having some sort of reaction . . . like you're shedding or something."

"Sunburn," I said. Again. "I fell asleep in the sun."

"Oh, okay. You should really avoid—"

"—doing that again," I said, finishing his sentence for him.

"Yeah, that's right." Kevin walked away, glancing just once more over his shoulder at the dog in the car. "It's sad, isn't it? They're going to . . ."

"Yes," I said. "They are."

I drove to the park, as far away from people as possible. Not only did I have to feed Prince if I was going to put off taking him down to the shelter, but I also had to walk him as well. I opened the door, sans armrest, and looked at him. He looked at me, his tail wagging and the remnants of some type of fiber from the armrest clinging to his muzzle.

He was so beautiful. He looked like the picture-perfect German shepherd you see in dog food ads. I unhooked his leash and he lightly hopped out of the car. I had put down a bowl of food already, and I grabbed a small metal bowl I kept in the car and filled it with water from the jug. He happily lapped away. I hooked the end of his leash onto the edge of the grill with the door open so he would have some freedom of movement, and so my hands could be free to finish the paperwork.

When I sat down in the front seat and started writing, I felt something brush my leg. It was Prince, sitting down next to me, having left his lunch to keep me company. I petted his enormous head and he looked at me, panting lightly. It sort of looked like he was smiling. I was starting to think I couldn't take this job anymore. I loved the animals and the people I worked with. I enjoyed the structure of a police department, and I even had the tuition deduction as an agreement between the city and the college for the space they rented out. All of that would be difficult to give up, but the number of times I went home in tears was starting to increase. Maybe I really couldn't handle this job—at least not this part of it.

"You're misunderstood," I told Prince as I was petting his head. He laid his muzzle on my knee, and I scratched behind his ears and under his collar, all the places that dogs loved to be scratched, hoping that wherever he was going after I brought him to the shelter would be better than the life he had had here. He certainly deserved that.

And I hoped he would remember that there'd been at least one human he could trust.

The Luckiest Duck

$\mathcal{I}$ always thought that the city sat along the most scenic part of the Hudson River. There would always be those who disagreed with me, but I was partial to it. Anytime I had a chance to take a break, I would often choose to go down to the park near the boat ramp and watch the river and the many different types of birds that called the riverfront park their home. The ducks were my favorite because they were friendlier than the geese. It got to the point where they seemed to recognize my car and would waddle over to greet me, knowing I probably had some bread for them. Hank, from the deli near my house, was always generous with the outdated bread. When I stopped by for coffee, he would often give me a loaf to take to the riverfront.

"Here you go, Lisa—take this with you for your feathered friends!" Hank owned the deli down the street from the high school. He was a generous man, and took good care of the teenagers who would stop by his deli during their lunch period. For a dollar, you could have a ham and cheese sandwich on a hard roll, a bag of chips, and a soda. I couldn't imagine how he made a profit this way, and I sensed that he didn't. He also never skimped on quality, making sure to buy only the premium cold cuts.

"Nothing but the best for my kids," he would say, and he meant it. I figured that there were more than a few kids growing up in Annesville who, for even that low price, had to sometimes eat on credit. I thought that Hank was partially responsible for helping quite a few kids who wouldn't have been able to eat lunch were it not for him.

I had been one of those kids.

"Just a coffee today, Hank—I have a lot to do, so I'm just going to drink it in the car. Thanks." I had about ten consecutive calls to go on, and my first appointment didn't start for about half an hour. I wanted to go down to the river, drink my coffee, and wake up a little bit before tackling the list.

"No problem; here you go. See you tomorrow," he said, handing me the coffee and a bag with a buttered roll. I shook my head at him, and he just laughed.

"Just because you're making the big bucks now, doesn't mean you're eating right. You know that breakfast is—"

"I know," I said. "The most important meal of the day." He laughed, handing me the loaf of bread as well. "Can't let those birds down the river get too hungry either."

I pulled up to my customary spot. It was still early enough so that a mist seemed to float just above the ground like a wayward cloud. The usuals were there, the people I noticed who sat in their cars or on the benches on nicer days and read the paper while feeding the birds. These were probably some of the most overfed birds in New York. Sometimes I would try to feed only the pigeons because they didn't seem to be as popular. I tried to do my part to fight pigeon discrimination one bird at a time.

I noticed a group of ducks near the dock. Usually, they would start up toward my car as soon as I pulled in. Something was different today; they were totally ignoring me. I felt sort of slighted. They were quacking loudly and seemed to be attacking something. Maybe they were fighting over some food. I grabbed the bread and got out of the car to find out why they were so distracted.

Most of them scattered when I got too close, but then seeing the bag in my hand, they changed their minds and started to walk over to me again. *Now you notice me*, I thought. Maybe this should be another feed-the-pigeons-only day.

I noticed that two ducks looked to be nipping at another duck that was squatting on the pavement. He had his head down and was doing nothing to fight back.

"Shoo! Get out of here," I said, waving my arms around, the bread falling out of the bag and flying in several directions. In a few seconds, it seemed that every bird in the vicinity was either waddling toward or diving for the bread. It didn't matter, as I'd brought it for them anyway, but I wasn't too happy about the bully ducks getting a meal after what they'd been doing to their brother, or sister.

I didn't know much about geese or ducks—or birds in general, for that matter. It was enough that I could tell the difference between them. Only domestic animals were in my job description; however, I was often sent out to handle calls that involved wild animals. I wasn't licensed for it, and anything I knew came from my own research and some limited experience. Wildlife rehabilitators were available, but they charged a hefty fee, and a lot of people couldn't afford it. When I came into contact with one once, I picked his brain for as much information as I could gather in a short time. There were certain limited situations where we would contact a certified wildlife handler, but for a municipality operating on a limited budget, it was something the city just couldn't afford to offer.

I knew I was overstepping my boundaries when it came to wildlife calls, but in most cases I was encouraged to do what I could. The exception was bats. I refused to enter anyone's home if they called about a bat. The department never forced me to handle these bat calls, even though they had attempted to send me on a few in the past. I had no idea what to do and no intention of learning. They finally gave up. I don't think they were too worried about me taking off my badge and walking out the door, as there were more than a few applicants who would've jumped at my job. No; it was more likely that I wasn't licensed for dealing with wild animals, and they knew it was pushing the envelope even to allow me to handle the calls I did take. They probably could've gotten into trouble with the state or something, which worked out fine for me. That's how strongly I felt about bats.

"Hey, little duck—what's wrong with you?" I didn't want to scare him, and for a moment I thought he was dead. But then I noticed him open his eyes and look at me. I looked around on the ground for a piece of bread. Those scavengers had pretty much cleaned me out. I found a piece next to my shoe, so I put it near his mouth (beak . . . bill?), close enough so he could eat it. He moved his head and picked up the edge of the bread, and then, in a quick flip, swallowed it whole. That was better. Things were looking up for this duck.

I heard my radio squawk from inside the car. It sounded like my radio number. I looked down at my belt and saw that the clip was empty. "What's wrong with me?" I said aloud. The duck turned his head to look at me again. Since he seemed to respond to my voice, I said, "I'll be right back." I got up and ran over to my car and answered my radio.

"Three Oh Six to Eight Forty-Four." Eight Forty-Four was headquarters; that one I knew by heart. There were some codes that applied to me, and some that I didn't learn until I started substituting on the dispatch desk. In the beginning I quickly learned the codes for "Where is your location," "Report back to headquarters," "Call headquarters by phone," "Taking a five-minute break," "Over and out," and "I'll be taking my lunch hour." There was a code for taking a bathroom break, but using that one was like opening yourself up to all sorts of nonsense. It was fun to call someone on the radio when they were, well . . . busy with the more private issues people deal with every day. This was why that code was rarely used. It was like announcing to headquarters, "I am now available for torment."

"You available on radio?" the desk sergeant asked. I knew what he really meant was "What's wrong with you; why don't you have your radio on?"

"Affirmative, Sarge, I am . . . now." I knew that he would translate my answer into "Yes, I didn't have it on before, and I left it in my car, but now I have it both turned on *and* clipped onto my belt, and I won't forget it again."

There were people listening to everything the police and fire departments said. Some of them were regular citizens with radios that were able to pick up police signals, who listened in as a hobby. In order to protect the privacy of the residents, most situations were referred to by code.

Other departments could also monitor our transmissions, and for a short time we'd had to share a signal with a neighboring town. This resulted in everyone getting frequently "stepped on," which meant that they would try to talk when we were trying to talk, or vice versa. Even though it would start off as an accident, it would sometimes turn catty, and people would press the transmit button simply to interfere with the communication of the other department. Eventually we had our own system, and all of that changed. It just made you realize that some people never outgrew the petty behavior they exhibited in the schoolyard.

The most important concern, however, was the Federal Communications Commission. The FCC had certain guidelines as to how to communicate on the police radio. You had to be aware that whatever you said was transmitted to a lot of places and to a lot of ears—some of whom were just waiting to have something to call the city and complain about.

Sometimes the funniest thing that would happen was something known as an "open mike." Someone accidentally leaning on their transmit button would be heard by every radio in the department, and then some. I had overheard some very interesting conversations this way. The few times it happened to me, I had been chatting to a dog or cat in my car. Once I had been singing some Christmas carols while I drove down to the shelter. It had been the only way to stop the dogs in the back of my car from howling. I was frequently reminded about that.

"Your nine o'clock canceled; they said to stop by tomorrow," the sergeant said.

"Ten-four," I replied. That was good. Now I had at least an hour to figure out what to do with this duck. When I got back out of the car, I noticed that the flock of ducks that had been antagonizing him before were back. And this time it looked like they were being joined by some Canadian geese. It was an avian riot!

I ran over to the duck, shouting, "Shoo, shoo . . . get out of here!" but got no reaction whatsoever. I looked around to see if anyone was going to get in on this and help me out, but nobody was paying me any mind. I stomped my feet and yelled as loud as I could. "GET AWAY FROM MY DUCK!" This seemed to work, and they quickly took off in different directions. I pulled off my jacket and wrapped it around the duck, which was still squatting on the ground. He hadn't tried to run away from them. I couldn't figure out what was wrong. He struggled a little when I picked him up, but only for a moment.

I tried talking to him. "I'm not going to hurt you . . . it's okay." I brought him over to my car and placed him in the backseat, looking around for something to put him in that would keep him from trying to flap all over the place should he get his energy back. I grabbed the box I kept the cat food in and dumped out all the dry food. I placed the box on the seat and gently picked up the duck to put him inside. That was when I discovered why he hadn't tried to run away from all of those crazed birds who had been attacking him. He had only one leg. One perfect leg with a webbed foot. Where his other leg should have been was a small hole. It appeared as though someone had done this intentionally and just pulled it off.

I looked at him, sitting quietly in the box looking up at me. I couldn't imagine how much that had hurt, having your leg torn off your body. I was surprised that he was still alive. I wondered if there had been any bleeding. Was he so quiet because he was in shock? I didn't know enough about this, and since I had just declared loudly enough for everyone at the riverfront to hear that this was "my" duck, I knew I had to find someone who did.

"He's so quiet. Are you sure he's all right?" Jim from the Records department asked, peering into the box that sat on the desk in the communications room. I was trying to find someone who would help take care of this duck, and so far, it had been a miserable failure. None of the local vets handled ducks, and even if they did, there was not enough money in petty cash or my budget for treatment. Maureen at the shelter had just laughed at me when I called, and then apologized for laughing and wished me luck. I could only imagine what they were all saying after I hung up.

"I don't know. I haven't heard him quack or make any noise yet." I was starting to feel discouraged.

"You know, I can keep an eye on him if you want to go to the pet shop. They might have an idea of what to do, or at least what to feed him while you look for a solution."

I smiled at Jim. He had retired from a large metropolitan police department years before, and now worked in the Records department here. I had a feeling that he really liked the duck, and since he had volunteered to watch him for me, I figured I would reschedule some calls and drive over to the pet store to see what I could learn.

When I got to the Pet Emporium, Lori came over to help me.

"What you need is poultry feed—much better than bread," she said, "and water—don't forget a bowl of water, and a soft towel for him to lie on. I'll go get you some poultry feed." She was very helpful.

This was a relatively new pet store, and it was actually within the city limits, which made it easy for me to get the supplies I needed. They didn't sell cats or dogs; they mostly dealt with ferrets, hamsters, fish, birds, and the like. They had some reptiles, too, from which I kept my distance. There was a small section for farm supplies, enough to keep the two farms still left in the area well provisioned. (Both farms were very small and off the beaten track.)

While Lori was always helpful every time I came in, the owner had decided that I was the enemy. The moment I walked in the door, he skulked into the back of the store to hide until I left.

It hadn't always been that way. Right after the store had first opened, when I was purchasing some dog food and new leashes for the department, the owner called me over to see something. "Check this out," he said, and led me into the back of the store where customers were not allowed. Jumping around in a little fenced-in area was an animal that looked like something I'd seen on TV, or at the zoo. It looked like a kangaroo.

"Is that a kangaroo?" I asked, astonished, thinking this was the last thing I'd expected to see when he brought me back here.

"Sort of," he said, walking over to pat the animal. It stopped leaping and let him scratch the top of his head. I wanted to touch it so badly, but I didn't know if it was a good idea.

"It's a wallaby," said the owner, "in the same family as a kangaroo, but smaller. His name is Max—you know, after Mad Max?"

"Aren't they from Australia?" I asked. I was still having a hard time wrapping my mind around the fact that this wallaby was leaping around the back of a store in Annesville, New York.

"Yeah, that's why I named him Mad Max—like that dude in the movie."

"Oh," I said. That seemed appropriate for an Australian wallaby in Annesville.

I finally felt like I had gathered myself together enough to ask to touch the wallaby. He seemed pretty calm at the moment. That was when I made my big mistake. "Is it legal to have a wallaby?" I asked. "I mean, uh, aren't they considered exotic animals?"

Well, it was like a door had closed in my face. He escorted me to the outside area of the store, and that was the last time I saw the wallaby. I forgot sometimes that the uniform made me appear much different than I perceived myself. As far as he was concerned, I was now "the Man." The next time I was there I asked about Mad Max, and the owner just looked at me like he didn't understand what I was saying. I never did get to pet that wallaby.

Lori didn't know of anyplace I could bring the duck, outside of the two farms I had already called, and they weren't equipped to deal with an injured duck. I bought the poultry feed and drove back to headquarters. It was getting late, and my shift would be ending soon. With all the running around trying to find out what to do with the duck, and attempting to handle a few other tasks I had to complete for the day, I was exhausted. And I still didn't know what to do with "my" duck.

"I got a number for you to call!" Jim told me as soon as I returned to headquarters.

"What number? What did you find?" I said. This was good news, and after this day so far, I really felt I could use it.

Jim handed me a card. "It's a wildlife rehabilitation center across the river, down near Rockland County. I called my wife, and she'd heard of it because she works near there. I was telling her about our duck and she suggested this place!"

Our duck. I was glad to see that I now shared joint custody of the duck. It was hard raising young ones alone these days.

"I called them, and they seemed a little standoffish. I get the sense they have more than they can handle right now, but maybe if you call, it might have more clout."

"Thanks, Jim, that's great! I'll call them and see if they'll take him."

He handed me the card, and I slipped into my shirt pocket. "I'll call as soon as I feed our duck."

I poured some of the poultry feed into a bowl and put it in the box with the duck. He was more alert now, looking around curiously, but still not making a sound. I saw that Jim had already made sure the duck had someone's flannel shirt to lie on. I thought it best not to ask where it had come from. My shift was almost over, and I was worried about our duck. He may have been more alert, but he still wasn't attempting to move or to quack, and I worried about his leg, or lack thereof. Infection? Blood loss? I had no idea what issues he might face because of what had happened to him. The sooner I could find someone who did, the better off he would be.

After what could probably be described as groveling (*begging* wouldn't be an adequate description), they agreed to take the duck and see if they could treat him. The only problem was, they were closing for the day, and they didn't accept any animals after 5:00 p.m. I looked at the clock. It was already 4:15, and the drive alone would take more than forty-five minutes, especially at rush hour. On top of that, I had not one, but *two* classes that night, and even if I brought the duck home with me, I would have to leave him alone with a cat, who, while very peaceful with other cats and the occasional dog, was absolutely fascinated with birds (and not in a good way). I wouldn't be home until 11:00, which would leave the duck alone with my cat for several hours—not to mention the fact that my landlord might be coming over to fix my hot water while I was gone. That would not go over well.

I looked at the duck. He seemed pretty content sitting on his soft shirt in a box with food and water. He didn't make any noise, and once I'd cleaned out some of the mess he had made in his box, he would probably be just fine until the next morning. I decided to keep him in the sally port overnight. The sally port was the garage entrance to the police department, where prisoners were brought in; it was also used to store a lot of equipment. There was a gated area there that would provide a perfect, safe little place for the duck to be kept away from anyone who would be using the sally port in the evening.

I would also feel better knowing that he wouldn't be alone for hours. Maybe someone could check on him for me. It was the middle of the week, so it probably wouldn't be too busy.

"Sarge, can I keep a duck in the sally port overnight?" The shifts were changing and people were walking in and out of the lobby. Sgt. Pierce was packing up his briefcase to leave at the end of his shift. He had been running late too. Without looking up, he said, "Sure." Then he shut his briefcase and left.

That was easy enough. Problem solved.

Later that evening, I was sitting in class, listening to the professor describe the failure of prime minister Neville Chamberlain's appeasement policy prior to World War II, when there was a knock at the door. The professor walked over to the door and opened it slightly. There was some whispering, and then he turned around and looked directly at me. "Miss Duffy, the police want to speak to you."

While a few people in class knew where I worked, the majority of them didn't. There was a gasp, some more whispering, and some pointed stares as I packed up my books and got up to go to the door. I turned around to face the class, thinking that maybe I would say something about my job, but then thought better of it. Let them think what they wanted to think; maybe it would add to my mystique, make me seem a little dangerous.

I walked out into the hallway and saw Steve, an officer who had been a few years ahead of me in high school. "What is it?" I asked.

"You're in trouble. Bennett is losing it. We had a raid; the cells are full, and all you can hear is this duck you have stuck in the sally port, quacking like crazy. It won't stop. We're trying to process and fingerprint everybody, and all you can hear is that duck going nuts. Now the prisoners are quacking, too. It's chaos. Bennett told me to come and get you."

This was not good. Sgt. Bennett was intimidating when he *wasn't* upset; the thought of walking in there to confront him now was something I was not looking forward to. "I got permission to leave the duck there; I asked Sgt. Pierce."

"Well, it doesn't seem like he remembers that, because Bennett called him, and Pierce said he had no idea that there was a duck in there. You're going to have to explain this to him yourself," said Steve. "I'm going on the road, and with any luck, I'll get to stay out there for the rest of the night." Steve turned and started to walk away.

"So, I'm going in there myself—you're not walking with me?" I called over. Sometimes guilt worked pretty well.

"Nope. Not on your life."

Sometimes it didn't.

Walking into headquarters was like walking into a circus. A bad circus. Steve had been right. Not only could I hear the duck quacking for all he was worth, but I could also hear some of the prisoners quacking as well. That, combined with the laughter coming from the cells, and the sullen look on the faces of the shift officers, was enough to cause my face to redden. This was not good. I thought that, looked at objectively, it was actually really funny. For the other officers, it was just going to be one of those things they'd look back on someday and think was funny—if I survived that long.

"Duffy. What the in the world is this?" Sgt. Bennett was really mad. I could tell because he wasn't loud. He spoke clearly, enunciating his words carefully, and his tone was serious. Deadly serious.

"I had no idea where to put him, and he only has one leg, so I asked Sgt. Pierce if I could keep him in the sally port and he said sure, but now I realize that maybe he didn't hear me, and I have to bring him to the wildlife place tomorrow, and he never quacked before, so I didn't think . . ."

Sgt. Bennett put his hand up to stop me. I just shut my mouth in the middle of my rambling.

"The sally port is for cars. It is used to transport prisoners. It is for equipment. It is *not* for ducks, one-legged or otherwise. Do I make myself clear?"

I nodded my head and then asked, "What do you want me to do?"

"Go get that duck and put it in the basement, in the locker room."

"Oh, okay," I said. That hadn't occurred to me before; it was so desolate down there that I probably wouldn't have considered it— but I should have.

I went into the sally port, and there was my duck. He looked a lot better. He was sitting up more, trying to balance on his one foot. He was quacking loudly until he saw me and then stopped.

"You got me in trouble, duck." He looked at me like he was expecting me to say something more.

I picked up his box and went back inside and then down the two flights of stairs to the basement, where I put him down on the bench in the locker room. I closed the door and hesitated for a moment. I opened it again and turned on the light, closed the door, and came back upstairs. The sounds of quacking were now reverberating in the empty stairwell. It seemed even louder than it had in the sally port.

I walked into the dispatch room and stood there. The sergeant was sitting at his desk going through all of the paperwork generated by the large amount of arrests that night.

"Sarge?" I asked quietly. "What do you want me to do now?"

He looked up at me briefly before going back to writing on a legal pad.

"Go back to class. You still have a lot to learn."

I sighed. Okay. I went back outside and walked down the sidewalk toward the college. Now I would get to walk back into the class that I'd just been escorted out of—by a policeman, no less. I was making good impressions all over the place.

Immediately upon walking into headquarters the next morning, I ran downstairs to the locker room to check on the duck. Someone had turned off the light, and when I turned it back on, the duck blinked at me like I had woken him up and gave one small quack. He seemed fine. More alert than he'd been when I'd found him at the park, but a lot less intense than he'd been last night. I picked up the box to put him in the car and was bowled over to discover that someone had refilled his water and food dishes during the night. Even with how busy it had been last night, and the cells full of prisoners, which meant that even the 12 to 8 shift had been busier then usual, someone had taken the time to make sure my duck had been cared for.

When I arrived at the wildlife center after navigating the dirt road with my rear-wheel-drive station wagon, I was impressed with how nice it was. It was located at the top of a hill so high, it was practically a mountain. The views from the fields that surrounded the building were amazing. I was given a tour of the "hospital," and saw tiny raccoons being bottle-fed by a young woman in a rocking chair. There were incubators and a few cages that had many different types of animals all sitting comfortably in different states of recovery. They were full, probably over capacity, and since they operated mostly on donations, I was grateful that they had accepted the duck for treatment.

The vet tech, a nice young man with a beard who was attending veterinary school, picked up the duck and put him on the table. "Yes, this was deliberate," he said. "Someone tore the leg off; otherwise, it wouldn't be such a neat wound. We'll make sure that there is no further damage or infection, but I don't think this duck can ever go home."

"Why not?" I asked. "He's not going to die, is he?"

The vet tech smiled at me. "Of course not. And actually, he is a she. This duck is a female. It's difficult to tell for someone who isn't trained, but one way to tell is that a female duck usually quacks louder than a male."

"Well, there you go. That makes sense," I said.

He raised his head from the duck to look at me. "I'm sorry, what did you say?"

"Oh, nothing important. Why can't she go home; what would happen to her?"

"She could be turned away from her flock. They might not accept her anymore, and they could hurt her, possibly kill her."

Now I understood what had been going on at the riverfront.

"Sometimes it doesn't happen, but every once in while it does. It's not worth taking the chance. Eventually she'll learn how to balance on her leg and she'll hop around so well, it will be like nothing happened."

"But where is she going to live?" I asked. After coming this far, I'd hoped that I had found my answer. I was fresh out of ideas about what to do with this duck.

"She can stay here. Look at that great pond over there." He nodded toward the window, and that was when I noticed a large pond several feet away from the field I had first seen upon arriving here.

"The staff can keep an eye on her to make sure she acclimates to her new environment, but I'm feeling pretty optimistic about it."

I felt as though an enormous weight had been lifted from my shoulders. The drama of the last two days had taken its toll on me, and I think the sleep deprivation was making me overly emotional.

"Do you want a tissue?" the vet tech asked.

"No, thanks, I'm fine . . . I just have allergies."

"Of course," he said, smiling at me. This had ended up much better than I thought it would. I was so choked up with gratitude that I had some difficulty holding myself together to get the words out.

"Thank you so much. This place . . . and you . . . you've been a lifesaver."

He smiled and nodded. He really had an engaging way about him. If it hadn't been so far away, I might have tried to find more reasons to come back.

Still smiling, he said, "I was just about to say the same thing about you."

Several weeks had gone by, and all the drama about the duck seemed to blow over. I was starting my first shift with Sgt. Bennett as my desk sergeant. I hadn't seen him since the whole duck episode. I had received a note from the chief asking me to please keep animals out of the sally port. I would have felt worse about the note except for the fact that he also told me they were purchasing a small metal building that would serve as a new storage facility for my equipment and supplies, as well as a mini-shelter down near the Department of Public Works. Now I would at least have a place with a roof and some protection from the elements in case I ended up in a situation like this again.

On my way out the door to start my shift, Sgt. Bennett called my name. "ACO Duffy."

"Yes, Sarge," I answered. He still made me a little nervous.

"What is the status of that duck?"

"She's great. She's recuperated completely and gets around well on her leg. She lives at the wildlife center now."

"Good. Glad to hear it. You know what that means, don't you?" he said, a small smile playing at the corners of his mouth.

"No sir, what is it?"

"That makes her one lucky duck!" He chuckled and went back to what he was doing.

Sometimes I just couldn't figure that man out.

I went outside to my car, smiling to myself while I walked over to the parking lot. Suddenly I had a pretty good idea of who had given the duck her food and water during the night shift she spent in the basement.

When It Wasn't Fate

Summer was usually a slower time for loose-dog complaints, at least in the very beginning of the season. It seemed that some of the usual suspects were happily preoccupied, busy with the kids now that they were home from school. They had someone to play with. People went away on vacations, and the nice weather seemed to put everyone in a good mood. With no school crossings to cover, I got the opportunity to catch up on some recordkeeping and license renewals that I had put off earlier in the year. The amount of physical exertion required seemed to calm down as well. While cat complaints would often go up, those required a different kind of effort. You really can't run after a cat (the cat always wins). Most cat complaints were for surrenders, found kittens, or trapping feral cats.

Although the animal control business seemed to slow down a bit during the summer, the polar opposite was true for the police. Their workload seemed to increase at this time of year. The warm temperatures, especially after dark, brought people out in droves to enjoy the night air. After a few weeks of this, it seemed familiarity really did breed contempt, because the amount of verbal and physical altercations seemed to rise with the temperature. Family get-togethers and barbecues started off well, but the combination of heightened emotion, elevated blood alcohol levels, and the heat added up to some volatile situations. This often resulted in call after call to mediate disagreements and domestic disputes. I often worried about the officers when they had to respond to these kinds of calls, because domestic disputes were the most dangerous of all.

Holiday parties were the worst. Sometimes it was just noise complaints or illegal fireworks, but we also received calls about too much smoke coming from barbecue grills. People who had just bought new grills and weren't sure how to use them added to the summer chaos. These complaint calls about smoke seemed to come one after the other. Often it was the combination of several grills going at once that angered people to the point where they called to complain. I thought sometimes it was because they weren't invited.

"Two Fifty-Four, report to a noise and smoke complaint at Mill Street. The locals are cooking!" Will was funny. He was the senior day-shift dispatcher and had been at the department for many years. He could handle several emergency calls at once and never break a sweat. His dry sense of humor helped to alleviate the number of callers who phoned for frivolous reasons. Sometimes a caller would hear his voice on the phone and just hang up. Days working with Will were always productive. He could tell when to invite people to come in and fill out a complaint in person, rather than sending a patrol to their home, knowing full well that they wouldn't come to the station unless it was truly a valid complaint. This discouraged the people who were just out to cause trouble for someone they might have been angry with. Will made the best use of everyone's time and had so much intuition, I sometimes thought he was psychic.

So it was with a great deal of surprise on a hot Friday afternoon that I was called to a noisy family barbecue at a house in the center of town. I wasn't even sure if it involved an animal; since the rest of the department was so busy (and loud), I couldn't hear why Will was sending me.

"Report to a noise complaint at one-oh-two Grant Avenue."

"Repeat. This is the ACO," I said into my radio, thinking that with all the background noise at the station, maybe Will thought he was sending a police officer. It took longer than usual for him to respond, as there were a lot of calls going on simultaneously, and Will was communicating with several people at the same time.

"Affirmative, ACO—one-oh-two Grant Avenue."

"Ten-four," I said.

Okay; maybe they were busy? I had been utilized before for calls that didn't involve animals. They had trained me as a matron, which I didn't like the sound of until they explained to me that I'd be trained on how to search a female prisoner. When there were no female officers available, they would often call me in to search and check on the prisoner every fifteen minutes until they either brought her down to the county jail, or a female police officer arrived for her shift. Sometimes when there were several females in custody, I would have to sit outside the cells with them until they were brought up to court.

One time, a group of female prisoners had been so loud and unruly that you could hear them all the way in the lobby. Some of the things they were yelling about were a bit inappropriate, so I had suggested we sing "Row, Row, Row Your Boat" in a four-part round. They seemed to like it, and I thought we sounded rather good. The lieutenant came in and just stood there looking at us, shaking his head. Finally, he muttered, "Okay, this works," and left. At least they weren't cursing and yelling anymore.

As time went on, more female officers were hired, and I was needed less often for this purpose. It was nice to have more women around, too—especially ones that were not behind bars.

I drove out to Grant Avenue and pulled up in front of the house. I couldn't find a house number anywhere; usually when this happened, I would just look at the other houses to figure out where to go. This time, I didn't need to do that. It was apparent from all of the parked cars in front of the house, the smell of burgers on the grill, and the music coming from the backyard where I needed to go.

I knocked on the door. There was no answer. Of course they wouldn't be able to hear me anyway. This was a loud party, but not any louder than average. I still wasn't sure why a dog warden was being sent to a noise complaint that wasn't about a barking dog. Maybe I was supposed to give them a warning? I wasn't going to call in and ask again. Will had sounded cranky enough already, and with good reason. The radio traffic was insane. This required me to do some independent thinking. I didn't have the power to write any summonses other than ones related to animals. Still, I had on occasion been sent to check-on-the-welfare calls when the department was very busy, a few car-blocking-the-driveway calls, and, once in a while, to provide an escort to the hospital. Those I liked. It was usually someone in labor, and I was allowed to use my lights and siren which I never used unless it was for a parade or a roadblock.

I walked toward the backyard where all the action seemed to be.

"Hello . . ." I called, cautiously entering the small backyard, where it looked like there were at least forty people playing music, drinking, eating, and laughing a lot. It didn't look so bad to me.

"Oh, here you are! This way . . ." A middle-aged woman gestured for me to come in the house through the back door. Maybe she already knew someone had called to complain? This was getting more confusing by the moment.

"Just follow me," she said casually, and led me in through the kitchen and down a hall toward the front of the house. "He's in here. He called you. Pop—she's here."

In direct contrast to the carefree party taking place outside, this place (which was probably a former living room) had been transformed into a dark, somber sickroom. There was a hospital bed in the corner and an IV pole set up next to it. An empty wheelchair sat next to the bed. I turned around to thank the woman for showing me in, hoping she'd give me an explanation as to why I was here, but she had already left. I heard the screen door slam behind her as she went back outside to join the party.

"Good afternoon, miss."

I looked around; it was so dark in the room that my eyes were having trouble adjusting. I looked toward the voice and noticed a man sitting in an armchair, surrounded by pillows. At first I thought he was an older man, but then I wasn't too sure; I couldn't place his age. He stood up slowly to extend his hand toward me. He was very thin and really tall, but the thing I noticed right away was that a large section of his skull looked like it was missing. His head was asymmetrical. I averted my eyes, not wanting to make him uncomfortable. I'm sure it was the first thing everyone noticed.

"Glad you could come. Name's Nate—Nate Busby. Have a seat." He sat back down and exhaled heavily. It was obvious that standing up had taxed him greatly.

I sat on the edge of the couch facing the armchair. All of the furniture had been crowded into a small area to make room for the hospital equipment.

"It's nice to meet you too, sir . . . It's just that I don't know why you called me here. They told me it was something about a noise complaint. If that's the case, then I should tell you that I'm only the animal control officer. Maybe there's been some sort of mistake?"

"No. I called you," he said, looking at me intently. On the table next to him were several amber-colored bottles of medication. He saw me looking at them.

"I'm dying," he said.

I wondered if I had heard him correctly. Looking around the room, it was apparent that I probably had. He had said it in such a matter-of-fact way, almost like *I'm going on vacation*. Why was he telling me this? I was trying to think of something to say.

"I'm so sorry."

"Thank you, but I'm fine." He smiled. This polite gentleman had just told me he was dying, and then he'd thanked me. He was resigned to it. I couldn't understand. I couldn't imagine ever being as calm about it if I'd been in his place. It was quiet in the room except for the thumping of the bass from the backyard. Why was there a party going on outside?

"I want you to take Smitty, my cat. He's about eight years old, but he's healthy; he's had his claws out, all his shots. I want you to take him so he can have a good home after I'm gone."

I hadn't noticed before, but blending into the blanket on top of the armchair was a small black-and-white cat. He opened his eyes at the sound of his name, yawned, and then went back to sleep.

"He's been fixed too. Smitty's been under the knife more than me!" he said with a laugh, which turned into a cough. Mr. Busby cleared his throat. "I had a tumor—you can probably tell. Sometimes these things just spread, and you can't stop them. But it's okay. I'm ready." He seemed almost cheerful.

"Mr. Busby . . ." I said, my voice cracking a bit. This entire situation was heartbreaking, but confusing at the same time. "If I take Smitty, it's considered a surrender, and I will have to bring him to the animal shelter. There's no guarantee that he will find a home." Even as I was explaining this to him I was running through the possibilities in my head. Who did I know who would take this cat?

"I know that. I called them already and explained everything. They're the ones who told me to call you. They're ready for him; they said that declawed cats like Smitty get homes really quick. I have the ten dollars over there on top of that dresser. You can take that with you too. I have one of his things, a toy he likes . . ."

He started to dig around behind him in the cushion of the armchair. I stood up, thinking I should help him, but then he fished something out and held it up.

"Catnip mouse . . . he'll need this. I told them about that too at the animal shelter."

I walked over to him and took the toy and put it in my pants pocket. "I'll make sure that this stays with him." I looked out toward the backyard. I could still hear the party going strong. Someone was laughing really hard. Someone else asked if a guest wanted cheese on their burger. The rest, I couldn't hear because of all the music and voices.

"Wouldn't you rather have someone in your family take Smitty, or maybe he can . . . stay here?" Even though I was weighing my words carefully, everything I said sounded awkward. Mr. Busby didn't seem to mind. Actually, he was taking all of this much better than I was.

"Them?" He looked over toward the back of the house, even though he couldn't see the yard from where he was sitting. "I wouldn't trust them to take care of a bug. If I'm not here, I don't want Smitty here either—not without me. He deserves to live with someone who wants him and will take good care of him. The kind of person that will adopt a cat from a place like the shelter—that's the kind of person who will take good care of him."

"That's true," I said.

It occurred to me that in all the years I'd been doing this job, I had never thought of it that way. I had always been fixated on trying to take care of everything myself, using the shelter as a last resort. I hadn't thought about the people who go to the shelter and deliberately choose to adopt a pet that didn't have a home. There were many of them. I saw them there all the time, yet I hadn't given them a second thought. There were many times that I would go to the shelter to visit a dog or cat that I had dropped off and found that someone had adopted them. In some ways I had blinders on, with the single goal of controlling everything myself. Even if my intentions were good, it was emotionally exhausting. It was selfish, even narcissistic of me to think that I was the only one who could make things better. It was suddenly apparent to me that maybe giving up control wasn't the worse thing in the world.

I told Mr. Busby that I would be right back. He nodded his head, saying, "Take your time; I'm not going anywhere." I looked at him curiously, wondering if this was another awkward moment, but then he smiled again and winked. He had been making a joke. I smiled back. I was so impressed by Mr. Busby. I just couldn't figure out what was wrong with his family.

I went out to my car to get my shelter booklet and the cat carrier. On the way back in, trying to navigate my way through the party guests, I saw the woman who had met me when I first arrived.

"Why are you having a party?" I asked. It seemed like a simple question, but it wasn't. I knew that I was really asking a lot of things. I was asking her why she was letting people have a party and play loud music when a good and intelligent man was dying inside her house. I was asking why she hadn't tried to include him in the festivities rather than allowing him to sit alone in the dark with his thoughts. I was asking her why, or really, *how*, she could sit out here laughing with all these people when time was quickly ticking away for Mr. Busby. Why was he sitting alone with his cat in a dark room that smelled of medicine?

I felt judgmental and bad about feeling that way all at the same time. I had never been here before, and I realized I didn't know the entire story. Nonetheless, everyone here seemed like they weren't even thinking about Mr. Busby.

"It's the Fourth of July weekend," she said matter-of-factly. "Want a Coke?" she asked, holding a can of soda out toward me.

"No, thank you," I said. I didn't understand this.

I went back inside, my face hot. I was angry. Maybe I didn't know the whole situation, but I still didn't think it was right.

Mr. Busby was holding Smitty, stroking his back. "Here," he said. "You can put him in there for me." I picked him up and he just lay in my arms, purring. He was a very agreeable cat. I placed him in the carrier and dug his catnip mouse out of my pocket and put it in there with him. I could see Mr. Busby looking at me while I pretended to take more time to shut the carrier door. I was trying to control my emotions before I looked at him again.

"It's okay, you know. Smitty and me, we have an agreement."

I waited to hear what it was.

"We're going to meet up again. It's one of those things that are meant to be."

"Like fate?" I asked softly.

He shook his head no and waited for me to look back. "No," he said. "Like faith."

They were waiting for Smitty at the shelter. They had a nice place all set up for him in the cat building, and when they took him inside for his checkup, I saw that they were careful to make sure they took his catnip mouse with them. It was one of the few times that nobody started teasing me the moment I arrived. Either they could see it on my face, or they were aware of the situation I had just come from, or maybe it was a little of both. When I got back to headquarters, it seemed that things had started to calm down. When I pulled out the drawer to get a complaint form to write up this case, I heard Will behind me.

"Nate Busby is a good man, isn't he?"

"Yes," I said. "He really is. You know him?"

"Known him for years. Most of us old-timers know him real well. He used to work for the city. He got sick right before he was supposed to retire—but isn't that always the way?"

What Will said was true. We had lost more than a few good people right before they could put in their papers and enjoy the retirement plans they had spent years working toward.

"I wish I'd known him," I said.

"You did," Will said gently. "Today."

And he went back to his typing.

The Randy Raccoons

$\mathcal{I}$nconsistency was the order of the week. What had literally started off with a bang at the Independence Day fireworks show at the riverfront park had slowly trickled down to a point where even waiting for the phone to ring was a source of excitement.

"You have to balance them like this . . . See? Twist the tops a little."

Officer Farrell and Sergeant Freeman were trying to build a tower out of the little plastic devices that the pizza place used to keep the cheese from sticking to the top of the box before it was opened. They looked like tiny little stools that would fit well in a dollhouse. Someone had suggested they looked like milking stools, so when it seemed like someone was taking too long filling out paperwork to avoid going back out on the road, that person was awarded the "Milking Stool Award" for milking an assignment as long as possible. I had won it once. I had thanked the Academy for this great honor—and then they took it back. Fame is fleeting.

My car was in the shop for repairs, and Sgt. Freeman had decided that I was "absolutely not" going to put animals in any of the other patrol cars, and since Sgt. Bennett had accused me of what they referred to as a "ticket blitz" when they had given me my own book of parking summonses a few months ago, I now had to limit the amount of summonses I wrote.

"So, Officer Duffy, I see that the chief saw fit to assign you your very own book of parking summonses," said Sgt. Bennett. He'd started packing up his briefcase to go out on the road. I had never seen a briefcase like this one before. It was brushed metal, possibly steel. A tank could drive over it and it would still look just as it had before. Rumors had been floating around the station that it was bulletproof.

On this particular day, there were enough staff members available to have a road sergeant *and* a desk sergeant on duty. Many times when a road sergeant was working, you wouldn't see or hear from them all day long. This was never the case with Sgt. Bennett.

"Yes, Sarge. Do you want me to go write some?" I was very excited about my new ticket book. I had learned how to chalk tires to figure out how long people were actually parking their cars on the streets that had no parking meters. I made sure to hit every handicapped parking spot in the city, including the ones at the shopping plaza in the north part of town. If you didn't have a handicapped permit, you'd better watch out. I was on the job!

Sgt. Bennett shut his briefcase with a snap. He peered up at me over his bifocals in that disconcerting way he had. His silver hair was always perfect, his uniform impeccable. His shoes were shined so well they looked brand-new. I looked down at my feet. Scuffed would have been an understatement.

"ACO Duffy, do you know what the word *revenue* means?"

"Isn't it another word for money, or income?" I said.

"Yes. In a way, that is the case. It's the money that a business receives from its activities, mostly from the sale of goods or services to its customers. Do you understand?"

"Yes." I wondered where he was going with this. With him, there were always more reasons than you thought there were.

"Businesses need customers. Customers drive cars. Customers park cars. Sometimes they park their cars in violation of parking regulations, and in some cases it is advisable to write them a summons." He looked at me to see if I was following him. I nodded my head. Of course I was following him. I knew all about parking regulations. I had written the most parking tickets that month, and the month before that. I was the new champion of parking tickets.

"However . . ." he said. He took off his glasses and rubbed the bridge of his nose before he continued. I had the distinct feeling that sometimes I gave Sgt. Bennett a headache. "If we write so many parking tickets that people decide to take their business elsewhere—like the mall, or down-county—then the businesses lose revenue. This means that the city loses businesses, which means that we also lose revenue. It's a cycle. Do you understand what I'm saying?"

None of that had occurred to me. I had been so consumed with writing parking tickets that I had lost track of the fact that it wasn't cars I was actually ticketing—it was people.

"Yes, Sarge, I understand," I said. "I have to stop writing so many parking tickets." There it was. In my quest to write the most parking tickets, I was single-handedly driving customers out of town, sending the city into an economic recession. I had been corrupted by power. Sometimes I felt like I could do nothing right in this job.

"Thank you. I appreciate it." Sergeant Bennett put his glasses back on and turned to walk toward the door.

I started to walk back to the communications room to grab a few complaint forms. I would stick to animals and leave the cars alone. At least I hadn't made too many mistakes in that area.

"Lisa." I turned around when I heard my name. Sgt. Bennett was holding the door to the lobby open with his foot. "Keep hammering the violators without handicapped permits. You're doing a good job with that. Those people deserve tickets." He put his cap on and gave me a quick nod before leaving.

"Thanks, Sarge," I whispered, even though he was already gone. Again, just when I thought I had figured him out, I realized that I hadn't.

As I was standing in the dispatch room, listening to Officer Farrell and Sgt. Freeman argue over who had the best tower of plastic stools, I actually wished that I had something else to do. With no parking tickets to issue, there was no reason to go outside and walk around town. Without a vehicle, there was no way to handle animal complaints. So, by default, I was stuck inside making calls for license renewals. This was probably the single most boring task in the world.

Yawning, I looked up from the counter into the lobby. Daryl had been washing the lobby floor. Now he was standing there, watching it, waiting for it to dry. It's important to supervise that sort of thing. What if one errant floor tile refused to dry? That could lead to others doing the same. Imagine the rebellion that could ensue! Who was I kidding? I had been on the same page of license expirations for over an hour. I was not the one to cast the first stone.

Just then, a woman walked in the door of the police department, bringing a rush of hot air behind her. Her high heels clicked purposefully as she strode over to the window where I was standing. She had that kind of platinum-blond hair that reminded me of movie stars from the 1940s. Her dark sunglasses and bright red lipstick added to the image. Since it was sort of dark in the lobby, I thought she would take her sunglasses off so I could get an idea of whether I'd ever seen her before. She didn't.

"I need to see an officer. I have to file a report about a Peeping Tom. *Two* Peeping Toms," she added with emphasis.

In what seemed like a millisecond, there were three police officers and the desk sergeant standing behind me, competing to take her complaint.

"I've got it," I said.

"No, that's okay, I can take this one."

"No really, I can take her complaint."

This, I had never seen before. I wondered if it was the boredom from the slowest day in the history of my career, or the fact that the mysterious complainant was very glamorous. I was going with glamorous.

"Thank you," she said, popping her purse open to take out some lip gloss and apply another layer onto her already highly glossed lips. I was feeling petty. I had been running late this morning and hadn't had time to put any makeup on.

It looked like Officer Farrell had won the competition. He grabbed his metal clipboard and walked out to the lobby. They sat down on the bench and I could see them talking, but I couldn't really hear them well because the sergeant had closed the glass panel, mumbling something about air-conditioning. Apparently he had lost the competition.

I could see her leaning in closer to Officer Farrell. He must have said something funny because she was laughing. Now he was laughing too. A good time was being had by all. Then, Officer Farrell got up and collected his paperwork. He waved over to the dispatcher and they unlocked the door to let him in. That was the fastest complaint I had ever seen.

"ACO, she needs to talk to you," he said to me, closing the cover on his clipboard with a loud click. "Good luck."

"She said she had a Peeping Tom; what does that have to do with me?"

"You'll find out," he said with a grin, and walked back into the other part of the communications room. Curious, I picked up my things and went out to the lobby.

"What can I do for you, ma'am?" I asked as I sat down next to her on the bench. Her perfume was a little overpowering, and the combination of that with the floor cleaner was starting to give me a headache. Daryl was still standing there, leaning on his mop, listening. I looked at him pointedly, and he started to wash the floor . . . again. He started whistling. He wasn't leaving. He had no intention of missing out on this.

"I have a Peeping Tom watching me through my bedroom window. There are two of them, actually; maybe they're brothers. I think it's terrible that the city does nothing about this kind of thing . . ."

I hadn't yet started to fill out the necessary information. Why waste a perfectly good complaint form? I was waiting for her to take a breath so I could tell her that I was the animal control officer.

"I want you to come to my house and do something to stop them . . . even though I can certainly understand why they do it . . ." She pulled at the neckline of her shirt and adjusted the, um, contents. Clearly she had no problem with self-esteem.

"Ma'am," I said. "You'll have to excuse me for interrupting you, but before I take your complaint, I think it's only fair for me to tell you that I handle animal complaints. I'm an animal control officer."

I could see some movement over at the window that separated the dispatch room from the lobby. The officers were watching. Of course they were; this was much better than stacking milking stools. Sgt. Freeman gave me a thumbs-up.

"I know who you are. That's why that sweet policeman over there"—she waved toward the window (I didn't have to look . . . I knew they were waving back)—"told me that I should speak to you."

"Okay," I said, still mystified, but ready to listen. "Tell me more about these Peeping Toms."

"They're raccoons, but that's no excuse for their behavior. It's unacceptable for them to get away with peeking in windows and watching me change at night."

"*Raccoons?*" I asked. I thought I had heard her correctly, but I wasn't sure. Did she really think that raccoons were interested in watching humans change their clothes? Perhaps if she was sitting on her bed eating out of a jar of peanut butter—then maybe I could understand it.

She nodded somewhat indignantly.

"Well, if they're not really causing any damage, I don't understand why this is a problem."

"I told you. They're looking in my windows at night, watching me. It's creepy."

"Have you pulled down the shades, closed the curtains?"

"No—why should I? I don't see why I have to change my habits just because of them!"

"Are you feeding them?"

"No, I would never do that!" She seemed genuinely insulted at my question. "Why would I reward them for being perverts!?" She was getting angry with me. She gathered her purse and stood up, and then she started yelling. "If you're not going to take me seriously, I am going to complain to the head animal control officer!"

"I am the head animal control officer," I said.

"Then I want to speak to someone else in the animal control department!" She was really mad now, and getting louder.

"I'm the animal control department. It's just me." I stayed seated. If she was going to scream at me, I wasn't going to deal with her. I was wondering at what point someone would come out to help me. I had a feeling it wasn't going to happen anytime soon.

"Well, then," she said, suddenly calm. "I will just have to call the city manager—he's a friend of mine, you know. I could walk over there right now . . ."

"Ma'am," I interrupted her, "I want to help you with this problem. Please, why don't you sit back down, and I'll collect some more information."

So I caved. She *had* pulled the city manager card, after all.

She looked at me disapprovingly. Even with her sunglasses on I could tell she was still considering going over to City Hall. The balance of power had shifted, and she sensed it. She sat down again on the bench and began to talk. I clicked the button on the top of my pen and began to write.

It seemed that several nights a week, two raccoons stood on their hind legs and propped themselves up against her window and watched her. It apparently coincided with the time that she was usually changing for bed. She had opened the window to yell at them and they would scurry away, only to return a few minutes later to reposition themselves and continue to watch. She hadn't attempted to go outside and confront them, which I thought was a wise decision. Raccoons are adorable, intelligent creatures, but they are wild animals, and are increasingly suspected of carrying rabies.

They are nocturnal creatures as a rule, which was why I wasn't too concerned that there was anything wrong with her Peeping Toms, who only came out at night. Rabid raccoons often experienced extreme personality changes. They could seem either overly friendly or extremely aggressive, and often roam about during the day (but that doesn't mean all raccoons spotted in the daytime have rabies).

Mother raccoons sometimes go out during the day to find food for their cubs. Raccoons in residential areas sometimes become used to humans and don't show any fear of them. When I used to get up before sunrise and jog through the city, I discovered that some of our local raccoons lived in the sewers. Even though my job had occasionally brought me into contact with wild animals, I knew that it was always wise to avoid them whenever possible.

Any bite from a wild animal needs to be dealt with immediately. Rabies is fatal unless you are given the vaccine as quickly as possible. I had once been given a series of several shots over a period of about a month after a receiving a bite from a feral cat. At first, I had been worried that I would have to have the twenty-something injections into my stomach, but luckily, times had changed, and a new vaccine and less-painful procedure had been developed. Even so, my hip and shoulder had been sore for weeks. The doctor had told me that soon there would be a preexposure vaccine for people like me who worked in "high-risk" occupations. But for the time being, another bite meant another series of shots. I didn't want to experience that again anytime soon.

I knew that I would have to handle this particular raccoon call as soon as possible. Her attitude and my crankiness had made this into a PR issue. Luckily, I had a few ideas.

Sgt. Freeman warned me before I left headquarters. Following me to the cabinet on the wall that held the keys for the patrol cars, he gave me an earful of directions. "Under no circumstances are you to put these raccoons in the car; no dogs either."

I nodded while I looked through all the keys hung on the wall. Which one did I want? I finally came across the keys to the newest patrol car. I didn't often get an opportunity like this.

"Hey—and no cats either."

"Yes, Sarge," I said as I walked over to exit the building. I couldn't wait to get my hands on this car. It even had a regular radio so you could listen to music. It had a bigger engine too. I bet it was faster than my car.

"Not even a . . . a gerbil!" he shouted out into the lobby. "You hear me?!"

I drove down to the Department of Public Works to get a Havahart trap out of the storage shed. I figured I would start with that. I wasn't that worried about actually trapping anything, least of all a raccoon. In my experience I had found that they were usually too smart to fall for that anyway. The trap was for Marilyn Monroe's benefit. It was a prop. I would leave it there with some bread inside so it looked as though I had baited it. I wasn't concerned that I would accidentally trap a different type of animal in the trap. No animal in their right mind was going to go near that trap. I knew that I had to make the area that the peepers came to every night as unappealing as possible. It suddenly occurred to me that in order to start this process today, all I had to do was to drive back to headquarters for a minute and get a bottle of ammonia, and I knew exactly where I could get that.

"Daryl? Daryl? *Daryl!*" I stood outside the supply closet door and yelled. I knocked on the door, and then knocked again, harder. I knew Daryl was in there; I could hear him, but apparently he couldn't hear me. The music was too loud. I opened the door a little and peeked in. Surrounded by shelves of cleaning supplies and equipment was Daryl, singing to a mop. He was really good too. I wondered why he kept his talent a secret. Why did he limit himself to a duet with a mop?

"Hey, Daryl, I didn't know you could sing that well!" I said, still at a high volume. Just then the song ended, and my voice now sounded like it was coming from a megaphone. Daryl swung around, gripping the mop like a baseball bat. It knocked into a few bottles of cleaning fluid and spray cans that started to fall into each other like dominoes. A gallon jug of bleach tipped over and started to drip onto the floor. I leaped out of the way of an empty paint can that was flying off the shelf in the direction of my head.

"*Damn, girl!*" Daryl yelled. He had dropped the mop and was covering his head with his arms to protect himself from the downpour of custodial supplies. After what seemed a pretty long time, it finally stopped. Daryl turned off the radio and stood there, shaking his head at me.

"Why you sneakin' up on me?" Daryl asked. I saw that there was a microwave on the shelf. I had never noticed before that it smelled like popcorn in here. Well, now it smelled like popcorn and bleach.

"I, uh . . . I just wanted some ammonia for a complaint I have. I'm sorry; I didn't mean to startle you."

I couldn't help myself; I had to look around a bit. I had never been in Daryl's supply closet before. Not many people had. Daryl was very protective of his domain. When he wasn't washing the floor, Daryl was often cleaning the weight room. We had the cleanest weight room around, and the cleanest floors. Daryl was also responsible for vacuuming and cleaning the police cars, but he refused to do mine. He had told the chief that he was allergic to dog hair.

"Is that a TV?" I asked, trying to get a better look.

"Here!" Daryl shoved a bottle of ammonia into my hands and shut the door in my face.

"Thanks, Daryl—I'll see you later," I shouted through the door, waiting a second to see if he would say good-bye.

He didn't.

The bottle of ammonia from Daryl's supply closet sat in a paper bag on the floor of the car. In order to get rid of the raccoons, I would saturate the area with ammonia. Raccoons couldn't stand the scent. The bread wouldn't be a draw either, because I planned to douse the bread with ammonia as well. Hopefully it would act as a sponge, absorbing the odor and serving to drive away any animal, raccoon or otherwise, that would be attracted to the trap. If I did this for a few days in a row, it would probably deter the raccoons from coming back, and they would be forced to find another source of entertainment.

I climbed the steps up to the porch and knocked on the door of the woman's apartment, but there was no answer. Good, she wasn't home. We had not started off well, and I wanted to set everything up when she wasn't there anyway. The trap was a tangible thing she could look at, so she could see that the city "was doing something" about her problem. I knew if I just left the ammonia, that wouldn't be enough for her. It had to look impressive.

I walked around the porch, looking for her bedroom window. I spotted it right away, as well as the place where the raccoons usually sat. It was an empty window box, devoid of flowers—front row orchestra seating for raccoons. It looked like there was no need for a concession stand, as they had brought their own snacks to the show, evidenced by the litter they had left behind. A remnant of a chicken wing and something that looked like pieces of eggshells lay in front of a large window. Someone around here didn't have a lid on their trash can. I would take a walk around the house and check for that, too.

Curious, I peered into the window. It was indeed a bedroom, but the better term for it would have been a boudoir. Everything was in red. Red velvet, red satin, even something wrapped around the bedpost that looked like a red feather boa. With all that going on, I couldn't figure out why she hadn't added some red curtains. Oh well, it wasn't my job to judge her interior decorating. I squatted down and opened the bottle of ammonia. I poured some on a sponge and spread it around the outside of the window frame. I started pouring it around the foot of the window.

"I wasn't aware that the police department did cleaning on the side." A deep male voice startled me. In an effort to stand up from my squatting position without dropping the ammonia bottle, I lost my balance and ended up sitting on the porch with a thump. I was always falling down and tripping over things; one time I had almost gotten stuck trying to coax a cat out of a large drainpipe. It was obvious that a career in ballet was not in my future.

"I'm sorry, Officer; I didn't mean to startle you. I own this place. My name's Joe Carroll. Let me help you." He extended his arm to help me up.

"No, but thank you. I'm fine." I picked myself up, trying to preserve what little dignity I had left. "Nice to meet you. I'm the animal control officer. We had a complaint about some raccoons that are . . . um . . . looking, or . . . watching . . . They're being a nuisance."

"Holly called you over?" he asked.

I looked at him blankly.

"My tenant, Holly. Very blond, very fancy, very . . . everything."
He laughed in a good-natured way. He was a little heavyset, with
dark hair going gray; the laugh lines around his eyes were deep, but
not in a bad way. It looked like he had spent a great deal of time in
his life being happy.

"She didn't give that name on her complaint. I think she said
it was Francie . . ."

"Yup, that's her. Francie; Holly; sometimes she's Dawn, too. She
can call herself whatever she wants as long as she pays her rent on
time. That's my philosophy." He opened a pack of gum and offered
me a piece. I took one.

"Well, your tenant has a problem with raccoons staring into
her room three or four nights a week. She claims that they watch
her change, and that it's intentional." I thought he would be shocked
at what I had to say.

"That makes sense," he said.

"It does?" Maybe I was the only one who thought this was
ridiculous. Maybe raccoons were famous for voyeurism, and I had
never known about it. Where would you look up information like
that?

"It does if you know Holly," he said with a smile. "That woman
needs a lot of attention. If there are raccoons looking in her window,
you can be damn sure she thinks they're looking at her."

"Well," I said, "they are looking in her window at night."

"Sure they are," he said. "They're waitin' for Mrs. DeKamp to
put out their dinner."

"Mrs. DeKamp? Is that another one of Holly's names?"

"No, no . . ." he chuckled. "Mrs. DeKamp was my previous
tenant. She had to move into a nursing home; it got to be too hard
for her to live on her own. She must be over eighty-five. Nice
woman. I stop by and see her on Sundays sometimes. She always
asks about those raccoons. She used to sit at that window and talk
to them."

"Oh, I see. They come by because they think she's still here."

Case solved. I felt very lucky that I had run into Joe Carroll.

Joe murmured something under his breath.

"Excuse me? I'm sorry, did you say something?"

"Yes, ma'am. I said, not exactly. I leave them scraps sometimes when I come by to check on things. I usually work during the day, so I have to take care of the property here in the evening—make sure the trash goes out on time, mow the lawn, fix this or that . . ."

"How often do you come out and do that?" I asked.

"Well . . ." he said in a smaller voice. He looked at me, smiled a little, and shrugged. "About three or four times a week."

I looked at him and shook my head. Then I put my hands on my hips, but before I could find the words to admonish him for his contribution to the peeping raccoon problem, he put his hands up like he was surrendering.

"I know, I know . . . I shouldn't be feeding them," he said. "I just saw them waiting out there one night for Mrs. DeKamp and . . . I thought well, just this once, then I couldn't stop because they're awful cute and, well, I just . . . "

"Hold on a minute," I said. I had an idea—and Joe Carroll was going to help me with it.

After my serendipitous meeting with Joe Carroll, I left the trap on the porch and stopped by every few days to make a big display of moving it, baiting it, and sprinkling ammonia on the porch. I stomped around, sighed a lot, and wrote down some notes on a legal pad. At first she wouldn't speak to me, but the more I came, the more she seemed to forgive me for not taking her seriously at first.

After a few weeks had gone by, I went over to pick up my trap because it was obvious that the raccoons were gone. There were no more scraps left behind and no reports of any unseemly raccoon behavior. It became clear that the raccoons had finally stopped their peeping.

"Thank you," said Holly, standing in her doorway. She was dressed in a really tight jumpsuit thing. As much as I didn't want to admit it, she could really pull it off.

"I feel much safer now. I enjoy my privacy, as you know."

"Oh, absolutely," I said. "Privacy is very important." I noticed that she didn't have curtains on her living room windows either.

"If you need anything further, or if the raccoons come back, just give me a call and I'll come right over," I told her as I gathered up my equipment for the last time.

"Oh, I'm sure you won't have to come back. If they were anywhere near here, they would still be staring in my window." Holly looked at her hands for a moment, admiring her manicure. Her nails were as red as her lipstick. I looked at my own hands clutching my equipment as I tried to juggle it all without dropping it.

I really had to stop biting my nails.

"Yes," she said, looking up from her nails. "I am very confident that those raccoons are far, far away."

But they weren't. They had just moved to the back of the house, near the basement window, where Joe Carroll still brought them their dinner several times a week. Except now it was just dinner, without a show.

Twilight Time

$\mathcal{I}$t was freezing outside. Literally. Last I'd heard, it was about 5 degrees, with the wind-chill factor making it feel like it was way below zero. I had been hopeful that most of my day could be spent in the car with the heat cranked up as high as I could get it, or better yet, maybe they would call me inside for some reason.

This was not to be.

"Eight Forty-Four to Three Oh Six. Report to forty-five Highland Avenue. Possible cruelty complaint."

"Ten-four," I responded, preparing to make a U-turn to head to the other side of town.

There were a few types of calls that I hated, and animal cruelty complaints were in the top two. Not only were they very sad, but they could also get really complicated. If it was a valid and serious complaint, I would have to contact the animal cruelty investigators from the enforcement unit of the ASPCA in Albany. While I always looked forward to talking with them when they came down-county, the reason for their visits overshadowed any enjoyment I might have felt from seeing them again. And even with weather like this, looking at a cruelty complaint meant that I wasn't going back inside headquarters anytime soon.

At first, the address didn't ring a bell. But as I approached Highland Avenue, I realized that I knew whose house I was going to. It was Hugh Vogel's house. Hugh was well known for his two beloved Alaskan malamutes. He would take them to the park and let the children pet them, always making sure to give them a lesson on when and how to approach an unfamiliar dog.

"Always ask permission first—that's important. Never, under any circumstances, go near a dog that's eating. Don't run up to him; walk normally. Hold your hand out, but upside down, like this." He would show the kids how to extend their hand palm down in a nonconfrontational way, and to let the dog sniff them first before attempting to pet them.

Hugh Vogel had every reason to be proud of his dogs. Not only were they gentle, well-trained, and well taken care of, but they were also truly beautiful. Unlike other malamutes I had encountered, his dogs never escaped from their yard to run loose all over the city. Generally, I felt that huskies and malamutes were not the best type of dogs for an urban environment. In the past, I had warned some people against getting Siberian husky and Alaskan malamute puppies. Sure, they were stunning to look at, but too often I received calls about them running away. As working dogs, these breeds had the instinct to run, but often seemed to lack the instinct to find their way home again.

They were also excellent escape artists. On two separate occasions I had spent over half an hour trying to untangle a certain Siberian husky from a tall chain-link fence that he had attempted to climb over. So although huskies and malamutes were great dogs, based on my experience, they were typically not well suited for city living.

Mr. Vogel's dogs were the exception to the rule. I felt some anxiety as I pulled over to park in front of his house. Hugh Vogel would never be cruel to any animal, let alone his own dogs. This was either a mistake, or something was very wrong.

The wind pulled the car door open so hard that I heard something pop. I pulled the collar of my coat up as high as I could regretting that I had removed the hood because I hadn't liked the way the jacket looked with it on. After three years at this job I finally realized that appearance meant nothing. It was all about substance, not style. (The hood had since vanished, taken by the same elves who stole many of my socks.) This had led me, at times, to resort to wearing the hat that I had been given when I was hired.

"You should wear the hat; it's part of the uniform. Next time I see you, I want to see that hat," the chief said, admonishing me a few weeks after I had started working at the department. Later that day, when I'd walked past his office wearing said hat, he'd stopped me in the hall.

"ACO . . . come here a minute." I turned around and walked over to him. He looked at me seriously, and then burst into laughter. "I'm sorry . . . I can't help it." He sniffled, trying to contain himself. "Now I see the reason you weren't wearing it. It's okay. You don't have to."

He was right. I looked ridiculous. The hat made me look like some kid trying to be a cop for Halloween. Even worse, it was enormous, and slid down over my eyes so that I had to keep adjusting it. Now, since I had lost the hood to my jacket, I had no alternative other than to use it when it was raining, or cold, like today. I wished I had left my jacket alone. Such is the high price of vanity.

"Over here," I heard someone calling. It was a couple standing on the porch next to Mr. Vogel's house, waving me over. Walking over to them, I had to fight the wind that was blowing against me. I stuck my hands deep into my pockets, numb in spite of my gloves.

"Come in, please. We're the ones who called." The woman led me inside, and she and a man I assumed was her husband stood across from me and started to speak at the same time. "It's so unlike him . . . He'd never hurt those dogs. Maybe it's neglect? We called and he just hung up. He's never done that before. Something's wrong . . . I knocked on his door . . ."

I put up my hand to stop them. I couldn't hear with both of them talking at once. I could tell they were concerned and that their intentions were good, but I had to hear their story one sentence, and one person, at a time.

Mr. Vogel's malamutes had always been well taken care of. They were more than pets; they were his family. As far as I knew, Hugh Vogel had never married. He had retired early after injuring his leg on the job, and from then on had devoted all of his time to his dogs. He, and a group of regulars that frequented the doughnut shop in town, would meet some evenings to laugh and tease each other with the familiarity of those who have shared decades of friendship. He often told stories about Jack and Bleu, passing around photos like a proud parent. I knew this because my uncle was one of the regulars, and when I was younger, he would sometimes bring me along. I would sit quietly on a stool, sipping hot chocolate and trying to make my apple-crumb doughnut last as long as possible.

I remembered asking Mr. Vogel about his dogs' names. "Why didn't you name them Jack and Jill—like the nursery rhyme?"

He had looked at me seriously and replied, "Because they wouldn't have liked that."

That must have been almost ten years ago, which meant that Jack and Bleu were now in their twilight years. I hadn't thought of it that way until this moment. I tried to recall the last time I had seen Mr. Vogel in the park with them. It had been several months ago, and they had looked fine—a little older, perhaps, maybe a little slower, but wasn't that true of everyone as they aged?

"Jack's been lying out there in the yard for hours. I walked over to see if everything was okay, and Hugh slammed the door on me. Told us to mind our own business. He said malamutes were arctic dogs; they like the cold."

She was genuinely upset. Her husband stood behind her, rubbing her shoulder as she spoke. It didn't appear as though this was one of those intrusive neighbor situations.

"Then I sent Buddy over," she said, looking up at her husband, "and Mr. Vogel did the same thing to him. I don't understand it. This isn't like him at all. That poor dog is lying out there in the freezing cold and he won't even talk to us about it."

"Well," I said, "he has a point, you know, about the cold. Malamutes thrive on it; they're built for cold temperatures. They originated in Alaska."

Even while I was saying this, I still knew that something was wrong. Sure, this breed was in its element on a day like this, but I didn't think that Mr. Vogel would let either of his dogs lie unattended in the yard for that long. Knowing that they were at an advanced age, and that the average life span of large dogs was around ten to fourteen years, I couldn't help but think that there was something not quite right about this situation.

"I'll go and see," I said, zipping up my jacket.

"Do you want us to come?" she asked.

"No, not right now. Let me see what's going on first."

I walked up to the front door, the frozen grass crunching under my feet. I stopped for a moment and decided that I would go around into the yard first. I had to separate my conflicting loyalties. I wasn't here to visit with Mr. Vogel; I was here to check on one of his dogs. The icy wind was hitting me directly in the face as I made my way back into the yard.

Then I saw him. Jack was lying on his side. He was bigger than Bleu, and had some sable in his coat. I knelt down on the ground next to him. "Hi, Jack. Are you okay, boy?"

He looked terrible. He looked at me for a moment, but then it seemed more like he was looking beyond me. He was bloated almost beyond recognition. I had seen this before. This was a result of kidney failure. Jack's organs were shutting down. I tried to pull him over to me so I could try and help him up, but when I put my hand under the side of his back, I could feel that he was partially frozen to the ground. His body temperature was dropping. Even with the double coat that protects malamutes from the elements, I thought that Jack might have hypothermia. He started to make a groaning noise. Arctic dog or not, he was lying outside in the cold not because he wanted to, but because he wouldn't be getting up again.

"What are you doing here? This is my property!" I looked up to see Mr. Vogel standing behind me. He didn't look well either, although he was obviously in much better shape than Jack was at the moment. But what else was wrong? Other than being angry, which I had never seen him before, I couldn't figure out what else was wrong with him. My mind was too clouded with concern over Jack, and also, with trying not to focus on the bitter cold.

Suddenly I realized that Mr. Vogel was standing outside in something that resembled a bathrobe. He had no shoes on. It was below zero, and he was standing outside in what amounted to his pajamas and socks. He wasn't okay either.

"Mr. Vogel, it's me, Frank's niece. Remember?"

He stood there looking at me blankly, no sign of recognition in his eyes.

Jack started groaning again. I had never heard him sound like this before. He rarely barked; it had always seemed more like he was talking when he tried. I used to enjoy listening to him because it sounded like he was singing. Now he sounded like he was in pain.

"Mr. Vogel, Jack needs to go to the vet; he's really sick."

I knew he was more than sick. It was obvious that there would be nothing a veterinarian could do to make him better, but at least they could give him some relief.

"Damn vet doesn't know anything. He's wrong. Jack's just old and tired. He likes the cold. He'll come in when he's good and ready. Now you should go too, and tell those busybodies next door to mind their own business!"

"Mr. Vogel, he's in pain. Can't you hear him?"

He just stood there glaring at me, the wind blowing his hair all over. He must have been freezing.

"What did the vet say, Mr. Vogel? Can you tell me that?"

I thought that maybe if I asked him some questions he would snap out of it. He was acting so strangely. I was driven between trying to get Mr. Vogel in the house and trying to get Jack into my car. I couldn't stand to see this beautiful dog suffering like this. It was one thing to watch an animal die peacefully—an aspect of my job that I'd had to learn to deal with—but this was different. I'd known Jack before I was an animal control officer, and seeing him lying there, obviously in pain, was breaking my heart.

I had to make a choice. I would take Jack to the vet myself. I couldn't handle Mr. Vogel on my own; I'd need some help for that.

I fumbled around under my jacket, looking for my radio. My hands were so numb I couldn't feel where I always clipped it onto my belt. My cheeks felt like they were burning. It was so incredibly cold.

I looked up at Mr. Vogel standing there. "You need to go inside or get a coat on. You can't stay out here like this!" I didn't know if I was yelling at him because of the wind, or because I didn't think he wanted to hear what I was saying. I was trying not to be angry at Mr. Vogel for being so unreasonable. He couldn't help it.

"Don't tell me what to do!" he shouted. "Who do you think you are?!"

"Mr. Vogel, please . . . we have to get him to the vet!" I was pleading with him now.

"Go away! Leave my dog alone!" he yelled. "He's just fine . . . he's a malamute . . . he's . . ."

"He's dying!" I screamed back at him.

All you could hear was the wind. It was starting to blow harder. I scrambled back over to Jack. His eyes were rolling back in his head; it looked like he was having some type of seizure. I wanted him to die, quickly, so it would be over . . . and yet I didn't.

I tried to take my jacket off to cover him up, but I couldn't find the zipper. My fingers were useless. I felt so powerless—something I felt often with this job. But I couldn't think about that right now. This wasn't about how *I* felt. It was about Jack, and about Mr. Vogel.

"Come here," I said, waving him over. He stood in the same place, watching me. What I had said to him about Jack dying had changed the way he looked somehow.

"Please . . . come here."

He walked over to us. His feet must have been freezing. He was looking at Jack, and as bad as it was, I really needed him to see.

"Jack," he said in a hoarse whisper. He squatted down closer to his dog. He put his hand on Jack's head and started to stroke his fur. For a moment Jack seemed to focus on him. His breathing slowed. He closed his eyes and seemed to relax at the touch of Mr. Vogel's hand.

"Do you see?" I whispered. "He needs you to make it okay. You can't do that by pretending it isn't real."

I had no idea where the words were coming from. I was over-whelmed at the responsibility of having to force this man to say good-bye to the dog he loved so much. I didn't want to be this person anymore. I wanted to be someone else, somewhere else, like the other people my age who were living in dorms and leading carefree lives, putting adulthood on hold. I didn't want to be here.

He was petting Jack steadily, like it could change what was happening.

"I know you love him, Mr. Vogel. But you have to love him enough to let him go."

He started to sob, continuing to stroke Jack at the same time. I put my arm around his shoulder. He was so cold he was shaking.

I heard the crunch of footsteps behind me, and I turned around to see the man and woman who had called me over to their house, standing behind us. The woman was trying to hold on to a blanket which was being whipped around in the wind. She looked at me and then over to Mr. Vogel, questioning me silently. I nodded.

She walked over to Mr. Vogel and wrapped the blanket around him. "Come on, Hugh. We'll follow her over to the vet's, and then afterward, you'll come back to our house for dinner."

Mr. Vogel nodded his head and slowly stood up.

"Bleu?" he asked her in a small voice.

"Of course she can come too. Come on . . . let's get you in the car and turn the heat on."

Mr. Vogel slowly got up, letting his neighbor help him to his feet. Then he stopped and looked at me, in a way that made me think he was seeing me for the first time that day. "You'll bring him?" he asked.

"Yes, I'll bring him. You'll be right behind me," I said.

He frowned a little and then squinted at me. "You're Frank's niece. You're all grown up now." I nodded at him.

Her husband walked up to me. "I'll help you get Jack in your car, miss . . . and then we'll follow you over to the vet's."

"Thank you," I said. Saying those words weren't enough to express how grateful I was that they had come over at that moment.

"You're shivering too," he said, looking at me. Then he looked over at Jack. I could feel myself shaking, but for some reason I no longer felt that cold. I'd read somewhere once, that when the body becomes too cold, when it's too much—you no longer actually feel cold, you start to feel numb. I wondered if that could happen to your heart as well. He gently touched my shoulder and said, "We have to get him over there in time so Hugh can say good-bye. Shall we go get him?"

"Yes," I said. "Let's go."

Karma and Get Me

$\mathcal{I}$t was going to snow. The Public Works Department was busy readying their plows and assessing how much salt might be needed. Roy at the city garage was getting the chains ready for the police cars, and the department was buzzing with preparations for a big snow event. This was the first time I had ever heard a snowstorm referred to as a *snow event*. In my head I pictured a large circus tent pitched outside in a snowdrift somewhere, with flags waving, music playing, and maybe valet parking. When I shared this thought with a few of my colleagues, they didn't seem to think it was as funny as I did. Apparently they were used to the term.

Everyone was running around, and the phones were ringing incessantly. There had been an altercation at the grocery store over some milk that had required two police units to be sent. You would have thought people were preparing for a nuclear holocaust instead of the first snowstorm of the season. It seemed that the entire city was focused on the weather. That was why I was a little surprised to get a call to report to the 200 block of Union Avenue to take a complaint about a dog sitting in someone's yard.

I pulled up in front of the house. It was a nice, well-cared-for older home with a front porch. Most of the homes in this part of town were all about the same age: early-twentieth-century, two-story houses with front porches and tidy little yards. I sometimes thought that when the time came that I could buy a house of my own, I would buy one right here.

I went up to the front door of the Oakley house and rang the bell. Waiting, I looked up at the sky. Heavy snow clouds were making it darker outside than usual for this time of day. It was really quiet. I thought about how people all over the area were running around preparing for this storm, buying shovels and fighting over groceries. Standing out here in front of the house, I felt far removed from all of the activity going on. I finally heard some footsteps.

"Hello, Officer," said Mrs. Oakley. She looked to be in her mid-fifties, trim and dressed in a pair of jeans and a sweater. The only thing that gave away her age was her silvery hair, which was cut in a modern spiky style. It looked great with her long, dangling earrings. I thought I'd be very lucky if I looked like her when I was older.

She squinted a little, looking closer to read the writing on my nametag. "Ack-oh Duffy. That's an interesting name. Is that Asian?"

I smiled at her. This wasn't the first time someone had thought "ACO" was my first name. I had already ordered another nametag that had just my last name on it.

"No, ma'am, it stands for animal control officer."

She touched my shoulder. "I am so sorry! You must think I'm ridiculous," she said.

"No, ma'am, not at all. A lot of people make that mistake. You have a complaint about a strange dog on your property?" I asked.

She ran her fingers through her hair and hesitated. "Yes. No. Sort of. Why don't you come inside—it's cold out there."

"Oh. Okay." I put my pen back in my pocket. Maybe the dog she'd complained about had already left her yard, gone to stock up on doggie treats before the storm.

I followed her into the house. Mrs. Oakley had candles everywhere. There were candles on the end tables, on top of the TV; a line of candles ran along the top of the piano against the wall. My eyes were still trying to adjust to the dark.

"Watch your step; I wouldn't want you to trip." I looked down and saw a black throw rug. It moved.

"That's Ebony . . . she loves to be underfoot," Mrs. Oakley said, continuing on ahead of me.

"Are you, um, conserving energy?" I asked, feeling my way down the hallway to the kitchen. It was literally the light at the end of the tunnel.

"Oh no . . . Actually, I'm channeling energy. Meditation. Burning candles of certain colors helps me to focus." I continued to follow her into the kitchen where there was more light.

"I've been tinkering with Buddhism. It's fascinating. A few friends and I are planning a trip to Japan this summer. I've never been out of the country before. Have you?" She pushed a stack of books and pamphlets out of the way and started putting out cups. People were forever offering me coffee or tea, one of the nicer perks that came with this job.

"Mexico once and the Caribbean. Not really that far," I told her. I didn't see myself going anywhere anytime soon, with school and work taking up all my time, except for when I was asleep. Sometimes I was even called into work in the middle of that too.

"So, you have a loose dog bothering you?" I asked, thinking that it might be wise to begin reining in this conversation.

"He doesn't really bother me," she said, pouring tea into the cups. "Would you like some honey?" she asked. I hadn't remembered her even asking me if I wanted tea, but I figured that it would be impolite not to drink it.

"No, thank you," I said. She pushed a plate of cookies toward me. They looked homemade.

"Please have a cookie," she said. I took one—for good public relations, of course.

She began to describe the situation with the dog. It seemed that she was semiretired, working part-time as a per-diem nurse to add to the pension she received from her late husband. Due to her unpredictable schedule, she was always leaving and coming home at odd hours. However, it seemed that regardless of the hours she worked, a mysterious black dog would be waiting for her in the backyard every time she came home. Sometimes it was there when she woke up. It never approached her, always sitting quietly under a tree, watching the house.

"I asked around to see if anyone had lost a black dog, but nobody has—at least, around this neighborhood. He doesn't look underfed. He never barks."

I tried to recall if I had received any phone calls recently about a missing black dog, but I couldn't remember any.

"Have you been feeding him?" I asked. This was usually the best way to get rid of animal visitors. Stop feeding them, and they would move on somewhere else. It never failed to amaze me how surprised people were at that fact.

"I wasn't at first, but then last week I thought I would leave him some leftovers from a little party I'd had. He didn't touch them. He's not interested in food."

A dog not interested in food. That was a rarity. However, if this was a dog that already had a home, and he was coming by for some other unknown reason, then perhaps he wasn't hungry. From my experience, dogs were motivated by two things: food and attention. Maybe this mysterious black dog was just lonely?

I couldn't help looking at the plate of cookies. They were delicious.

"Please, have some more. I'm so used to making them, even though my children are all grown up now. My grandson is coming up to visit over break, so I have plenty."

"School vacation?" I asked, politely taking another remarkable cookie. I promised myself I'd stop after this one.

"Yes, he's in his third year of college, in Georgia. You'd think that he would want to stay in a nice warm climate during this time of year, but he likes the winter. He called me earlier to ask if it had started snowing yet."

"You have a grandson—in college?" That would have made him around my age. She must have started her family when she was very young.

"Yes. A granddaughter, too. She was here for Thanksgiving." She was holding her cup of tea, staring into it like she was looking for something.

I looked around the kitchen. As dark as the rest of the house was, the kitchen was the opposite. Everything was bright and modern. It looked very contemporary for this type of home, but it was appealing. I noticed that there were stacks of books everywhere. I glanced at the books on the table. There were books on spirituality, Eastern religions, northern Italian wines. Travel brochures lay on almost every flat surface in the room.

She looked up again. Something had changed about her; she looked troubled.

"This will be the second holiday season without Neil . . . my husband."

"I'm so sorry," I said. I wondered what had happened to him. "Was he a great deal older than you?" I asked, and immediately regretted it. "I'm sorry, I shouldn't have asked that."

"No, it's fine. It's good for me to talk about it. He was only about five years older than me."

"So young," I said.

Mrs. Oakley raised her eyes from her tea and looked at me quizzically. "I suppose."

"Well, even though this dog isn't bothering you, it's still a violation of the municipal code for dogs to run loose. If you want to call me the next time you see him, I could come over right away and take him out of your yard. He might be missing from another area. The shelter keeps that kind of information; if he is missing, they can possibly reunite him with his owner."

"I don't know if I should do that." She got up from the table and walked over to the kitchen window.

"If you can give me a more detailed description of him, I could come by when you're at work as part of my routine patrol. Is he a large or medium black dog? Any markings that you noticed?" I was ready to write her description down on a notepad, so I'd be able to identify this dog when I saw him.

"He's out there now, if you want to see him," she said, still calmly peering out the window.

Why hadn't she said something when I arrived? I pushed my chair back and walked over to the back door. It was a small yard, surrounded by a cast-iron fence that looked to be as old as the house, but had been restored perfectly.

Sitting in the middle of the yard was a medium-sized black dog. He looked like he was part Lab, with maybe a little terrier mixed in. From a distance, it looked like he might have been wearing a collar. He sat there watching us watch him. There was no barking, no running around in circles. He was just sitting in the yard staring at the house.

"Well, since I'm here now, let me try to get him and put an end to the problem." I took my jacket off the back of the chair and started to put it on. Mrs. Oakley seemed very conflicted. "I don't know. Maybe I should just let him stay." She looked so anxious and upset.

"Well, at least let me go out there and see if he has a license tag so I can get the number. If he does, I can use that to trace his owner."

Mrs. Oakley started to take deep breaths, rubbing her temples with her fingertips. She started humming. I couldn't understand why she was getting so worked up about this.

I opened the door slowly so as not to scare the dog away, but when I stepped out onto the patio, he was gone. There was no rustling of bushes, no jingling from a collar and tags that would signal in what direction he had fled. Everything was silent and still. I walked out into the yard and looked around. There was no sign of him. Walking over to the gate, I pulled on it to see if it was easy to open. It didn't open. It didn't even move. How was he getting in the yard? I supposed he could have jumped; the fence wasn't that high. It was still odd.

Walking back into the kitchen, I could see that Mrs. Oakley seemed better. She smiled at me. "He's gone again, right?"

"Yes, like he vaporized or something." I didn't know if it was the candles, the amazing disappearing dog, or the eerie stillness before the storm, but I shuddered. This was a little spooky.

"Well," she said, standing up and starting to clear the table, "maybe that's for the best then."

"Have you ever seen the dog open the gate out back?" I asked.

"That gate never opened. My husband painted the fence a few years ago and was planning on replacing the gate, but he never got around to it."

"Oh," I said. "I'm sorry." I felt like I had put my foot in my mouth, again.

"No, no . . . nothing to worry about. It's okay. I meant what I said about talking about it. I don't mind. I keep very busy, between work and my friends and my reading group and the classes I'm taking in . . . I told you, right? Eastern religions?"

"Yes, you did mention that," I said.

She seemed a lot less agitated than before I had gone out to get closer to the vanishing dog. She walked me to the door, blowing out a few candles on the way. She turned the light on. I looked out and noticed that it had finally started to snow. The flakes were coming down fast; a dusting already covered the road.

Mrs. Oakley opened the door for me and then asked me a question. "Are you familiar with the concept of reincarnation?"

"Yes," I said. "It's a Hindu belief, right? That when you die, you come back in another form."

"Buddhists believe that too," she said, looking at me, weighing her words carefully. "I think I know why that black dog comes here to sit in my yard."

"Why?" I asked.

"Because I think it's my husband. I think Neil has come back to keep an eye on me."

"Oh, I see." I stood there looking at Mrs. Oakley, and she stood there looking at me. I realized that I was probably supposed to say something. "So, Mrs. Oakley, it was nice meeting you. Thank you for the tea and the cookies. When you see the dog again, you can give me a call if . . . if you decide you . . . um, want to . . . um, you can call me." The words were stumbling out of my mouth like a rock slide. She didn't respond, just nodded. She seemed so matter of fact about it.

"Okay then, well . . . bye." I was really taken by surprise. I didn't have an appropriate response for this kind of thing. Reincarnation?

It wasn't every day that I had a reincarnation complaint. Actually, it wasn't any day.

I walked toward the car. Getting in quickly, I started it and put it in gear. It was already hard to see out of the windshield, with the snow coming directly at me. I was glad that I only had a few blocks to drive to get back to headquarters.

Mrs. Oakley was nice, and I didn't think she was crazy. After a few years at this job, I knew crazy, and Mrs. Oakley didn't fit the bill. Granted, I hadn't expected her to say what she'd said. But just because I wasn't completely convinced that Mr. Oakley had come back in the form of a black dog, didn't mean it wasn't true. It wasn't my role to make any determination on that. If this was her husband, in canine form, she might want him to stick around, which would explain her ambivalence about the situation. Maybe I would investigate some more and try to find out if anyone in the city owned this dog, or if anyone was missing one of this description. If not, maybe Mrs. Oakley would be interested in formally adopting him? It was a strange thought—adopting your reincarnated husband-now-dog, but I'd heard stranger. Maybe.

Back at headquarters everyone was in full emergency mode. It seemed that this snowstorm was turning into a serious blizzard. The chief had decided to send the civilian staff home early. I had to find a place that was relatively quiet to finish my daily reports before I could go home. Sometimes there was an empty desk in the Records office around that I could use. Actually I was supposed to be sharing a desk with one of the Record's staff, but that didn't work out. My job took me outside most of the time and her job had her behind a desk most of the time. It made no sense to intrude on her neatly organized system with my haphazard mess. So, I usually just grabbed a spot wherever I could. Today I was lucky enough to use the desk of one of the women who had already left due to the weather. With all the activity going on at the moment, I thought the Records office would be a quiet place to get my paperwork done—and it was, until I mentioned what Mrs. Oakley had told me about the black dog.

"That's blasphemy! You should refuse to go back into that house!" said one of the women who worked in Records. She had some very strong opinions about reincarnation.

"I can't *refuse* to go on a call. Besides, I like Mrs. Oakley, and if she believes her husband has been reincarnated into a dog, who am I to say it isn't true? That's her belief!"

"Because it's a sin, that's why! It's just plain sinful!" She was getting angrier.

I didn't see the big deal. There were many different religions in the world. Who was I to tell someone which one they should believe in? I wasn't one of those people who felt compelled to inform people about my beliefs, but even if I had, it certainly wouldn't have been appropriate for me to do it on the job.

"You're judging someone by your own rules," Jim chimed in. That surprised me. He usually kept to himself, but I was glad he was there today. "There are millions of Buddhists in the world. Why, the population of China alone—"

"Then they're all sinners and blasphemers!" she shouted.

"You are so intolerant! How can you say you're a religious woman if you won't give others the respect they deserve?!" said Jim.

I don't think they noticed when I slipped out. This had not turned out as I had planned. But if I'd really thought about it, I would have remembered what December was like in that office. Between the small Christmas trees on some desks, the Hanukkah decorations on one side of the room, and the tension you could cut with a knife, let's just say that the holiday season in there was definitely *not* the happiest time of the year.

It was several weeks later that I happened to run into the mysterious black dog again. This time he was sitting in the middle of Union Avenue. Cars were swerving to avoid him, beeping at him— and he didn't move. I pulled over to the side of the road and grabbed my leash. There was quite an audience watching me, so I had no choice but to pick him up. As I approached, he started to back up. "Oh no . . . don't do that!" I said under my breath. Just because I was standing in the middle of the road trying to seize a dog, who was also standing in the middle of the road, didn't mean that people would stop driving around us. This wasn't a main road, and there were alternate routes, but that didn't matter. They kept coming.

I always felt that there was something about driving a car that made even the most mild-mannered people more aggressive. Actually, they were the ones who worried me the most. The only time I had been almost run over by a car during a school crossing, the driver had been an elderly woman in a massive 1970-something car, using all of her eight cylinders to come at me like I had a target painted on my chest. It was bad enough that she did this once, but after returning from whatever errands she had run, she came at me again from the other direction. This time I was smart enough to memorize her license plate right before I'd scrambled for the sidewalk, and I called in her plate number on the radio. Thank goodness there had been no children crossing the street at the time. Later, the lady said she hadn't been wearing her eyeglasses, but even if she had, I would bet money that her last prescription had been filled sometime during the Nixon administration. Still, I didn't buy that it was her vision. I had heard her accelerate, and that hadn't had anything to do with her vision.

The black dog was watching me carefully. I was hoping that he would let me slip the leash around his neck without trying to make a break for it. I could hear the traffic around us as I got closer to him. *Please don't back up, please don't back up.* That was when it occurred to me that maybe I could put him at ease if I said his name. I had nothing to lose.

"Neil, I'm going to just take you out of the road so you're safe. Good, uh, Neil. Good dog." He seemed to hesitate at this and stopped backing up. Either he recognized his name, or he liked the sound of my voice. It didn't matter to me, just so long as he wasn't putting himself in danger. I slipped the leash around his neck, and he didn't try to resist. I had thought he was entirely black, but up close I could see that he had a white triangle of fur on his chest. He wasn't that young, but he wasn't that old either.

I walked him back to the car and opened the back door. He jumped into the car like it was something he did every day. Maybe this dog really did belong to somebody. I would have to bring him down to the shelter, just in case he was missing from his home. At some point before I did this, I had to stop at Mrs. Oakley's house and tell her what was going on.

"So he has to stay at the shelter for at least seven days before they can let him be adopted. This way they can make sure that he isn't missing from somewhere." Mrs. Oakley hadn't been home when I'd stopped by before driving the dog down to the shelter. It wasn't until I was on my way back to headquarters that I saw her car in front of her house.

"Seven days. I see." She seemed upset again. Maybe if she knew that she could permanently adopt Neil, she would feel better.

"Here's the number to the shelter." I scribbled the number on the corner of my notepad and ripped it off. "After the seven-day period is over, you can go down there if you want to make it official—you know, bring him home with you."

She took the paper and looked at it. "Thank you, dear. I'll put this somewhere where I won't lose it." She folded it and put it in her purse.

"Well, I have to go. It was nice seeing you again." I walked back to my car. Mrs. Oakley was waving from her porch. Soon Mrs. Oakley wouldn't have to be lonely anymore, and the black dog would have a new home—or, perhaps, his old home.

"Your friend has to make up her mind." Maureen had called me from the shelter. She sounded frustrated. Even over the phone I could easily visualize how irritated she must look at that moment. I was glad that I wasn't there. "There's a nice couple that wants to adopt this dog, and I can't hold him any longer. It's been at least two weeks now. You must realize how lucky this dog is, don't you? He's about eight years old, which I notice is what you actually put down on the shelter sheet. This may be the first time you got that right."

"Let me just make sure that Mrs. Oakley doesn't want him. She lives just down the street. I'll call you right back."

I just had to make sure Mrs. Oakley knew that someone was going to adopt Neil. I knew that she often worked odd hours; maybe she hadn't had the time to go down and get Neil during shelter hours.

"All right. But I'm warning you—I can only give you an hour. After that, it's out of my hands. I just hope that these people don't change their minds. I'm holding you responsible for this," she said.

"Fine . . . I accept the responsibility. I'll call you back. I promise."

"Good." She hung up.

I looked at the clock. I had to get over to Union Avenue right away. I grabbed my keys and drove to her house. Once I'd arrived, I rang the bell twice. No answer. I saw Mrs. Oakley's car parked outside, so I knew she must be home. She was probably sleeping. I felt bad about waking her up, but time was of the essence. In less than an hour, Neil, who was possibly her husband (or, at least, Mrs. Oakley believed he might be), would be going home with someone else. I had to let her know.

Finally she opened the door, rubbing her eyes. She was wearing a kimono. "Oh, hi, Miss Duffy. Come in. I was going to make some coffee. Would you like some?" She went inside and I followed her.

"I don't have time for coffee right now, and neither do you. A family is going to adopt Neil in less than an hour unless you do something."

She walked into the kitchen. "Come in and sit down. I don't have any cookies today. Would you like a sandwich?"

"No, thank you. Mrs. Oakley, did you hear what I said?"

She poured water into the coffeemaker and then opened the cabinet to reach for the cups. She turned around to look at me. I must have looked as frustrated as I felt.

"Have a seat, dear. I have something to tell you."

I sat. I looked up at the clock. I had thirty-five minutes left.

She walked out of the room for a second and came back in and put a photo album down on the table in front of me. She flipped through it and then showed me a photograph of an older woman and a man. It looked like they were with a group of people at some type of party.

"That's Neil," she said, pointing to the man. I remembered that she had told me he was only about five years older than she was, but the man in the photograph looked a lot older than his late fifties or early sixties.

"And that's me." She looked at me while I examined the photograph. How could that be Mrs. Oakley? The woman in the picture was quite a bit overweight and looked a lot older than Mrs. Oakley. There were no jeans or trendy haircuts. The woman in the photo looked like she could have been Mrs. Oakley's mother.

"Very different, right?" she said, closing the album.

"You look so much . . . younger in person." Again, I felt like no matter what I said, it could be considered insulting. Mrs. Oakley didn't seem to think of it that way. She laughed.

"How old do you think I am?" she asked, pouring me a cup of coffee.

"I don't know . . . um, maybe fifty-six, fifty-seven?"

This seemed to make her laugh harder. She pulled out the kitchen chair and sat down across from me. "I'm going to be seventy this year."

"Wow," I said, once again wondering if that was the right response. I couldn't help it. The woman in the picture and the woman sitting in front of me looked like two entirely different people. It was more than age. It was her style and her hair, or her exercise regime, and something else I couldn't put my finger on.

"Now, don't get me wrong. What I am about to say may sound terrible to you, but I don't want to go back to that woman you see in the picture. I had a good life. I love my children, and I have some happy memories, but . . ."

I looked at her, waiting for her to continue.

"I never felt like . . . *me* . . . until now. I never had the time to pursue my own interests, or even take care of myself before. I was married very young, but that's what you did then. Do you understand?"

I did. My own parents had married when my mother was barely out of her teens. I couldn't imagine doing that myself. I couldn't imagine doing it now, and I was already past the age my mother had been when I was born.

"I wouldn't change anything. But the way my life is now makes me feel like I'm really living . . . for the first time. I have my friends over and I don't have to chase them out of the house because my husband doesn't like any noise. I can read as many books as I want. I can explore new recipes and new interests, and now I'm even going to travel.

"So, even though I think this dog may be Neil, I don't want to adopt him. I've had a lot of time to think about this since you were here last," she said, leaning in toward me. "I don't have enough time to take care of a dog. A cat is easier, and Ebony spends a lot of time at my daughter's house anyway. My hours at work are unpredictable, and even though I'm planning on retiring in a few months, I hope to be traveling . . . a lot."

She picked up her spoon and stirred her coffee. "This may sound selfish, but this is the only way I can put it. It just wouldn't be fair—for either of us."

I nodded my head. None of this had occurred to me. I had completely expected her to be thrilled to have her husband back, even if he was a dog. But after talking to her, I understood. I didn't think she was being selfish at all. Mrs. Oakley had waited years to be able to truly be herself. She had raised a family and taken care of everyone to the point where she had stopped taking care of herself. It wasn't time to be responsible for a dog. It was time for Mrs. Oakley to have wine and cheese parties, study philosophy, and travel to the Far East. It was *her* time now.

Neil went home with his new family; a quiet couple with no children. They wanted a dog for companionship, but one that wouldn't jump on the furniture or bark a lot. As far as I knew, it was a perfect match.

I saw Mrs. Oakley a few times around town. The last time I ran into her, she told me all about her trip to Japan, and invited me to stop by sometime to see her photos—but to come soon, because she was leaving for Italy in a few weeks.

After the religious war I had started, I thought it best to go back to Records and try to smooth things over. A box of fresh muffins from the bakery seemed to do the trick. I had no intention of changing anyone's mind; that wasn't what I was worried about. I just wanted to make sure everyone was okay with each other, and that I hadn't caused a major rift in the office.

After all, if what goes around comes around, you can never be too careful.

Sometimes It Chooses You

"*I*t's called PR—public relations. It's a way of maintaining a positive relationship with the community. I was thinking that they could interview you on the cable channel," said the chief. "What do you think of that?" He seemed excited at this idea, and he was looking at me like I should be equally as excited.

"Sure, um, I guess so," I said. What I really wanted to say was *No . . . it's a bad idea. Bad, bad, bad!* I definitely did not want to be on TV, even if it was only cable. I didn't photograph well. I could only imagine the damage a TV camera would do. My throat would close up, and I wouldn't be able to talk. It could get ugly.

"You know, on second thought, um, I don't think I would be very good at that sort of thing. I mean, thank you for considering me, but I don't think I would represent the department all that well . . ."

"That's just one idea I had. The other one you could do sooner."

The chief was coming up with lots of ideas. I sensed that he was having a slow day.

"You can go talk to some of the high school kids," he said. "The head of Special Education up there called to ask if someone from the department could talk with some of the students. It's perfect! You could talk about civil service careers, what you do on a daily basis, bring some of your equipment."

"In the auditorium?" I asked, knowing that if he said yes I would have to come down with something highly contagious.

"No, I would never ask you to do that—unless you wanted to, of course." He looked at me, raising one eyebrow a little higher than the other. Great. Now I was giving him ideas. I shook my head no a few times, then some more just in case he hadn't noticed the first time.

"Okay, no large venue. It's just some kids in a classroom."

"Uh, okay . . . I could do that." I figured at this point I had to agree to something.

"Great! I'll call and set it right up." He immediately turned and walked into his office, and I suspected, right over to the phone. He was very decisive about everything, and even though I usually admired him for that, this was a little different. He was making decisions that involved me.

I had never been comfortable talking to groups of people. Since I had started at the department, I had slowly grown in confidence, and felt more capable when dealing with the people I came in contact with each day. But I preferred talking with one or two at a time, at most. The idea of standing up in front of a room full of teenagers was intimidating. I knew it was either this, or talk to a camera. I wasn't sure which was worse. Maybe the chief would just let me talk to a reporter from the newspaper? Maybe I could suggest that to him and he would forget about trying to send me out like some sort of public relations missionary.

I stood in the hallway, trying to hear what he was saying on the phone. Maybe I would just go and get in the car and get back out on the road. The chief didn't think I wrote enough loose-dog tickets anyway. I shifted from one foot to another and looked toward the door to the lobby. The chief wasn't coming back out of his office. This was a good thing. Maybe he had been distracted by something more important. What we really needed right now was a good riot or something—maybe a nice oil spill. Yes. I should definitely go out to the car. I pulled out my car keys.

The chief poked his head out of his office. "Oh good, you're still here."

Oh, good, I thought. *I'm still here.* I should have run when I'd had the chance.

"Next Tuesday at ten. You're to report to the principal, and she will bring you to the room where you will talk with the students." He waited for me to say something.

"Yes, sir," I said. He looked at me seriously for a moment, finally noticing that I seemed to have some reservations about all of this.

"You'll be fine . . . I know it. Don't worry. It'll be great." He gave me a little salute and went back into his office. I stood there thinking that now I would spend the entire weekend worrying about this. His head popped out again.

"Maybe we should combine this with the cable show—have them tape you up there at the high school!"

I stood there and opened my mouth. No sound came out.

"Just kidding!" He winked and vanished back into his office.

My stomach hurt.

On my way back outside to the car, I passed by Daryl who was washing the floor in the lobby.

"So, I hear you might be on TV," he said.

Well, *this* must break the record. It had only taken about two seconds for this information to spread all the way out into the lobby.

"Didn't you already do this today?" I asked. It seemed to me that when I had come in for lineup that morning, I had slipped trying to navigate my way around the WET FLOOR signs.

"Nope. You must be thinking of another day," Daryl said while chewing on his ever-present toothpick.

"No . . . I don't think so. I remember coming in this morning and tripping over one of your signs."

Daryl slowly stopped mopping the floor, wrung out his mop, and set it back in the bucket. He crossed his arms in front of him and smiled. "Well, you do seem to trip on things a lot."

"What has *that* got to do with anything?" I asked.

"No offense, but you are mighty accident-prone."

"Hmmph," I said. He was the one washing the same floor over and over, just so he could be out there in the middle of things all the time, getting an earful of everything that was going on. Either that, or he was hiding out somewhere under the radar. At some point this conversation had gone awry. We had been talking about him, not me.

Whistling, Daryl took a bottle of glass cleaner off his cart and started spraying the window on the door. I sighed. I knew I really didn't have any reason to be angry at him. It wasn't Daryl who was bothering me. He really did do a great job, and would drop everything to help you if you needed it. I was just frustrated at my situation. He stopped washing the window long enough to open the door and hold it for me.

"Thank you," I said.

"So, like I said before you got all huffy—the chief's putting you on TV?"

"No, he's not," I said. "He's sending me to the high school to talk to teenagers instead."

"Well, that sounds . . . interesting." Daryl was looking at me the way you'd look at someone who was being wheeled into surgery. "Good luck with that."

"Thanks," I said as I strode quickly toward my car. I would need it.

I kept staring at the course catalog my advisor had spread open in front of me. He was crossing out certain courses with his pen.

"You have to commit to a major soon," he said. "First, you chose political science, then English . . . then back again. And now nursing . . . There is no possibility that you can handle Organic Chemistry." He looked up at me abruptly. "Oh, I'm sorry. No offense."

Mr. St. James was my advisor. He was originally from Jamaica. I always enjoyed listening to his accent; even his insults had a lovely rhythm to them. He probably hadn't realized that he had said the last part of that sentence out loud until it was too late. It was okay; he was right. My nursing career goals had taken many paths through the years and had finally come to a dead end. The name of that dead end had been Organic Chemistry.

"No offense taken," I said, looking back at the catalog. It seemed to me that when someone said "No offense," it was really a disclaimer for the opposite. This was the second time today some-one had said that to me. It was also the second time today that I had deserved it.

"All the journalism courses are offered during the day. That doesn't work for you, though."

"No, it doesn't." I sighed. I could only take classes at night.

"You did very well in the history courses you took last semester."

I nodded my head. I had really enjoyed those classes.

"Think about this, my dear: At some time in the near future you will have to make a decision. Promise me you will take some time and really think about this." Mr. St. James looked tired. He had been pushing me to make a decision for months. There were no more electives left to take.

"I promise . . . really. I'll think about it," I said, knowing as I said those words that I still wasn't sure what I was going to be when I grew up. The problem being, I was already grown up.

Tuesday morning I pushed the stretcher to the back of the animal control wagon. I had to make room for the Havahart trap, the snare pole, and the cat carrier. I had a small photo album filled with some photos of different dogs I had taken about a year ago when I had been experimenting with a friend's camera. Which of these things should I bring inside? I didn't want to walk in the front door hauling all of this into the high school, past scores of teenagers standing around watching. Even though it had only been six years since I'd walked these halls, it felt like a lifetime ago.

I got in the car and looked in the rearview mirror. The chief had said to make sure I had my tie on. Maybe he thought it would help me look more legitimate. I readjusted the rearview mirror, started the car, and pulled out of the parking lot on my way to what I was sure was going to be a public relations nightmare. Maybe after I crashed and burned, the chief would give up on sending me anywhere else to talk to the public, and he'd leave me alone with my cats and dogs.

"Good morning, Lisa," said Mrs. Eichler, the secretary in the main office. She remembered me. "Thanks for coming today. Look at you—so professional! Mrs. King is in a meeting, so I'm going to bring you downstairs to Mrs. Willis."

"Thank you," I said, looking around. Everything looked smaller. I had decided to bring in the snare pole and the trap, thinking that I could explain how they worked. That would eat up at least ten minutes. Then I could take questions. (What if there were no questions?) I had grabbed the photo album at the last minute, too.

"Did Mrs. Willis tell you about the class you're going to be talking to today?" asked Mrs. Eichler, who was walking down the steps very quickly. I was struggling to catch up to her, dragging all the equipment I had brought with me. Maybe bringing all of this had been a mistake.

"I think she spoke to the chief, and he made the arrangements. He did mention that she was the head of the special education department." I remembered Mrs. Willis. Even though she had never been one of my teachers, anytime I had come into contact with her, she had always been kind and helpful. Mrs. Eichler made a left, and I followed her. I had never been in this part of the building before.

"These are some of our students who have different developmental issues. Some have had neurological problems or other conditions that make it necessary for them to have a different program.

Some of the students . . . well, they may be a little difficult due to some behavioral and emotional issues." She looked at me from the corner of her eye, never slowing down on her way to the classroom. "I just don't want you to take it personally if they don't respond to you."

"Oh, of course. I won't," I said as I labored behind her, clutching my snare pole a little harder. The chief had told me that these were kids who weren't likely to pursue college after high school, and that I should talk about types of jobs in civil service that didn't require a degree. He hadn't said anything about emotional and behavioral issues.

I arrived at the door and stood there watching Mrs. Willis talk to the class. There were about twelve students in the room. A few of them had their heads down; one was facing the window, and the others seemed to be listening to Mrs. Willis. She turned to me and smiled. I looked behind me to ask Mrs. Eichler if I should go in now, but she had already left. I looked down the hallway. There was no sign of her anywhere. She was fast.

"Come in, Officer Duffy. Class, this is Animal Control Officer Duffy from the police department. She's here today to talk to you about what she does. We would like to thank you for coming today. We've been looking forward to this since last week." She nodded to me to come closer, and I walked to the front of the room. I looked around. Nobody appeared overly enthusiastic. I wondered who the *we* was in the "We've been looking forward to this."

It was time for me to say something. I had sort of practiced what I might say in front of the mirror that morning while brushing my teeth. I hadn't impressed myself.

"Good morning. I'm really glad to be here," I said in a way that I hoped sounded like I meant it. There was silence. Two of the kids who'd had their heads on their desks lifted them up to look at me. The boy staring out the window hadn't moved.

I took a deep breath. Maybe Mrs. Willis could help me start this. I turned to look over at her, and she was gone too. How did they do that?

I looked back at them. I could swear I heard crickets.

"How many of you like dogs?" I figured I would start with an easy question. A few hands went up. "How many of you have a dog or a cat at home?" More hands went up. This wasn't so bad. I asked the girl in the front, "Do you have a dog or a cat?"

"I have both. I have a puppy named Bobo, and my cat doesn't have a name. She just comes when you say 'Cat.' She likes me the most."

"Well, that makes her a very smart cat," I said.

She smiled.

Where was all of this coming from? I found I didn't have to struggle to find the words I had planned on saying. Not only that, but I had better words, and I wasn't sure why it was so easy.

Another hand went up. I said "Yes?"

"Why do you have to take people's dogs away?" asked a girl in the back of the room. The boy looking out the window looked like he was trying to listen without making it too obvious.

"I don't really take them away for good. I just take them out of dangerous situations, like when they are running in the road and they could get hit by a car. If their owner promises to take better care of their dog, I can bring them back."

"What happens if they don't?" she asked.

"Well, I can write them a ticket, and they would have to pay a fine before they could get their dog back. That's one way to make sure they follow the law next time."

"Has that ever happened—where the people don't listen, and the dog gets hit by a car?"

This was actually something I saw too often. Sometimes when it happened, it made me think that I couldn't do this job anymore. I was here to tell them about my job, but I hadn't thought that I would have to explain this part of it.

"Yes, it happens sometimes. I have to go and help when it does . . . and sometimes it's really sad."

A tall boy with long hair sitting in the far corner raised his hand. His voice was really deep. He sounded more like a man than a high school student.

"Do some of them die?"

"Yes," I said. "Sometimes they die."

"Do you cry?"

I looked at him, and there was something about the way he'd asked the question that made me feel like this topic hit close to home.

"Yes, sometimes I cry. No, actually, I cry a lot. But I also get to see a lot of happy things, and I try to focus on those, because if you just think about the bad things all the time, it just gets to be—"

"Too much," he finished.

"Yes," I said. "Exactly. It gets to be too much. So instead of thinking about all the sad things that happen, I do everything I can to make sure it doesn't happen again. If I can do something about it, then I don't feel so sad anymore. Although some people think I'm mean for taking their dogs away, it's my job to protect them."

Another hand went up. "What's that stick for?"

And then another. "Can I see it?"

And then a flood of questions: "Is that a trap?" "Have you ever caught anything in it?" "How did you get this job?" "Is it hard to get a job in the police station?" "Where do you bring the dogs you catch?"

I answered all of the questions to the best of my ability.

Another student asked, "Do you ever catch any other kinds of animals?"

"Sure," I said. "I've had complaints involving ducks, turkeys, groundhogs, raccoons, ferrets . . . lots of different types of animals."

"How do you know what to do?"

I laughed. "Sometimes I don't know what to do. I have to look it up or ask someone. Sometimes I only learn what to do after I totally mess up the first time. Actually, that's how I think I learn most things."

A girl in the front row cried out, "Me too!" and laughed. The sound of her laughter made me feel, well . . . there were no words for what I felt.

"Would anyone like to see how the snare works?" I looked around the room for a volunteer. The boy looking out the window said, "Yeah!"

"Okay. Why don't you come up here and you can help me show everyone." He stood up and made a big deal of cracking his knuckles and stretching like he was going into the big game as a pinch hitter. He was really funny.

Soon, all of the kids had come forward from the back of the room and were sitting up closer, getting involved. There were kids inspecting the trap; one was trying to pick up a sneaker with the snare; another boy was filling out a copy of a voided parking ticket I had brought to show them. I started showing them some of the photographs of the different dogs I had taken pictures of while I was working. They were passing them around. I wished I had taken more.

This visit to the school hadn't been anything like I thought it would be. I had built these teenagers up in my mind to be something they were not. They were just kids, even if a few of them were much bigger than I was. I heard the bell ring. I couldn't believe the class was over so quickly. It seemed like I'd only been there for twenty minutes at most. I heard Mrs. Willis from behind me. She was standing by her desk. When had she come back in?

"Okay, everyone—let's thank the animal control officer for coming today."

"Thank you!" "Bye!" "When are you coming back?" "Can you bring some dogs next time?" They were all talking at once except for the boy who had asked me if I cried when a dog was hit by a car. He stood there silently behind everyone else.

"Let's go, ladies and gentlemen. Miss Sanchez is waiting for you outside the gym."

I bent down and started to pack up some of my equipment.

"Thomas, you have to go to gym now." Mrs. Willis was gently trying to guide him out of the room.

"I wanted to ask the animal officer a question—real quick, okay?" he asked.

She nodded her head. "Sure, Thomas, go right ahead. I'll write you a pass so you won't be marked late."

Mrs. Willis went over to her desk and took a pad out of a drawer and started to write.

Thomas walked over to where I was standing. He was at least a head taller than me. "Do you ever get, like kittens . . . you know . . . when nobody wants them?" He was talking so softly, and his voice was so low that I had to really listen carefully to make out what he was saying.

"Yes, I do. I can't tell when it's going to happen, but this is usually the time of year when I start getting the most calls for that."

"If you get some, can I maybe have one? I'll take good care of him. My cat lived a really long time, but he got old and . . . he died. Can I call you or something?" He looked so grown-up with his slight beard and serious expression, but he wasn't. He was a boy who missed his cat.

"You know what I'll do . . . If you give me your phone number, as soon as I get any kittens that need a home, I will call you right away, and you and your mom—"

"My grandma. I live with my grandma."

"Okay, you and your grandma can come down and pick one out." I took out my pen and wrote his number down on the back of my shelter book. "As soon as I get any, I'll call you."

"Thank you," he said softly. He took the pass Mrs. Willis handed him and left.

I picked up the trap and then grabbed the snare, tucking them under my arm along with my photo album. I felt a lot less clumsy than I had when I had arrived earlier that morning. I didn't understand why I had thought everything was so heavy before.

I turned around to thank Mrs. Willis. She was sitting behind her desk, looking at me intently. Maybe I had done something wrong? Maybe I shouldn't have let them examine the equipment . . . But nobody had been hurt, and they had been really interested in how things worked.

"Is everything okay, Mrs. Willis? Did I do something wrong?" I must have screwed this up somehow. Great public relations representative I was. I had really felt like everything had gone so well. I had found that after a few minutes, I hadn't been uncomfortable at all.

"No, no, Lisa, that's not it. What are your plans?" she asked, crossing her arms and waiting for an answer.

"Plans?" I asked. Did she mean, what were my plans for the day? I had an appointment to take a complaint later on, and then probably a school crossing to cover.

She stood up and asked again. "What are your plans—for your life? Your career? Are you planning on going to school?"

"Actually, I am in school. I've almost completed my third year, but I haven't chosen my major yet. It's funny that you should ask me that today, since last week I had a similar discussion with my advisor. I have to decide soon."

"I'll walk with you," she said, getting up from her desk. "I have until next period when they come back from gym."

We walked down the hallway toward the stairs. I could hear some of what was going on in the classrooms we passed by. Bits and pieces of lectures, someone was showing a film, the sounds of some wind instruments from behind the auditorium doors. All of these sounds brought back memories of when I had been a student here.

Mrs. Willis spoke while we climbed the stairs.

"The students in that class don't usually talk to people they don't know. I've had guest speakers before, substitute teachers . . . Except for Lizzie in the front, they either ignore them or misbehave. They interacted with you. Especially Thomas, and he rarely speaks to anyone."

I was surprised. After a few short moments, these kids had been engaging, friendly, and curious. They asked so many questions I couldn't even answer them all. They seemed to really have a great time. Each one of them had made an impression on me. I didn't think I would be able to forget any of them anytime soon.

"I really enjoyed meeting them, Mrs. Willis. It was a privilege. Thank you for inviting me to your classroom." What had started off as involuntary public relations duty had turned into one of the best days I could remember having in a very long time.

Mrs. Willis walked with me over to the front doors of the high school. She had such a serious expression on her face. "I want you to listen to me carefully," she said. "I don't say this lightly. Sometimes people choose a career, and sometimes it chooses them. Do you understand what I'm saying?"

I nodded my head.

"I think you should seriously consider becoming a teacher."

I was flattered. Mrs. Willis had been teaching for almost thirty years, and hearing this from her really meant a lot to me. She gave me a quick hug and said good-bye.

As I walked out into the sunshine, I stopped and looked around for a second. I needed to memorize exactly what everything looked like in this very spot, at this very moment. I wanted to be able to look back someday and remember it all clearly when I told people about the moment I realized what I was going to do with my life.

About a month later I received a call from a gentleman on Congress Avenue who wanted to surrender a litter of kittens. Rather than the purebred Himalayans he and his wife were expecting, Stewart's Victoria of Dunmore Cliffs had surprised them all with a diverse litter of very fluffy tiger-Himalayan mix kittens. It seemed that someone had gone slumming.

"I don't know how this could have happened," the man said while I placed the box of kittens gently on the passenger seat in my car.

"Of course you know how this happened!" his wife admonished him. "I told you not to let her out on the patio until after . . . um, you know . . . after!"

It looked like this was going to erupt into a major argument any second. I thought I had better distract them. "Excuse me, but do you call her by that long name all the time?"

"My goodness, no. That is her call name. It's the name on her pedigree," Mrs. Stewart-of-Dunmore-Cliffs said.

"Oh, of course. I'm sorry. What do you call her for short?"

"We call her Victoria," said the woman, at the same time her husband said, "We call her Vicky." They began bickering again. I noticed that the entire time they were arguing, Vicky or Victoria, oblivious to all the drama going on, sat calmly in the window, giving herself a bath.

As I got in the car and started it up, the couple continued arguing. I looked over at the box next to me. Inside, there were five beautiful six-week-old kittens cuddled together, sound asleep. I figured they must be used to loud noises.

"Thanks. Good-bye." I waved. There was no response. So I pulled away from the curb and drove off down the road. I didn't have the time to sit there waiting for them to stop arguing. I wanted to get back to headquarters as soon as possible. There was someone waiting for one of these kittens, and I had an important phone call to make.

It had been quite a while since I'd been back to the high school. This time there was a chill in the air. The leaves had already started to turn, yet it would be a few weeks more before they were at their peak. I took a deep breath and pulled open the front door and made my way to the main office. Mrs. Eichler greeted me again.

"Good morning, Lisa. Are you ready?" she said, while pulling open a drawer from behind the counter.

"I think I am."

She removed a folder from the drawer and pushed it toward me. "Don't forget to sign the substitute list."

I picked up the pen on the counter and signed.

"Here," she said, and handed me a key. "You're in for Mr. Gardner. He's Global Studies, so that's right up your alley."

I shifted a bit from one foot to another. I was going to have to get used to wearing heels. I smiled at her. "Thanks," I said.

"You're going to be just fine." She smiled back and then turned around to answer the phone.

I walked over to the teachers' mailboxes and took the attendance forms I would need. On the way downstairs to the classroom, I passed by the large wall of windows that looked out over the city. I saw a police car sitting at a light. The light turned green, and I watched as it made a turn and drove away. For a moment, I felt a lump in my throat. While this was a transition that I had worked very hard to make, it was bittersweet.

I was going to miss the animals and the camaraderie of the police department. I would also miss so many of the people I had come to know and care about while working as the animal control officer. They were more than my colleagues, they had become like my family. I was four years older now, and in some ways I felt that I'd experienced more in that period of time than I had in my entire life before. Yet I remembered the day I walked into headquarters on my first day of work like it was yesterday. And, inasmuch as I had grown tired of braving the elements and dealing with the cold in the winter, there was much to be said for having a job where you could be outside to smell the rain in the spring and watch the first snowflakes fall at the beginning of winter—a job where your break room is the Hudson River, and your office is an entire city.

While many people go off to work in a building in some other town, I was given the opportunity to be part of something bigger—the privilege of being invited into the lives of the people in this community. Sometimes I was with them at their weakest moments, and sometimes at their best. There is something about how people interact with their animals that strips away their facades—the walls that most of us keep up in order to live according to the way we think adults should behave.

I had observed that most people, like their pets, just want uncon-ditional love. I had learned that irritating and irrational behavior is sometimes just a by-product of loneliness; that even though there are people who can be cruel and inhumane, there are more who are compassionate and kind. I had shared in the joy of reuniting lost dogs with their owners, and experienced the anger and sadness of holding dying animals in my arms, my futile efforts to change what was happening having met with failure. I had laughed a lot and cried a lot. In some ways I had grown cynical, but in others, I had grown tolerant.

Most of all, I had grown up.

I fumbled a bit with the key, my hands shaking a bit as I opened the door. The sun streamed in on the rows of empty seats. I put my folder on the desk and walked over to the board. Picking up a piece of chalk, I held it between my fingers for a moment and looked at it. Carefully, I wrote my name on the board.

I heard a voice behind me and turned around.

"Are you our teacher today?" A pretty young girl, her hair braided with beads, stood quietly, holding her books against her chest and waiting for my answer.

"Um . . . yes," I said quietly. I looked down at the chalk I was still holding, and then back up at her. I smiled, and this time, my answer was confident and clear.

"Yes, I am."

~ The End ~